Marxist Theories of Imperialism
A Critical Survey

This seminal account of Marxist theories of imperialism is now appearing in a revised and expanded edition.

Covering figures as diverse as Hobson, Luxembourg, Hilferding, Bukharin, Lenin, Frank, Wallerstein, Emmanuel and Warren, as well as Marx himself, it analyses how Marxists have accounted for the role of imperialism in the spread of world capitalism.

Marx had expected the spread of capitalism to lead to full capitalist development everywhere (unless anticipated by socialist revolution), while Lenin and his contemporaries concentrated on the role of monopoly and inter-imperialist rivalry. More recently, the focus of theory has shifted to the explanation of underdevelopment, which has prompted a renaissance of Marxist thought.

This book provides a clear guide to this important body of theory, establishing how the competing theories relate to each other and assessing them in terms of their logical coherence and their relevance to real problems.

Anthony Brewer is senior lecturer in Economics at the University of Bristol. He is the author of *A Guide to Marx's Capital*, 1984, and of a number of articles in learned journals.

Marxist Theories of Imperialism

A Critical Survey
Second Edition

Anthony Brewer

London and New York

First published 1980 by Routledge & Kegan Paul
Reprinted 1982, 1984, 1986 and 1987

Reprinted 1989 by Routledge

Second edition published 1990 by Routledge
11 New Fetter Lane, London EC4P 4EE

Simultaneously published in the USA and Canada by Routledge
a division of Routledge, Chapman and Hall, Inc.
29 West 35th Street, New York, NY 10001

© 1990 Anthony Brewer

Printed in England by Clays Ltd, St Ives plc

British Library Cataloguing in Publication Data
Brewer, Anthony, *1942–*
    Marxist theories of imperialism : a critical survey. – 2nd ed.
    1. Imperialism. Marxist theories, history
    I. Title
    325.3201

    ISBN 0–415–04468–5
    ISBN 0–415–04469–3 pbk

Library of Congress Cataloging-in-Publication Data
applied for

In memory of Iris Brewer

Contents

Preface

My aim in this book is to survey Marxist writings on imperialism and, more broadly, on the emergence and development of the world capitalist economy. I have tried to maintain a sympathetic but critical position; critical because Marxist theories have often suffered from being accepted or rejected wholesale, rather than being subjected to detailed scrutiny and constructive criticism, and sympathetic because I think there is a lot to be learned from them.

In revising the book for the second edition, I found few major new ideas to incorporate; the last decade has been one of consolidation and reassessment. Dependency theories were still alive ten years ago, but the criticisms I and others made then have now been generally accepted, so I have gathered the story of the rise and fall of dependency theory into one (long) chapter. I have also added a chapter on Hobson which should, with hindsight, have been there all along.

I have benefited greatly from constructive criticism from others. Roger Berry, Martin Browning, Aidan Foster-Carter, and Andrew Friedman all gave me helpful advice when I was writing the first edition, but are not to blame for the results. Karen Snodin helped with translations. Gillian Baker, Pat Shaw, and Marjorie Lunt typed the first edition. The new edition, for those who are interested, was written and laid out in Microsoft Word, to produce a PostScript file, effectively using the typesetter to produce camera-ready copy as if it were a printer attached to my microcomputer. I owe a special debt of thanks to Emma Waghorn for firm but sympathetic editing, and to Alan Jarvis, David McCarthy, and others at Routledge who have guided me through the process. Finally, Janet Brewer has given invaluable support throughout.

Chapter 4 is based on a paper presented at a conference on imperialism at Catania, Sicily, September 1987, to be published in the conference volume, *Italia e Inghilterra nell Eta dell' Imperialismo*, edited by Professor E. Serra.

Abbreviations

Some books that are referred to repeatedly are cited in the text by an abbreviated form of their title. They are listed below; for full details see the bibliography.

Accumulation	Luxemburg (1951), *The Accumulation of Capital*
Alliances	Rey (1973), *Les alliances de classes*
Anti-Critique	Luxemburg (1972), *The Accumulation of Capital – an Anti-Critique*
AWS	Amin (1974), *Accumulation on a World Scale*
Capital	Marx (1961, 1957, 1962), *Capital*, vols I-III
Colonialisme	Rey (1971), *Colonialisme, neo-colonialisme et transition au capitalism*
CULA	Frank (1969a), *Capitalism and Underdevelopment in Latin America*
CWE	Wallerstein (1979), *The Capitalist World Economy*
DAU	Frank (1978), *Dependent Accumulation and Underdevelopment*
EPEA	Arrighi and Saul (1973), *Essays on the Political Economy of Africa*
FC	Hilferding (1970), *Finance Capital*
Imperialism	Lenin (1950), *Imperialism, the Highest Stage of Capitalism*
IUD	Amin (1977), *Imperialism and Unequal Development*
IWE	Bukharin (1972a), *Imperialism and World Economy*
LAUR	Frank (1969b), *Latin America: Underdevelopment or Revolution*
LL	Frank (1972), *Lumpenbourgeoisie: Lumpendevelopment*
Manifesto	Marx and Engels (1950), *Manifesto of the Communist Party*
MWS	Wallerstein (1974a), *The Modern World System*
PEG	Baran (1973), *The Political Economy of Growth*
UD	Amin (1976), *Unequal Development*
UE	Emmanuel (1972), *Unequal Exchange*

1

Introduction

The last two or three centuries have seen two interconnected developments that have transformed the world. First, production and productivity have increased to levels that would previously have seemed not so much impossible as inconceivable, and the whole nature of industry and of many of the goods produced has altered beyond recognition. How could earlier generations have conceived of live colour television pictures from the moon, broadcast to a mass audience in their own homes, or flocks of aircraft carrying northern Europeans on their annual migration to the resorts of the Mediterranean? Second, inequalities of wealth and power between different parts of the world have grown to an equally unprecedented degree. Americans and Europeans sit in comfortable homes, watching televised reports of famine in Africa. These are facts that everyone knows, but we tend to take them for granted and to ignore the extent to which they determine the whole character of the modern world. They can only be understood and analysed by looking at the historical process by which they have evolved, on a world scale, over a period of centuries.

The same period has been marked by a third development, the rise to dominance of the capitalist mode of production, in which production is carried out by many distinct, privately owned enterprises which sell their products on the market and employ wage workers. Capitalism has almost completely supplanted earlier forms of organization (peasant agriculture, feudal estates, slave plantations) in the advanced countries. In the underdeveloped countries, peasant agriculture still supports a large part of the population, but these areas have been drawn into a world market and a world-wide system of specialization which has completely undermined traditional economic and social structures.

The colonial empires hacked out by European powers, and the whole system of European and American military and political dominance over the world, which reached its peak in the early twentieth century, can only be understood in the context of this process of uneven development. The basis for military supremacy was economic. Superior technology meant superior armaments and a capacity to transport armed men to any part of the world. Superior economic organization made it possible to finance the overhead costs of military forces, and to deploy them to devastating effect. The motives for imperial expansion were also predominantly economic. Some historians now seek to deny it, but the men of the East India Company, the Spanish conquistadors, the investors in South African mines and the slave traders knew very well what they wanted. They wanted to be rich. Colonial empires were exploited ruthlessly as sources of cheap raw materials and cheap labour, and as monopolized markets. The romantic image of empire (flags fluttering over distant outposts, and the like) may be appealing, but a serious study must concentrate on more fundamental economic issues.

I do not claim that every incident in the history of empire can be explained in directly economic terms. Economic interests are filtered through a political process, policies are implemented by a complex state apparatus, and the whole system generates its own momentum. Much of the history of the British empire, for example, pivots on the need to safeguard the route to India; British policy in, say, the Mediterranean should not be explained in terms of the economic gains to be made in that area alone, but in terms of the maintenance of empire as a whole. The drive to imperial expansion must be explained as one element in the whole process of capitalist development.

Equally, the creation of formal empires, under a single flag and a single political authority, is only part of the story, and perhaps not the most important part. Formal political independence, with a flag, an airline and a seat at the UN, does not guarantee real equality, though it may be a necessary condition for real independence and development. Some countries have never been formally annexed, and most Latin American states have been formally independent for a century and a half, but they have been drawn into a system of inequality, exploitation and dominance almost as deeply as if they had been subjected to direct colonial rule. Under-developed countries still participate on very unequal terms in a world system of trade and investment.

My purpose in this book is to survey the various accounts of the development of the capitalist world economy that have been put forward in the Marxist tradition. I shall not discuss non-Marxist theories (except where they are relevant to the main theme), pre-capitalist empires or Soviet expansionism. This is not to deny the importance of these topics (especially the last); it is simply a matter of drawing a line around a reasonably coherent subject area. I shall not attempt to define 'imperialism' at this stage; indeed, I shall not present a final definition at any stage. Different writers used the word differently, and I shall follow the usage of the writer under discussion. Some of the authors discussed in the book did not use the word 'imperialism' at all. The set of topics set out in the preceding pages – the emergence of capitalism, its spread through the world, the unequal development of different areas, the dominance of some countries over others – all hang together, regardless of which elements we choose to label 'imperialism'.

I have argued that imperialism (in any of several different senses of the word) must be seen in the context of the whole history of capitalism on a world scale. Correspondingly, any theory of imperialism can only make sense when seen as a whole. This dictates the structure of the book. The work of each major writer must be seen as a whole, since a 'vision' of the whole system determines the treatment of particular aspects of it. The main body of the book will therefore be devoted to an examination of the work of a succession of major theorists in (approximate) chronological order.

1.1 HISTORICAL OUTLINE

As background, I start with a very brief, selective, and inevitably inadequate outline of the historical record. The fifteenth century is as good a starting point as any. At this time, Europe was not particularly rich or technically advanced compared with, say, India or China. The Arabic

3

cities dominated what long-distance trade there was, controlling the trading links between Europe and Asia, and the main Indian ocean routes. Certain parts of Europe had, however, a crucial lead in weaponry and shipbuilding, and the ability and incentive to take advantage of it. This was the basis for the explosive expansion of the Spanish and Portuguese sea-borne empires at the end of the fifteenth and the beginning of the sixteenth centuries.

During the first part of the 'mercantile' period (roughly 1500-1800), Spain and Portugal dominated. The Spanish empire was based on precious metals mined in central America and the Andes, funnelled through Panama to Spain, running the gauntlet of piracy in the 'Spanish Main' on the way. The mines, and the agricultural estates that fed them, were worked by forced labour. The Portuguese empire was more a string of trading posts controlling the traffic in spices and, later, in African slaves, but leaving social systems and systems of production relatively untouched. At the same time the expanding mercantile cities of western Europe came to depend on grain produced by serf labour on the estates of Prussia and Poland, shipped from Baltic ports.

In the seventeenth century, the emphasis shifted to the production of sugar in slave plantations in the Caribbean and Brazil, while Spain and Portugal progressively lost control of the seas and of key parts of their empires, first to the Dutch and then to the English and French. Labour was scarce in sugar-growing areas, and the 'Atlantic triangle' was born; manufactured goods (especially guns) were shipped to Africa, slaves to the Americas, and sugar back to Europe. As the eighteenth century went on, English, French, and Dutch trading posts in Asia expanded into territorial possessions, and there were signs of the more profound changes in Europe that developed in the following century.

In the mercantile period, then, European commerce came to dominate much of the world, though the goods exchanged in inter-continental trade were still mainly luxuries (sugar, spices, tobacco) together with slaves and precious metals. The organization of society and of production in South and Central America was totally and forcibly transformed, with whole populations exterminated and replaced, while in Africa and Asia the impact of Europe was in general either superficial or wholly destructive (the slave trade, the looting

4

of India). How this pattern of trade and production should be described is controversial. Frank and Wallerstein (chapter 8 below) insist that it was a capitalist world system, while others such as Banaji, Brenner and Rey (chapter 10) would describe it as a system of mainly pre-capitalist societies, linked by exchange, with an evolving capitalist centre in Europe. This disagreement is part of a larger debate over the definition of capitalism.

By the eighteenth century, capitalist relations of production, characterized by the employment of free wage-labour in privately owned businesses producing for the market, were well established in England and, to a lesser extent, elsewhere in north-west Europe. Productivity was rising fairly rapidly (though not as rapidly as later), and was already well above levels in the rest of the world. One factor in this general technical advance was the 'scientific revolution', which was closely linked to military and mercantile needs. Astronomy and the measurement of time, critical to navigation, were at the heart of Newtonian physics, and thus of a wholly new view of nature.

The decades around 1800 were a critical turning point, separating the mercantile period from the classical epoch of capitalist development. In the political sphere, the American and French revolutions created a new conception of politics. Britain supplanted France as a major colonial power and took effective control of India, which became the linchpin of the British empire. Even more significant, the industrial revolution, centred in Britain, marked the start of a new era. It was a protracted affair, but taken as a whole it was one of the most important events in human history. Its short-run effects on the mass of the people were probably retrograde, but it became possible to conceive of the abolition of poverty and drudgery through mechanized production. Marx's vision of socialism was based squarely on the potential created by industrialization.

The industrial revolution happened where and when it did because of a conjunction of external and internal factors (whose relative importance is a matter of debate). The organization of production in Britain was by this stage wholly capitalist, based on firms that were relatively large (by previous standards) but numerous, flexible, and driven by fierce internecine competition. They could recruit workers with the necessary skills from a substantial urban proletariat, and lay them off again equally quickly when market conditions changed or when labour-saving innovations made them redundant. Britain controlled the markets of the world, a vital advantage since the most important raw material, cotton, had to be imported, while a large part of the produce was exported. The profits of empire contributed to the ready availability of funds for investment. This was a new kind of society, which the rest of the world regarded with amazement. In a wider sense, the industrial revolution went on for much of the nineteenth century, a period of sustained development in the main centres of capitalism. The new industrial methods were introduced into industry after industry, and spread to other parts of Europe and North America. This was the context in which Marx wrote. By the end of the nineteenth century, Germany and the United States had emerged as major industrial rivals to Britain, and Japan had started on the process of industrialization.

The case of Japan is important, since it is still almost the only example of complete capitalist development outside Europe and areas of European settlement. Those who argue that subjection to Europe caused the failure of development elsewhere can point out that Japan was one of the few areas that remained outside European control, while those who argue that the success or failure of capitalist development depends primarily on internal social structures can point out that Japan started from a social structure that had much in common with European feudalism.

The area effectively integrated into the capitalist world economy expanded throughout the nineteenth century. Most of Latin America achieved formal independence, but came under informal British control. Asia, the largest and most populous continent, was opened up for capitalism. The British established effective control of the whole Indian subcontinent, and forced China, at gunpoint, to permit the import of opium. The French got Indo-China and the Dutch already controlled the East Indies. Russia was steadily pushing back its frontiers in Siberia and central Asia. Parts of Africa were colonized, setting the scene for a scramble for the rest at the end of the century. North America and Australasia were opened up. It was in this period that the world was definitely divided into 'advanced' and 'underdeveloped' areas, and the basic patterns of the present world economy were established. A new pattern of trade emerged, replacing the trade in luxuries of the mercantile period: advanced capitalist centres exported manufactures and imported food and raw materials. The physical bulk of goods traded expanded colossally, but transport had been transformed along with the rest of industry and was able to cope.

The end of the nineteenth century marks another major turning point, the beginning of what Lenin called the 'imperialist stage' of capitalism. Following his lead, many Marxists reserve the term 'imperialism' to describe the twentieth century, using other terms for the expansionism of earlier periods. I will follow the usage of whichever writer is under discussion. There was a rapid increase in the size of firms and a spread of monopoly in the form of cartels, trusts and so on. The twentieth century is often said to be the period of 'monopoly capital'. Exports of capital had increased rather earlier, augmenting rather than replacing trade in goods, at first in the form of loans to governments and public utilities, but increasingly as 'direct' investment in productive enterprises. In the early twentieth century investment was mostly in resource-based industries and related infrastructure. The natural resources of the whole planet were opened up for exploitation.

At the same time there was a scramble for control of the few remaining areas not already brought under colonial control, especially in Africa. Latin America passed, more gradually, from the British to the American sphere. Once the division of the world was complete, any further territorial expansion had to be at the expense of rival colonial empires. There was a sharp increase in tension between the main powers, especially between Germany (the rising power) and Britain (with the largest empire), which culminated in two world wars. That the rise of monopoly, the export of capital and the outbreak of inter-imperialist rivalry are connected is generally agreed among Marxists, though the exact nature of the connection is more disputable. This is the subject matter of the theories of imperialism worked out at the time by Hobson, Hilferding, Bukharin and Lenin (chapters 4-6).

The twentieth century has seen a number of developments. First, the area covered by the world capitalist system has contracted, with the subtraction first of Russia, then of China,

Cuba, much of south-east Asia and so on. In all cases these areas broke away as a result of war or of violent internal struggles. The nature of the systems installed in these countries will not be discussed here, but the fact of their existence has had important effects on the world balance of power. Second, international trade has grown more rapidly than total production, while international investment by major firms has grown even faster, making them into 'multi-nationals' operating on a world-wide basis. Markets for liquid money capital have also been internationalized. The world capitalist economy is much more tightly integrated than ever before, despite the achievement of formal in-dependence by most underdeveloped countries. The system cannot possibly be understood by looking at particular nation states in isolation. Third, the capitalist world became very clearly divided into advanced and underdeveloped countries, differing not only in income levels, but in almost every other aspect of their economic and social structure. There are, as in all previous periods, a few doubtful cases, but it is notable how small a fraction of the world's population they contain. In almost all cases there is no difficulty in assigning a country to one group or the other. This cleavage is clearly a major structural feature of the twentieth-century world system, though it may be breaking down as the end of the century approaches.

The advanced countries (Europe, North America, Japan, Australasia) went through a bad patch in the two world wars and the depression of the 1930s, but then experienced the 'long boom' of the 1950s and 1960s. Overall, levels of productivity have increased enormously over the century and the capitalist form of organization has almost completely displaced others. Trade and investment flows within the advanced 'centre' have grown especially rapidly, so trade with the underdeveloped 'periphery' is now a relatively small part of the total. The economy of a typical advanced country has a relatively large industrial sector, and an even larger service sector organized on modern capitalist lines. Agriculture employs a small fraction of the labour force, using modern capital-intensive techniques. (In some cases, a peasant sector survives with the help of subsidies.) The majority of the population are wage earners, and trades union organizations, if they have not fundamentally altered

the nature of capitalism, have at least ensured that the
benefits of increased productivity have been shared with the
working class. Democratic institutions have become well
established, with free elections and guarantees of personal
freedom. The advanced countries contain the headquarters of
the main multinational companies and are the main centres of
technological development. They produce and export a very
wide range of manufactured and primary products. They
import some primary products and a growing volume of
labour-intensive manufactured goods from underdeveloped
areas.

Turning to the underdeveloped world, there are important
differences between the 'three continents' (Latin America,
Asia, Africa). In Latin America, indigenous societies were
almost wholly destroyed centuries ago, white or creole ruling
classes with a European culture were established, and the
institutions of the modern state were installed at almost the
same time as in Europe. The larger Latin American countries
have average income levels well above those of Africa and
Asia, though equally far below those of Europe. At the same
time, they have all the structural features of underdevelopment. In Asia, major pre-capitalist civilizations were
drawn into the capitalist orbit more gradually and at a later
date. The larger Asian countries have well-established local
ruling classes, a considerable technological capacity, and
industrial sectors which are quite large in absolute terms,
though small relative to population. Average income levels,
however, are very low, with an enormous mass of peasants
and workers reduced to near starvation level. Some smaller
Asian countries, on the other hand, are relatively industrialized, and have experienced very rapid economic growth,
while Japan is, of course, in another category altogether.
Africa suffered the destructive effects of the slave trade over
several centuries, but actual European penetration into most
of the continent did not come until the 'imperialist' stage,
much later than in Asia or Latin America. It is, in general, the
least developed continent, with tiny industrial sectors and
low levels of income, and is still ravaged by famine and
disease.

Despite these differences, one could still talk, in the middle
of the twentieth century, of a 'typical' underdeveloped
country, with a small proportion of the population employed

9

in modern industry, and large, low-productivity, agricultural and service sectors. Wages and incomes are low (except for a small elite). Agriculture mainly consists of small peasant holdings, except where there are plantations producing for export. These peasant farms are no longer self-sufficient 'subsistence' holdings, but are integrated into the market system. Foreign trade generally accounts for a rather large fraction of total national income, with imports of capital goods, intermediate products and raw materials paid for by exports of primary products or labour-intensive manufactures. Export earnings also have to finance outflows of dividends, interest and royalties. Underdeveloped countries generally trade with advanced countries and not with each other. This pattern is clearly quite unlike that of an 'untouched' pre-capitalist economy, and is the result of incorporation into the world capitalist system. By the last quarter of the century, some underdeveloped countries were industrializing rapidly, and moving towards the structure of a typical advanced country, while others were stagnating.

The class structure of underdeveloped countries in the mid-twentieth century was distinctively different both from that of a pre-capitalist society and from that of the advanced countries, though in some places it was changing fairly rapidly towards the pattern of the developed capitalist countries. The small scale of industry and its domination by foreign firms with labour-saving production methods meant that the industrial working class and local industrial capital, important forces in advanced countries, were small. In their absence, the system was dominated by local representatives and affiliates of multinational companies, by trading interests and by landlords. The largest popular classes were the peasantry and the urban 'lumpenproletariat' of unemployed or casually employed workers.

Advanced and underdeveloped countries, then, are complementary halves of a very unequal world system, the product of a process of development stretching back centuries. At different stages in its evolution, and in different areas, it has taken very different forms. A complete theory of imperialism must account for all of them.

10

1.2 HISTORICAL MATERIALISM

The writers surveyed in this book share a common set of assumptions. All assigned a central role to the evolution of the economic system, and all agreed that imperialism must be explained in terms of the development of capitalism. This approach derives, of course, from Marx. In this section I will briefly summarize some of the elements of Marx's method, *historical materialism*.

Marx observed that production is always social; Robinson Crusoe is a myth. Seen from a technical, physical point of view (*the forces of production*) or in terms of the actual activity of work (*the labour process*), production is the activity of human beings working in the natural environment to modify it to meet their needs. As a social process, however, it also involves relations between people, the *(social) relations of production*, which govern access to the means of production and the use of the product. These relations are not a matter of deliberate choice; the organization of production in, say, Europe today is not the result of a conscious decision that wage-labour in capitalist factories is a better system than the serfdom of the Middle Ages or the slave system of Antiquity. It is the product of a long process of historical evolution. Marx argued that the analysis of society must start from the structure of social relations, not from individual choices or motivations:

> In the social production of their existence, men enter into definite, necessary relations, which are independent of their will, namely relations of production corresponding to a determinate stage of development of their material forces of production. The totality of these relations of production constitutes the economic structure of society, the real foundation on which there arises a legal and political superstructure and to which there correspond definite forms of social consciousness. The mode of production of material life conditions the social, political and intellectual life-process in general. (Marx 1976: 3)

Marx's assertion that the economic 'foundation' ultimately governs the 'social, political and intellectual life-processes in general' is one of the most controversial aspects of his work.

It does not seem to me to be useful to discuss it at a general level; the test is whether it can be justified by detailed analysis in particular cases. I propose to treat it as a working hypothesis, adopted for purposes of argument.

Marx insisted on the need for abstraction. Society is too complex to be grasped as a totality, an integrated whole, in a single step. Instead, we must isolate the simplest and most fundamental social relations and build up an abstract representation of how they work and how they fit together. Concepts developed in this way can then be used to construct an analysis of the real (or 'concrete') world. However, a single set of abstract concepts will not serve for the analysis of all societies. Marx praised the classical economists (of the late eighteenth and early nineteenth centuries, notably Smith and Ricardo) for recognizing the need for abstraction, but criticized them for applying concepts appropriate to the analysis of the capitalist economies of their time to all periods of history, failing to recognize the historical specificity of capitalism. Different stages of development are characterized by particular, different structures, and a separate process of abstraction is needed for each. A *mode of production*, in the abstract, is a simple, basic structure of social relations that is the starting point for the analysis of a particular stage of history. It is essential to Marx's approach that there are only a limited number of these basic forms.

Each mode of production (except the simplest, the primitive-communal, and the highest, the future communist mode) defines a pair of opposed *classes*, a class of producers exploited by a non-producing class. The relation between these two classes is the central, defining feature of the mode of production. At this level of abstraction, classes should not be thought of primarily as groups of people, but as opposing positions within a structure of social relations. In particular, a class cannot be conceived of in isolation, since it only constitutes a class by virtue of its relation to another class; there cannot be employers without employees, slave-owners without slaves, and so on.

Marx's original idea was simple and elegant. The various modes of production are successive stages in the history of human society. Each has its own structure and can 'reproduce' itself, that is, it can maintain both the forces of production (by replacing used-up means of production, and

12

so on) and the relations of production (by perpetuating the subordination of one class to another). The mechanisms of reproduction differ, of course, between different modes. The stability of each mode, however, is only relative; each generates development of the forces of production and, in the process, brings about changes in its own functioning that lead in the end to a breakdown of the existing structure and its replacement by the next in the sequence.

> At a certain stage in their development, the material productive forces of society come into conflict with the existing relations of production. . . . From forms of development of the productive forces these relations turn into their fetters. At that point an era of social revolution begins. . . . In broad outline, the Asian, ancient, feudal and modern bourgeois [capitalist] modes of production may be designated as progressive epochs of the socio-economic order. (Marx 1976: 3-4)

Society, in this account, has evolved from a (rather nebulous) primitive-communal stage, through the ancient and feudal periods, into the capitalist societies of Marx's (and our) time, which will in turn be replaced by communism. The ancient mode is defined by the opposition between slaves and free, slave-owning citizens, while the feudal mode, in its classic form, involves production for local use by a class of unfree peasants or serfs who control their own subsistence plots, but are compelled, by extra-economic coercion, to support a class of feudal landlords.

The most frequently studied mode of production, the only one that Marx analysed in detail, is the capitalist mode, characterized by (1) generalized commodity production, production for the market by many distinct and unco-ordinated units of production, together with (2) polarization of wealth, so a class of owners of the means of production confronts a class of free but propertyless workers. Ownership of the means of production excludes non-owners (workers) from production, except on terms acceptable to the owners. Workers have to sell their labour-power (their capacity to work) to capitalists in return for wages, which they spend on the goods they need to live. Marx's analysis of capitalism is discussed in more detail in chapter 2.

Marx recognized that non-European history could not be fitted into this 'Eurocentric' succession of stages, and he introduced the Asiatic mode (discussed further in chapter 2) to deal with this problem. The point of the Asiatic mode is that it does not develop in a way that leads on to further stages, but tends to persist unless disrupted from outside. He also admitted that the succession of stages could be broken by outside influences, especially by conquest.

> In all conquests there are three possibilities. The conquering nation subjects the conquered nation to its own mode of production . . .; or it allows the old mode to remain and is content with tribute . . .; or interaction takes place, which gives rise to a new system, a synthesis. . . . In all cases the mode of production – whether that of the conqueror or of the conquered nation or the one resulting from the fusion of the two – is the determinant of the new distribution that occurs. (Marx 1976: 27)

A real society cannot, in any case, be reduced to a single abstract mode of production. Marx argued that: 'In every social formation there is a specific kind of production that predominates over all the others, and whose relations therefore determine their rank and influence. It is a general illuminant tingeing all other colours and modifying their specific features' (1976: 39). Relations characteristic of several modes of production may be combined in a 'social formation' with one predominating. This idea has been revived recently (see chapter 10). Among other advantages, it makes a place for the 'petty-commodity' mode of production (production for the market by independent producers who own their own means of production), which has never predominated, and therefore cannot appear in a list of stages.

Once we regard modes of production as basic forms of organization which can be combined and elaborated in many ways in different historical circumstances, the range of possibilities becomes almost infinite. A limited number of modes can be analysed carefully in (conceptual) isolation, then complications can be built in to analyse a rich variety of real situations. This is the scientific method; the discovery of simple ideas to elucidate complex problems.

What Marx left, in short, was not a complete interpretation of history, but a fragmentary outline of European history, an analysis of the capitalist mode of production, and some tantalizingly brief indications of how his analysis could be extended. It would be foolish to treat Marx's writings as holy writ. In the study of imperialism, a central problem is to analyse the interactions between initially very different societies, with different dominant modes of production. Marx's few writings on India and Ireland (discussed in chapter 2 below) are not particularly helpful, but his method has proved very fruitful, as I hope to show.

In an analysis of imperialism, the actions of (capitalist) states must play an important role. It is almost an axiom of Marxist theory that the state acts to defend the interests of the ruling class (the dominant exploiting class). There are many statements to this effect in Marx's writing, although he presented very little detailed analysis to support it. The state was one of the (many) topics he planned to work on and write about, but never managed to reach.

It is fairly easy to see why the state should act to preserve the broad outlines of the existing social system. The ruling class is normally well organized to defend its interests, and the higher level personnel of the state (politicians, bureaucrats, military officers, etc.) have a clear interest in preserving the existing state organization, which could hardly hope to survive a wholesale change in the social order. In any case, a failure to meet the essential needs of the dominant mode could only result in chaos and economic regression in the absence of a positive alternative. Support for the existing order does not imply unthinking conservatism. On the contrary, it requires constant adaptation to changing circumstances, and may mean acting against the interests of particular sections of the ruling class. It does not follow either, that the state will succeed in this task; circumstances may overwhelm it, and the historic role of stupidity and error should not be underrated.

There remain many alternative policies consistent with preserving the system. An assertion that the state acts in the interests of the 'ruling class' is not self-evident, and may not even be meaningful. There are always, in practice, divisions of interest within the capitalist class, so the interests of the class as a whole are not clearly defined. Some Marxists appear to believe in a special providence which ensures that state policies always coincide with the 'objective requirements of expanded reproduction', or something of the sort. This is ridiculous; policies are the outcome of clashing sectional interests within and across class boundaries, in a particular political and ideological structure. The state, it is often said, has a certain 'relative autonomy'. Some work has been done on these lines, but the construction of general theories is at a very early stage, leaving something of a gap in the theory of imperialism. In most of the theories discussed below, the focus is on an economic analysis which 'explains' policies by showing that they serve the interests of (major sections of) the capitalist class. I shall concentrate on the economics of imperialism, following the general trend of the literature. Economic issues are, at the least, an important part of the story.

1.3 THEORIES OF CAPITALISM AS A WORLD SYSTEM

Marxist theories of the development of capitalism on a world scale fall into two groups: those that concentrate on the progressive role of capitalism in developing the forces of production, and those that present capitalism as a system of exploitation of one area by another, so development in a few places is at the expense of the 'development of under-development' in most of the world. Capitalism, according to the first approach, creates the material preconditions for a better (socialist) society, as well as the class forces that will bring it about, while the second approach suggests that it is precisely the failure of capitalism to generate economic development that makes revolution necessary. The historical record suggests that there is an element of truth to both of these opposed positions; capitalism has generated massive technological and economic advances and also enormous geographical disparities in economic development.

The first of these views is broadly that held by the 'classical' Marxists, from Marx to Lenin and his contemporaries. It has been strongly revived in recent years. According to this account, the development of each country is determined primarily by its internal structure, specifically by the nature of the dominant mode of production. Capitalism, a system in which free wage workers are employed by competing firms, tends to generate economic development, while other modes do not (at least on the same scale). External forces have their effect primarily by altering the organization of production. Competition is at the heart of a classical Marxist analysis of capitalism. The largest, most efficient firms with the newest capital equipment are the most profitable, and can increase their lead, while weaker firms fall behind and the weakest are eliminated by bankruptcy or takeover. The threat of failure forces firms to maximize profits, to reinvest profits for expansion, and to seek out new methods of production, new markets, and new sources of supply. In pre-capitalist modes of production, by contrast, the exploiting class must, above all, maintain the basis of the extra-economic coercion which they exercise over the producers. As a result pre-capitalist systems are relatively static, dominated by custom, with the (potentially investable) surplus redirected into non-productive channels.

The expansion of capitalism constantly expands the demand for natural resources (minerals, land, etc.); this is one motive behind the geographical expansion of capitalism. Even with a static demand, development of transport and the search for cheaper sources of goods will tend to draw new areas into the capitalist orbit. The search for cheap labour is yet another motive for geographical expansion.

In the classical Marxist account, grossly oversimplified, capitalism emerged first in a few centres, generating capital accumulation and development there, and opening up a lead over the rest of the world without necessarily taking anything from it (though capital will always take what it can get). Capitalism spread, starting the same process in other areas. Different parts of the world are runners in the same race, in which some started before others. Any advantage gained by one at the expense of others is incidental.

The alternative view has been developed since the Second World War, notably by Frank and Wallerstein, as a response to the apparent failure of capitalist development in many parts of the world. In this view, the unit of analysis must be a world system, with differing geographical areas or nation states as mere component parts. Capitalism is not defined by a specific relation between classes, but by production for profit in a world system of exchange, and by the exploitation of some areas by others. The 'metropolis' or 'core' exploits the 'satellites' or 'periphery' by direct extraction of profit or tribute, by unequal exchange, or by monopolistic control over trade. In the periphery, ruling classes owe their position to their function as intermediaries in the system of exploitation, so they have an interest in preserving it and in preserving the corresponding patterns of production. Underdevelopment is not a state of original backwardness; it is the result of the imposition of a particular pattern of specialization and exploitation in the periphery. Within the world system, different forms of 'labour control' may be used: forced labour, wage-labour, slavery, and so on. The class structures of different nations, and particular forms of exploitation in production, are merely results of the place of the areas concerned in the world system, not the key determining factors (as they are in a classical Marxist analysis).

In this approach, oversimplified, capital accumulation is seen not as a precondition for genuine, qualitative advances in the level and methods of production, but rather as a redivision of a fixed magnitude, a transfer of resources from the exploited periphery to the centre. Development in some areas and the 'development of underdevelopment' in others are opposite sides of the same coin.

These two views involve quite different readings of history. In the classical Marxist view, capitalism started off in a few places and has since spread out geographically in a process of internationalization of capital, and has evolved through a succession of stages, with key turning points in the industrial revolution and when large-scale export of capital (not goods) started. According to Frank and Wallerstein, by contrast, capitalism as a world system dates from the sixteenth century, and has remained essentially unchanged ever since. The classical Marxists saw capitalism in dynamic terms, while their opponents saw it as a basically static system of exploitation.

The contradictions between these two views should not be overstressed, though they are very real. The world economy is a complex whole in which relations of production and exploitation exist both within and between nations. It may not matter much whether we say that underdevelopment is the product of external influences (which also determine a certain class structure and organization of production), or that underdevelopment is caused by a certain class structure and organization of production (which may be in whole or part the result of external influences). When we get to a more detailed level of analysis there are many theories that cut across this simple classification. It is, nevertheless, a helpful preliminary way of ordering the material.

The definition of the term 'underdevelopment' differs according to the approach adopted. In the classical view, underdevelopment is synonymous with backwardness, with an early stage of development. Frank and his followers, on the other hand, argue that an isolated country could not be called underdeveloped, as underdevelopment is defined by incorporation into a world system in a subordinate position. Whichever definition is adopted, there is little doubt as to which category to put any particular country in, so there is not likely to be much confusion. I shall use the term descriptively; an underdeveloped country is one that shows the general structural features of underdevelopment described in section 1.1 above.

Marx (chapter 2) concentrated on a closed and wholly capitalist economy in his main theoretical work. In a rather less formal way, he analysed the origins and expansion of capitalism within a single nation state. His importance to the theory of imperialism is primarily that he established a basic framework of analysis that other writers have built on. His articles on India make it clear that he saw British rule, however brutal, as ultimately progressive, because it laid the foundations for subsequent capitalist development.

Luxemburg (chapter 3) developed Marx's picture of the expansion of capitalism into the pre-capitalist societies that surround it. She advanced two explanations for this expansion. The first is that capitalist economies suffer a chronic problem of 'realization', that is of selling the products produced for sale, and must therefore seek markets abroad. This idea recurs in a variety of forms in the history of imperialism, and I shall refer to it as 'under-consumptionism' (though Luxemburg's variant of it does not exactly fit the term). I shall argue that under-consumptionism is mistaken. She also argued that competitive pressures lead to expansion, in search of raw materials and cheap labour, and here I think she is right. In either case pre-capitalist 'natural' (non-market) economies cannot be penetrated by simple market

19

competition, for lack of markets to compete in, and must therefore be broken open by force.

Hobson (chapter 4) was not a Marxist, but he deserves a mention in a survey of Marxist theories because his work has influenced many Marxist writers. He presented one of the first coherent accounts of imperialism (before Luxemburg). His version of under-consumption is the prototype of many, and he was one of the first to link the scramble for Africa and the intensified inter-imperialist rivalry at the end of the nineteenth century to the development of monopoly; this became a major theme of Marxist writing on imperialism.

Hilferding, Bukharin and Lenin (chapters 5 and 6), the main authors of what I will call the 'classical Marxist theory of imperialism' (since Marx did not discuss imperialism as such), wrote immediately before and during the First World War. In economic life, the main change since Marx's time had been the development of monopoly, fulfilling his prediction that the competitive process, with its constant elimination of smaller and weaker firms, would generate a tendency to monopoly. It remained, however, to analyse the results of this development. At the same time, there was a scramble for colonies, and intense antagonisms emerged between the main capitalist powers. All three writers stressed the formation of monopolies on a national basis, and the intensification of competition on a world scale between national groupings of capital. At the same time, they predicted an acceleration of capitalist development in backward areas of the world.

Hilferding's main contribution (chapter 5) was the concept of 'finance capital', the fusion of industrial and financial capital into huge interlocking groups. These groups do not compete with each other by price cutting: they enlist state support to gain control of whole industries by financial and political means. Most of the elements of a theory of inter-imperialist rivalry were worked out by Hilferding, but his main focus was on the internal development of capitalist economies.

Bukharin (chapter 6) transformed Hilferding's analysis by setting it in the context of a world economy in which two tendencies were at work. The tendency to monopoly and the formation of groups of finance capital is one, and the other is an acceleration of the geographical spread of capitalism and its integration into a single world capitalist economy. Blocs of finance capital form on a national basis, because of their links with national states. Competition thus becomes competition between 'state capitalist trusts', with annexation and war as means employed in the competitive struggle. Lenin's pamphlet on imperialism (also discussed in chapter 6) follows Bukharin in most respects while avoiding the main issues of theory, and adding elements taken from Hobson. Lenin insisted that imperialism should be regarded as a stage of capitalist development, the monopoly stage, rather than being a policy of capitalist states or an aspect of the relations between capitalist states. This terminology can cause some confusion, since other writers (following everyday usage) used the term to refer specifically to international relations of dominance and exploitation. His rather obscure treatment of the reasons for capital export, which could be interpreted in terms of Marx's theory of the falling rate of profit, or in terms of under-consumptionist theories, has also caused confusion. Altogether, Lenin's pamphlet has been treated with a reverence it does not deserve.

The work of Baran (chapter 7) represents a turning point in the theory of capitalist development on a world scale. The classical Marxists, from Marx to Lenin, had expected full capitalist development, in due course, throughout the world. Baran argued that the destiny of the underdeveloped countries was distinctively different from that of areas that developed at an earlier date. Monopoly, he argued, leads to restriction of output and investment, and hence to low growth (in all parts of the world). In advanced countries output is high, and high monopoly profits depress workers' consumption, so there is a chronic shortage of demand (this is almost identical to Hobson's argument). In underdeveloped countries the 'surplus' is partly absorbed by the luxury spending of the ruling class, but much of it is transferred to the advanced countries (as profits), where it contributes to the problem of absorbing the rising surplus. Monopoly thus transforms capitalism from a force for development into a cause of stagnation, both in advanced and in underdeveloped countries. In underdeveloped countries, however, there was no competitive stage, so they are 'frozen' at a low level of production and income.

Marxist and radical writings of the 1960s and 1970s were dominated by the idea that capitalism blocks development in

21

the Third World, because the countries of the 'periphery' are dependent on the countries of the 'centre', a line of argument that became known as dependency theory (chapter 8). Frank was a central figure in the resulting debates. I shall argue that his theories have crucial weaknesses. Frank's conception of capitalism as a world-wide system of monopolistic exchange and exploitation has already been described. The main criticism of this approach is that it ignores the role of relations of production in determining both the dynamics and the class structure of the system. Amin incorporated a formal analysis of international exchange into an account of accumulation on a world scale. He argued that the impact of developed capitalism on less developed or pre-capitalist areas imposes a pattern of specialization that limits future development. His version of dependency theory improves on its predecessors by including an explicit treatment of 'unequal specialization'. Important weaknesses, however, remain. The determinants of the development of productivity in different areas remain unclear, and his version of dependency theory, like others, has under-consumptionist elements which seem to me to be mistaken.

Emmanuel's theory of 'unequal exchange' (chapter 9) has started a new line of its own. He too saw capitalism as a world system of exploitation through exchange, but in his model surplus can be transferred through trade in competitive markets, without monopoly. An essential component of Marx's theory of a closed capitalist economy is the establishment of a single general rate of profit and a corresponding set of 'prices of production'. Marxist theories of the world economy had no corresponding linkage between the analysis of production and of exchange, until Emmanuel provided a theory of the determination of prices of production in a world economy. The main assumption is that capital is mobile internationally, while labour is not. The main criticism of his analysis is that certain key variables (the pattern of specialization, productivity, wages) are not adequately explained. He made a useful contribution to a theory of the world economy, but claimed too much for it.

There have also been a number of debates on more specific issues, generally revolving around the differences between the Frank–Wallerstein position and the newly revived classical Marxist approach. One major area of debate surrounds the concept of a mode of production, and its application to contemporary underdeveloped countries (chapter 10). The central point at issue here is whether the ① internal structure of underdeveloped countries can be conceptualized in terms of the persistence of pre-capitalist relations of production and, if so, whether this is cause or consequence of their backwardness. A second area of debate ② centres on trends in the relative standing of different capitalist states (chapter 11). In the post-war period, most Marxists assumed that the United States would maintain or increase its dominance as the principal imperialist power, and that underdeveloped countries would inevitably become relatively, if not absolutely, poorer and more thoroughly subordinated as long as they remain part of the world capitalist system. Capitalism was seen as a stable, self-reinforcing global system of inequality. This view has now been undermined by experience; American hegemony has crumbled, and there has been rapid capitalist development in some parts of the underdeveloped world. — *like what?* ③

Taken together, the writings surveyed in this book seem to me to provide most of the makings of a coherent theory of the *the Asian* evolution of capitalism on a world scale, though such a *miracle"-* theory has yet to be worked out in detail. What follows is my *Singapore,* guess at the form it might take. It is only a tentative outline; *Taiwan, etc* to go further would go beyond the scope of this work.

The 'mercantile' period was characterized by very loose integration of the world economy, so developments in different parts of the world were determined primarily by the dominant mode of production in each area. Transport costs were high, long-distance trade was mainly in luxuries and both capital and skills were relatively immobile. Europe advanced because Europe was becoming capitalist. Elsewhere, European military power had its effect mainly by transforming the mode of production, either installing (pre-capitalist) forms of exploitation from the outside (as in Latin America) or clearing the ground for future capitalist development (as in North America).

The nineteenth century was a period of transition. The emerging world economy was still rather loosely integrated, and the emergence of new centres was still possible where internal conditions were ripe and resolute state support was forthcoming. At the same time, the development of capitalism in Europe and North America was breaking up mercantile monopolies, bringing down transport costs, and inaugurating a new stage of development. As the world economy became more closely integrated, the developed industrial centres had a crucial advantage, since productivity levels were rising while wages remained relatively low. As a result, they had a crushing cost advantage in all the main lines of industrial production, and relatively backward areas were confined to natural-resource-linked activities. The advantages of the more developed areas could not easily be transferred, since skills were mainly in the hands of the workers, and capital tended to flow towards concentrations of skills. The need for a network of specialized services and suppliers had a similar effect. These 'external economies' were especially important in the epoch of competitive capitalism, but remain important now.

Monopoly capital, however, tends to 'internalize' external economies by taking over external suppliers and by codifying and routinizing skills. Modern multinational firms are able to transfer technology to new locations with relatively low additional costs. At the same time, wage levels in advanced countries have been rising. The cost advantages of established industrial centres have been eroded on both counts. There is now a clear tendency for production to be shifted to low-wage areas in underdeveloped countries, although it will take a very long time for this tendency to work its way through the whole range of industries.

It does not follow that the whole of the Third World can look forward to complete capitalist industrialization, since the emergence of new poles of development will intensify competition and eliminate weaker competitors. Equally, the mass of the population in newly industrializing countries may not gain much for a long time. Capital-intensive methods of production hold down the demand for labour and the resulting unemployment holds down wages. The prospect is one of uneven development as between different areas, accompanied by working-class poverty – very much what Marx predicted over a century ago.

2

Marx

Marx did not use the word 'imperialism', nor is there anything in his work that corresponds at all exactly to the concepts of imperialism advanced by later Marxist writers. He did, of course, have a theory of capitalism, and of its development, and his work contains extensive, if rather scattered, coverage of the impact of capitalism on non-European societies. Unlike many of his successors, Marx saw the relative backwardness of the non-European world, and its subjection to European masters, as a transient stage in the formation of a wholly capitalist world economy. Marxist writers have drawn on various elements of Marx's theory in their work on imperialism. They have not, in general, based their analysis of imperialism on Marx's writings on colonies.

I shall first set out, very briefly, Marx's theory of a wholly capitalist system. Marx argued that capitalism could in principle exist and develop on its own, without needing to expand into surrounding pre-capitalist societies. In fact, however, capitalism emerged in a wider pre-capitalist world, so the next step will be to look at Marx's theory of the origins of capitalism, and of its expansion at the expense of other modes of production. Finally, I shall survey Marx's writings on colonies, and in particular the famous articles on India. The first two sections, then, deal with the capitalist mode of production in the abstract, the rest of the chapter with its insertion into social formations that are not wholly capitalist.

A preliminary comment on terminology: Marx did not have a generic term to describe the rule of a more advanced nation state over a more backward area. I have used the term *colonialism*, which has been widely adopted since. When Marx himself used this term it was usually to refer to European settlement in areas from which the indigenous inhabitants had been expelled (such as Australia and America).

2.1 CAPITALISM

The heart of Marx's life work was the analysis of the capitalist mode of production, contained in *Capital*, volumes I-III (Marx 1961, 1957, 1962, cited below by title and volume number). The centrepiece is a theory of a closed, homogeneous, capitalist economy. Labour-power has a single price, governed by the value of labour-power, and, when prices of production are introduced (in the third volume), there is a single general rate of profit which accrues to all capitals. This is an abstraction, of course, and throughout the three volumes Marx used examples to link the abstract theory to a far more complex reality. Within the theory, though, there is no space for any differences in economic conditions between different countries. Marx's conception of the capitalist mode of production is diametrically opposed to that of dependency theorists like Frank, for whom the centre–periphery relation is an essential feature of capitalism.

In this section, I shall outline the basic theory very briefly, with the focus on key concepts used by later writers. This is not a text on Marxist economic theory: there is a substantial literature on the subject for those who wish to read more (e.g. Brewer 1984; Foley 1986; Howard and King 1985).

Capitalism is a particular form of *commodity production*, production of goods for sale on the market. This form of economy exists where there are many independent producers who produce goods for sale rather than for their own use. Marx distinguished between the *use value* of a commodity, the use to which it can be put, and its *exchange value*, what can be got in exchange for it. The production of use values is absolutely essential to the survival of any society, but in a commodity-producing system this is obscured by the fact that the producer is interested only in the exchange value of the product.

Marx argued that exchange values are explained and determined by *(labour) values*, where the value of a commodity is defined as the *socially necessary labour time* (measured in hours), directly or indirectly required to reproduce it. The labour theory of value has been the subject of much debate (e.g. Morishima 1973, 1974, 1976; Steedman 1975, 1977; Himmelweit and Mohun 1978; Wright 1979). The difficulty in using labour values is that goods do not, in fact, exchange at their values in a developed capitalist economy; they exchange at market prices which fluctuate around prices of production (see below). In cases of joint production and in any but the simplest cases involving fixed capital, values are hard to define satisfactorily, and are liable to come out negative, or to fail to add up correctly (Steedman 1975, 1976, 1977). Very few theories of imperialism depend heavily on the labour theory of value, so labour values can be treated simply as a convenient way to set out Marx's theory. The main propositions could be restated in terms of other theories of price, but I shall use labour values, since that was how Marx did it. The heart of Marx's theory, his account of the social relations of capitalism, does not depend on the labour theory of value.

Marx then asked: what is the source of the *surplus value* (roughly, profit) which accrues to a capitalist? He found the answer in the specific social relation which links a wage worker with a capitalist employer. The worker, he said, sells his *labour-power*, his capacity to work, rather than his labour. The distinction between labour-power and labour is crucial to the labour theory of value (the labour value of labour would be a nonsense), but it also reflects a central feature of capitalism; the actual work process, the conversion of labour-power into actual work itself, is carried out under the authority of the new owner of labour-power, its buyer, the capitalist. The capitalist also buys *means of production* (materials, equipment, etc.) for the worker to work with.

The value created by labour corresponds to the number of hours worked in (say) a day (given average conditions of production), but the wage paid by the capitalist corresponds to the *value of labour-power*, that is, the labour required to reproduce a day's labour-power, which is, in turn, the value of the commodities needed for the subsistence of the worker (and his family, since the worker must be reproduced). If the value created in a day exceeds the value of a day's labour-power then there is surplus value which the capitalist can pocket when he sells the product. In terms of the relationship between the workers as a whole and capital as a whole this amounts to saying that profit (or surplus value) exists when the workers produce more than they get. Surplus value, in other words, corresponds to a *surplus product*. For an individual capitalist, however, profit (or surplus value) depends on prices (or values), since the commodities individual workers get are not the same as those they produce; where the goods produced and consumed are not the same we cannot subtract the one from the other unless they can be reduced to a common unit. For an open economy the same problem exists when workers produce goods for export and consume, in part, imported goods.

Marx's theory of the wage (or value of labour-power) is something of a difficulty. He stated that the commodities needed by workers are not determined by purely physiological needs, though these set a minimum, but also contain a 'historical and moral' element. In other parts of his work, notably the pamphlet *Wage, Price and Profit*, there are elements of a theory of the determination of wages by bargaining power. What is clear is that if wages rise so far as to reduce profits below some minimum level, there will be a cessation of production and a crisis. This sets an upper limit to wages which ensures the existence of profit.

Capital, in this framework, is 'value in process', money or commodities being used to produce surplus value. An individual capitalist's wealth is first in the form of money, then of means of production and labour-power, then of the commodities produced, and finally in the form of money, from the sale of the product, ready to start the cycle again. (In practice these stages overlap.) Capital is defined by the cycle as a whole. In measuring the capital involved we count the value of money, work in progress, means of production and final commodities. This differs from the definition of capital used in non-Marxist economics in two ways: the latter is narrower, in only including means of production, but wider in including means of production regardless of the social context. For Marx wealth is only capital if it is used by capitalists to produce surplus value in a capitalist system. I shall use this definition throughout. To put it another way, conventional economics treats capital as a technical requirement of production. Marx saw it as a social relation which defines a specific *mode of production*.

We should pause here to consider the status of the two 'spheres' of *production* and *circulation* (exchange). Both are integral parts of the *circuit of capital*, the cycle described above. A capitalist economy consists of many separate enterprises, each controlled by a capitalist owner, linked together by market exchange, which is not controlled by anyone; capitalist production is anarchic and is governed by the blind working of economic laws independent of the will of any individual. The circuits of different capitals intertwine with each other: each buys means of production from others, while workers buy means of subsistence from one capitalist with wages paid by another. Capitalist production as a whole includes many separate production processes and the processes of exchange that link them. Both are integral parts of production as a social process. Some Marxists have tried to argue that production (narrowly defined) is in some sense the primary element and circulation secondary. In view of the discussion above, this view will not stand up.

It is possible for part of production to be carried out under capitalist relations of production and part under pre-capitalist relations, linked by exchange, as in the relation between slave plantations in America and the Lancashire cotton textile industry at the time of the industrial revolution. Some writers describe this as wholly capitalist production (with an unorthodox form of labour discipline on the plantations), others as a relationship between two different modes of production. The question seems, at least in part, semantic. The important point is that there is a social process of production encompassing both capitalist and pre-capitalist relations of production, an important possibility in systems of commodity production. This, however, is to jump ahead; my concern at the moment is with a wholly capitalist system.

The essential character of a capitalist system comes out most clearly in Marx's discussion of the *reproduction* of the system. For simplicity, he used the device of *simple reproduction*, in which the system is reconstituted exactly as before after each cycle of production, before moving on to *reproduction on an extended scale* (also called expanded reproduction, reproduction on a progressively increasing scale, and so on), where part of profit is accumulated, as new capital, and the system grows. Note also that the idea of a simple 'period of production', starting with means of production, wage goods for workers' consumption, and so on, and ending when they have been used up and replaced by newly produced goods, is another analytical fiction which simplifies the story without affecting the principles involved.

Consider first the relation between workers and capital. At the start of a period of production, workers have no wealth, 'nothing to sell but their labour-power', and therefore have no option but to look for a job. They cannot produce on their own account, since they cannot afford to buy means of production. The capitalist pays them a wage, enough to cover their (socially determined) needs. At the end of the period of production the workers have spent their wages, and are back where they started, forced once again to seek a job. Throughout, Marx assumed that there is a *reserve army of labour*, a pool of unemployed workers competing for jobs and keeping wages down. If expansion of the system absorbs all these unemployed workers, the threat of unemployment no longer holds down wages and maintains labour discipline; a crisis follows, reducing production, promoting labour-saving investment, and reconstituting the reserve army. Capitalists, on the other hand, start with purchasing power (*money capital*) sufficient to pay wages (*variable capital*) and buy means of production (*constant capital*). At the end of the process they get enough revenue to replace the outlay, plus a surplus (profit), which can be used entirely for their own consumption (simple reproduction) or partly for new investment (expanded reproduction). Starting, then, from a situation in which owners of commodities (capitalists) confront propertyless workers, the cycle of production ends with the reproduction of the same confrontation between the same two classes, ready for the cycle to start again. Where capitalism came from in the first place, is a different question, to be taken up later.

To ensure the reproduction of the system, it is not enough that capitalists should get surplus value. Capitalism is a species of commodity production, so production is carried out by many separate capitals with no central co-ordinating plan. The right mix of use values (means of production, necessities of consumption and so on) must be produced. Marx analysed this problem in the final chapters of *Capital* II, in terms of the exchange between two *departments* of social production: department 1, industries producing means of production; and department 2, producing consumer goods. He showed, using numerical examples, or *schemes of reproduction*, that there is a certain relation between the outputs of the two departments consistent with simple reproduction, and another relation, depending on the rate of accumulation, consistent with extended reproduction. It is easy to see how this analysis could be pursued in more detail to determine the necessary proportions between different branches of production within each department.

One aspect of Marx's analysis of reproduction which is very relevant to the theory of imperialism and which has caused endless debate is the question of markets. How can capitalists hope to sell all the goods they produce? There is an argument used by many Marxist theorists, which I shall label *under-consumptionism* (see Bleaney 1976; a number of variants of under-consumptionism will be discussed in later chapters, especially chapters 4, 7 and 8). In its simplest form it goes like this: if the workers cannot afford to buy the whole product, who can the capitalists sell it to? In simple reproduction, Marx's answer was that the capitalists consume the surplus product themselves. This entails selling to each other, since each specializes in the production of a particular product, but wishes to consume others. In a growing economy, capitalists still exchange the surplus product among themselves, but buy means of production for new investment instead of means of consumption, and the proportions between the two departments, 1 and 2, must be correspondingly different. The argument is slightly complicated by the assumption that wages are paid in advance; some of the new investment takes the form of wage payments to additional workers, who spend the money on consumer goods. The money used to carry out transactions is not a problem either, since it passes from hand to hand without being used up. At the end of each cycle it has returned to its starting point, ready to circulate again.

The core idea of under-consumptionism is that consumer demand is somehow more fundamental than demand for means of production, that the latter only exists to provide for the former. It is often argued (Hobson 1938, is a classic case) that if consumption is (say) static, because wages are constant, then there will be no incentive to invest. This is simply wrong, since investment can be directed to industries producing investment goods (means of production) as well as

31

to the consumer goods industries. Consumer demand has no special status in a capitalist framework; the bulk of it is from workers, who will only be employed if they contribute to profits, so both consumption and investment derive primarily from profit-seeking decisions by capitalists. If capitalists save and invest, more workers are needed, and total workers' consumption goes up.

It is possible that investment will be insufficient if profit prospects are poor. In this case, capitalists cut back on investment and employment, reducing demand and setting off a chain reaction. On the other hand, when high profits are expected, the chain reaction works the other way round. Marx expected capitalism to evolve through a series of booms (which ensure the development of the forces of production) and slumps, or 'periodic crises'. The schemes of expanded reproduction show that it is possible in principle for demand to expand in line with supply, though it is equally possible for the system to suffer crises (as it does in practice). The explanation of crises must be sought in the determinants of profitability, not in any inherent problem of demand. I shall discuss particular variants of under-consumptionism as they arise, notably those of Luxemburg, Hobson, and Sweezy. Under-consumptionist arguments are important in the theory of imperialism because they can explain a search for external markets to make up for the deficiency of demand at home.

2.2 THE DYNAMICS OF CAPITALISM

In Marx's theory, surplus value is generated by the gap between the value produced by a worker, which is simply the length of the working day, and the value of labour-power. Marx called the part of the working day equivalent to the value of the commodities the worker can buy with the wage, *necessary labour*; the rest is *surplus labour*. Surplus value can be increased by lengthening the working day. This is called *absolute surplus value*. It can also be increased by increasing productivity in the industries producing wage goods (or means of production used in the wage goods industries), thus reducing the value of labour-power (in hours of labour equivalent) without reducing the actual commodities the worker gets. This is *relative surplus value*. Looking at it

32

another way, the surplus product that workers produce can be increased either by making them work for longer (absolute surplus value) or by improving production methods so more is produced in the same time (relative surplus value). Absolute surplus value has a limit, set by physical exhaustion, while relative surplus value does not. Absolute surplus value is important in the early stages of capitalism, and in colonies, where working hours are forced up to the maximum and wages down to the minimum, while relative surplus value dominates in advanced capitalism.

Constant efforts to cut costs are forced on capitalists by competition, the primary driving force in capitalism. Any new method of production which reduces costs (a technical improvement, or an 'improvement' in labour discipline) will bring extra profits to those who introduce it quickly, before the general price level has been forced down. Once it is generally adopted, competition forces prices down in line with costs, wiping out any remaining high cost producers. Marx assumed (in general rightly) that large-scale production is more efficient than small-scale. Competition, therefore, forces capitalists to accumulate and reinvest as much as possible in order to produce on a large scale. Marx called growth through reinvestment of profits, *concentration of capital*. Bigger firms will be better able to survive, especially in slumps, and will be able to buy out smaller firms. The growth of the scale of production by amalgamation of capitals is called *centralization of capital*.

Despite the constant increase in efficiency produced by these processes, Marx asserted that there is a *tendency for the rate of profit to fall*; many Marxists have suggested that imperialism is a response to falling profits. Marx's argument is as follows: let c stand for the value of means of production used, v for the value of labour-power and s for the surplus value generated. Then s/v is called the rate of surplus value: surplus labour divided by necessary labour. The rate of profit, however is: $s/(c + v)$, since capitalists relate profit to the total capital invested, in means of production and in the purchase of labour-power. Now the profit rate, $s/(c + v) = (s/v)/((c/v) + 1)$, dividing top and bottom by v. The fraction c/v which appears on the bottom of this expression is called the *value composition of capital*.

Marx defined the *technical composition of capital* as the ratio of the mass (physical quantity) of means of production to the mass of labour employed. The *value composition of capital* is the ratio between their values. Marx said (*Capital* I: 612): 'I call the value composition of capital, in so far as it is determined by the technical composition and mirrors the changes of the latter, the *organic composition* of capital.' However, he often seems to have used the term 'organic composition' interchangeably with 'value composition'.

He claimed that c/v will rise as capital is accumulated, outweighing any rise in s/v (as a result of productivity increase), so the rate of profit will tend to fall. This is the law of the tendency of the rate of profit to fall. He then introduced a number of counter-tendencies; s/v may rise, wages may be depressed below the value of labour-power, and so on. The most important is the fact that if productivity is rising, the value of any given quantity of means of production will fall, since less labour is required to produce it. For this reason, the value of the means of production used need not rise even though the mass (physical quantity) does, so c/v need not increase in value terms. The 'falling rate of profit' theory depends, essentially, on rapid technical progress in consumer goods industries, using an increasing mass of means of production, without corresponding technical progress in the production of means of production. Another counter-tendency is foreign trade (*Capital* III: 232). Marx argued that capital invested in foreign trade may make high profits, for several reasons, including the possibility that the home country is more advanced and gains a super-profit just as the first firms with an innovation do, the possibility that labour may be more productive in the home country without being higher paid (the opposite of Emmanuel's argument, to be discussed later), and the high rate of exploitation in colonies. These are a ragbag of reasons with little theoretical backing; without an adequate theory of the world economy they can be nothing more. In any case, the theoretical argument is at the stage of analysing a closed and homogeneous capitalist economy, in which these factors have no place.

The decisive argument is the cheapening of the means of production, discussed above, since this cheapening is inherent in the process of capitalist development. There is no special reason to expect the value composition of capital either to rise or to fall. It can in any case be shown that capitalists will only adopt new techniques if they *increase* the rate of profit at the existing level of wages. Any technical innovation that reduces costs will also raise the general level of profits once it is in general use. (The classic proof is by Okishio 1961, 1963; see also Himmelweit 1974; Hodgson 1974; Bowles 1981; Roemer 1981; and Shaikh 1982.) Rejection of the falling rate of profit is still controversial, though the arguments cited above seem decisive to me. It has large implications for Marxist theory, since many Marxists have predicted an automatic collapse of capitalism because of falling profits. The alleged tendency for the rate of profit to fall has also been used to explain capital export and hence imperialism, sometimes regarded as part of a process of 'mobilizing the counter-tendencies' to falling profits. The falling rate of profit is quite unnecessary to these arguments, since they amount to saying that capital seeks cheap labour and high profits, which is sufficient explanation by itself.

Another quite distinct effect of competition is the formation of *prices of production* (which will be dealt with in more detail in chapter 9). The basic idea is that competing capitals move from one industry to another in search of higher profits. Where profits are high, an inflow of capital lowers them by increasing supply and depressing price. Relative prices must then deviate from values, since if prices were proportional to values, the rate of profit would be high in industries with a low value composition of capital, and vice versa. Mobility of capital leads to the formation of a single general rate of profit.

This analysis enabled Marx to deal with *commercial capital* (or *merchant's capital*), a specialized part of capital which takes over functions of buying and selling from industrial capital. According to the labour theory of value, surplus value arises in production, not exchange, so commercial capital does not produce surplus value. It does, however, perform a necessary function, since purchase and sale of commodities are essential parts of the circuit of capital, and must, therefore, receive a profit (from a difference between buying and selling prices) equivalent to the general rate of profit. Commercial capital played a much more important role in the origins of capitalism than in Marx's analysis of a pure capitalist system.

35

Another functional fraction of capital is *financial capital*, which performs a rather heterogeneous collection of functions unified by the fact that all involve handling money (as opposed to commodities), and by the fact that they permit a centralization of money capital. Industrial and commercial businesses frequently find themselves holding idle money balances. If a bank can collect idle money together it can economize on the actual money held, and put the rest to use by lending it out to other capitalists who are temporarily short of money. The savings of individuals (retired capitalists, members of non-capitalist classes and so on) can also be collected and put to use.

The importance of these different fractions of capital (industrial, commercial, financial) is that they define different sections of the capitalist class, which may have different interests. There are other divisions within the capitalist class, for example between small and large businesses and between capitals in different branches of production (agriculture, industry, etc.). One of the functions of political activity and of the state is to arbitrate between these different interests.

Summarizing the argument so far, Marx defined the capitalist mode of production in terms of the relation between two classes, wage workers and capitalists, and demonstrated how a closed capitalist system can reproduce itself on an expanding scale. Competition leads to capital accumulation, rising productivity, and concentration of capital into ever larger units. The next step is to analyse the emergence and development of capitalism in a previously pre-capitalist world, and the functioning of the capitalist mode of production in social formations which contain other modes as well.

2.3 THE ORIGINS OF CAPITALISM

Capitalism, once in existence, has a logic which can be captured by abstract theory, but its origins are a once-for-all process that must be explained in terms of specific historical circumstances. Since the defining feature of capitalism, for Marx, is the relation between a class of propertyless, free workers, and a class of private owners of the means of production, the essence of the problem is to explain how these two classes came into being.

Capitalism first emerged in Europe. It was transplanted, partly grown, to colonies of European settlement (America, Australia, etc.) and developed independently in Japan. In the rest of the world capitalism came from outside as an alien growth introduced, frequently, at the point of a gun. Marx did not regard this geographical pattern as accidental. He argued that the prospects for the development of capitalism depended crucially on the previous structure of society, which differed in different parts of the world. Europe (and Japan; *Capital* I, ch. 27: 718n) was dominated by the feudal mode of production, and most of Asia (particularly India and China) by the Asiatic mode of production.

The decay of the feudal mode of production created a fertile environment for the growth of capitalism, while the Asiatic mode did not, because feudalism involved a form of private property in land (the main means of production in a principally agrarian society), while the Asiatic mode of production was based on communal ownership of land. 'Bernier correctly discovers the basic form of all phenomena in the East – he refers to Turkey, Persia, Hindostan [India] – to be the *absence of private property* in land. This is the real key even to the Oriental heaven' (Marx 1969: 451). Since this aspect of Marx's thought is controversial I quote here some extracts from *Capital* to demonstrate Marx's view of the importance of the pre-existing social structure in determining the prospects for the development of capitalism.

> Usury has a revolutionary effect in all precapitalist modes of production only in so far as it destroys and dissolves those forms of property on whose solid foundation and continual reproduction in the same form the political organisation is based. Under Asian forms, usury can continue a long time, without producing anything more than economic decay and political corruption. Only where and when the other prerequisites of capitalist production are present does usury become one of the means assisting in establishing the new mode of production by ruining the feudal lord and small-scale producer, on the one hand, and centralising the conditions of labour into capital, on the other. (*Capital* III, ch. 36: 583-4)

To what extent [commerce] brings about a dissolution of the old mode of production depends on its solidity and internal structure. And whither this process of dissolution will lead, in other words what new mode of production will replace the old, does not depend on commerce, but on the character of the old mode of production itself. . . . The obstacles presented by the internal solidity and organisation of pre-capitalistic, national modes of production to the corrosive influence of commerce are strikingly illustrated in the intercourse of the English with India and China. . . . [In India] this work of dissolution proceeds very gradually. And still more slowly in China, where it is not reinforced by direct political power. (*Capital* III, ch. 20: 325, 328)

Both the Asiatic and feudal modes of production, in their pure forms, involve production for local use by peasant families, producing agricultural and handicraft goods for their own subsistence, and also supporting a ruling class who extract a surplus by extra-economic coercion. In the feudal mode of production, the key social relations link individuals (or families; succession to both rights and duties is normally hereditary); an individual lord has rights over a certain territory, and can exploit the peasants of that territory by extracting rent in labour services, in kind, or in money. Correspondingly, individual peasants are tied to particular plots of land, having the right to till that land and the corresponding duty to perform surplus labour for the landlord. In the Asiatic mode of production, the link is between a state (representing a ruling class) and the village communities which occupy the land, distribute it among their members according to customary rules, and are exploited by 'tax-rent'. The political organizations corresponding to these two modes of production mirror the difference in their economic organization; feudalism is characterized by 'parcellized' sovereignty (the phrase is from Anderson 1974) divided between many semi-independent feudal lords, while Asiatic society is 'despotic'. (For discussion of the concept of an Asiatic mode see Krader 1975 and Anderson 1974.)

There are difficulties with both concepts. The concept of the feudal mode as applied to Europe is well established, but there are disputes over its definition, deriving mainly from the problems of analysis posed by societies outside western Europe (e.g. are Latin American *haciendas* feudal?). The concept of an Asiatic mode is even less well established; Anderson (1974) rejected it forcefully. Part of the problem is that the distinction between feudal and Asiatic modes is not as clear as it seems, since there are many intermediate forms of land tenure. In any case, the real history of forms of economic organization in Asia before capitalist penetration is both complex and little understood, so the differences between Europe and Asia remain to be explained.

As the feudal order in Europe disintegrated it broke down into a society of independent peasant producers, generally paying rent to landlords. Production was a mixture of subsistence peasant production, handicraft production for local use, and small-scale production for the market. Feudal landlords, however, had some claims on the land in the form of rents, and ill-defined rights over common lands.The crucial stage was the conversion of these (privately owned) feudal rights into full private property in the land, including the right to dispossess the occupiers, a right that generally did not exist in the classic feudal social order.

Capitalism is defined by the relation between propertyless, free workers and the owners of the means of production. By expelling peasants from the land, the means of production were concentrated into the landlords' hands while at the same time the expelled peasants became a proletariat, and markets were created by splitting up activities previously carried out in self-sufficient units. What follows is Marx's description of the logic of this process (*Capital* I, part VIII, especially ch. 30). Lenin worked through a rather similar analysis (Lenin 1974) in his polemic against the *Narodniks*.

The story starts with peasant farmers who largely produce their own subsistence (including the products of rural handicrafts) and exchange only a surplus on the market. They trade, on a small scale, with an urban handicrafts sector, while landlords spend their rents on the products of peasant farmers and on urban handicrafts, as well as on maintaining servants, and so on. After the expulsion of the peasants, food is produced in much the same quantities, on the same land, by a smaller number of agricultural workers suffering a lower standard of living; the surplus in agriculture has thus increased. A substantial part of the dispossessed peasants are employed as wage workers in urban or rural industry, fed from the agricultural surplus. Their products can be sold (by their employers), because pre-capitalist rural craft industries have been largely destroyed, creating a vacuum into which capitalist producers can move.

The process, as Marx described it, could in principle be carried through without any fundamental changes in the forces of production: much the same goods go on being produced, in the same way, using the same land and the same means of production. What has happened is that the social relations of production have been completely reorganized. Previously production was largely for direct use. Now, industry and agriculture, urban and rural production have been separated, and production is largely for sale. Previously the producers possessed their own means of production; now they are propertyless wage earners. Marx called this process the *primitive accumulation* of capital. It is not accumulation in the sense of the creation of means of production that did not exist before. From the point of view of society as a whole it is not accumulation at all. It is primitive accumulation *of capital*, because means of production and labour-power that were not previously part of capital are transformed into capital. To quote: 'We know that the means of production and subsistence, while they remain the property of the immediate producer are not capital. They become capital only under circumstances in which they serve at the same time as means of exploitation and subjection of the labourer' (*Capital* I, ch. 33: 767). In practice, of course, this process occurred over a long period of time, in which methods of production were changing and other forces were at work undermining pre-capitalist forms of organization. The account given above is an abstraction.

One aspect of the transition that needs more explanation is the origins of the capitalist farmer. Typically, in England, landlords did not operate all their land themselves, but rented it out to capitalist tenant farmers, who employed agricultural wage labour. Marx's account here was rather unclear (as are the historical facts), but it seems that he saw the origins of the capitalist tenant farmers primarily in the better-off peasants, who allied themselves with the landlords in the struggles over enclosure of common lands, a class that came later to be called by their Russian name, the *kulaks*. The description given by Marx applies mainly to England, the first fully capitalist society. In France, for example, the revolution of 1789 established a system of free peasants owning their own land, and capitalist agriculture was slow to develop. The transition from feudalism to capitalism depends very strongly on specific circumstances.

Marx described other factors at work in the transition from feudalism to capitalism (while always placing the main stress on the creation of a proletariat): the influx of plunder into England from India and other colonies, the establishment of a world market, the massive growth in mercantile wealth, and so on. The exact role of these external factors is not very clear. The influx of wealth presumably made it easier for prospective capitalists to start businesses and build them up, and it promoted a turnover in the actual personnel of the landowning class, with *nouveau riches* buying out declining and indebted feudal magnates. All this must have acted as a sort of lubricant for the still very slow progress of the capitalist juggernaut. Many recent writers have reversed Marx's emphasis, making the flow of plunder into Europe the main factor in the origins of capitalism (and the failure of capitalist development elsewhere). Marx certainly discussed internal and external factors in primitive accumulation, and the interpretation given above is only one possible reading. I think it accords both with the logic of Marx's case and with the weight of his arguments. A stress on external factors is consistent with a picture of capitalism as a world system divided into centre and periphery, but that was not how Marx saw it.

Finally, Marx emphasized the role of the state. Its main function during the process of primitive accumulation (apart from providing legal backing for the expulsion of peasants) was to repress the newly forming working class, and keep their wages down.

> The organisation of the capitalist process of production, once fully developed, breaks down all resistance. The dull compulsion of economic relations completes the subjection of the labourer to the capitalist. Direct force, outside economic conditions, is of course still used, but only exceptionally. . . . It is otherwise during the historical genesis of capitalist production. (*Capital* I, ch. 28: 737).

2.4 THE EXPANSION OF CAPITALISM

Once capitalism is established, capitalists are driven by competition to find new methods of production which raise productivity and lower costs of production. In pre-capitalist modes of production, by contrast, labour-saving changes generally bring no benefits (since redundant producers cannot be expelled), and increased output is only useful if it can be consumed by the ruling class or used to maintain unproductive servants, soldiers, and the like. Competition in a capitalist system generates cumulative development. Each advance is soon copied, laggards go bankrupt, and the leader's advantage can only be maintained by repeated expansion and innovation.

As early as 1848, in the *Communist Manifesto* (Marx and Engels 1950, cited below as *Manifesto*), Marx insisted that the development of the forces of production was the essential historical function of capitalism:

> The bourgeoisie cannot exist without constantly revolutionising the instruments of production, and thereby the relations of production, and with them the whole relations of society. . . . The bourgeoisie, during its rule of scarce one hundred years has created more massive and more colossal productive forces than have all preceding generations together. (*Manifesto*: 36, 37)

At the same time, capitalism expands, and draws all other societies into its orbit. In some places, Marx argued that this outward expansion was driven by a need for markets. In the *Manifesto*, for example: 'The need of a constantly expanding market chases the bourgeoisie over the whole surface of the globe. It must nestle everywhere, settle everywhere, establish connections everywhere.' I have argued that Marx was not an under-consumptionist, and did not see capitalism as dependent on external markets; I do not think that this quotation (and others like it) is a real difficulty for my reading. Capitalism does not develop evenly; where one industry (such as cotton textiles in the industrial revolution) develops ahead of others, it can find itself hampered by a shortage of demand relative to a greatly expanded supply. Competition forces capitalist firms to seek out the markets in which they can get the best prices for their products, and to seek out the cheapest sources of supply for the goods that they buy. The search for cheap raw materials is particularly important, since their availability depends, in part, on natural conditions (such as climate and mineral deposits) which are to be found spread all over the globe. In addition, though there is no inevitable shortage of demand, there is, equally, no guarantee that demand will always be adequate. Capitalist economies progress through a sequence of booms and slumps, so there are always periods of glut in which sellers search desperately for markets.

Another factor driving the capitalist sector to expand at the expense of pre-capitalist production is a need for fresh supplies of labour-power. It is true that the reserve army of labour is constantly replenished by workers made redundant by advances in productivity, but Marx always assumed that a healthy capitalist system would tend to expand more rapidly than the growth of productivity in itself would permit, and would thus periodically run into shortages of labour. In the absence of any external source of labour-power this would cause an increase in the wage (as demand outpaces supply in the market for labour-power) which would both stimulate labour-saving innovations and provoke a crisis, reducing demand for labour. Any external sources of labour-power would be eagerly raided in order to stave off the crisis.

The competitive process meets both of these needs; the need for markets and the need for labour-power, so long as capitalist production is surrounded by pre-capitalist producers of commodities, especially small-scale individual producers. The technical advances enforced by competition allow capitalist firms to undercut the prices of pre-capitalist producers, eating into their markets and at the same time ruining the producers and forcing them into the proletariat. Since capitalism emerged in a decaying feudal society in which commodity production was already well established, conditions were favourable for it to expand and dominate economic life in western Europe (though it took a long time).

When capitalism first emerged, and the first capitalist empires were established, the dominant form of capital was merchant capital, and the methods of production used were still essentially those of pre-capitalist times. There is a long first period in the history of capitalism in which these two special features predominate, before the period which was Marx's main subject, when industrial capital had come to predominate and when methods of production had been revolutionized by the rise of modern industry. In England, the leading capitalist centre, modern industry originated in the late eighteenth century, but did not come to dominate until well into the nineteenth.

Merchant capital can develop wherever exchange takes place on a sufficient scale. In a pre-capitalist world, only the surplus over the needs of reproduction is sold, and, where this surplus is gathered by a ruling class in the form of rents in kind or as the product of forced labour, its 'cost of production' is not clearly defined. There can be huge differences in prices between different areas, and many opportunities for monopoly profit. In addition, natural conditions are responsible for great differences in the costs of production in different areas. With a large enough volume of trade, differences in prices would be eliminated, but when long distance trade was very costly and risky, there could be large profits in trade, and very large profits from monopolizing trade. 'The independent development of merchant's capital, therefore, stands in inverse proportion to the general economic development of society' (*Capital* III, ch. 20: 322).

At the same time, the emergence of commodity exchange and large-scale trading constituted a basis for the emergence of financial capital. In his writings on India, Marx placed great stress on the political power of the 'moneyocracy' during the period of transition, a power gained largely by corruption. The period of transition from feudalism to capitalism and the early stages of development of capitalism are thus marked by a massive efflorescence of merchant's capital and financial capital, cut down later by the rise of industrial capital. The commercial empires of the sixteenth to eighteenth centuries were driven mainly by attempts to monopolize trade (though a simple desire for plunder, a motive that is as old as the existence of societies worth plundering, was also an important element). In some cases (such as the sugar plantations of the West Indies) these essentially commercial activities extended into the organization of production, where indigenous sources of supply proved inadequate. In general, the production systems set up were not capitalist, for the simple reason that no proletariat existed in the areas concerned.

Rightly or wrongly, Marx was very clear that participation in a world economy dominated by merchant capital did not necessarily make the mode of production capitalist.

> Independent mercantile wealth as a predominant form of capital represents the separation of the circulation process from its extremes, and these extremes are the exchanging producers themselves. They remain independent of the circulation process, just as the latter remains independent of them. . . . Money and commodity circulation can mediate between spheres of production of widely different organisation, whose internal structure is still chiefly adjusted to the output of use values. (*Capital* III, ch. 20: 322)

The whole chapter from which this quotation is taken, 'Historical Facts about Merchant's Capital', is of great importance in understanding Marx's view of the emergence of a capitalist world economy.

Where the preconditions for capitalist production exist, however, merchant capital tends to move into (capitalist) production, typically in the form of the dominance of merchants over small-scale independent producers, which can develop into 'outwork', a system in which the workers work in their own homes with materials and other means of production provided by the merchant. This is, however, according to Marx, only a by-way in the development of capitalism:

> The transition from the feudal mode of production is twofold. The producer becomes merchant and capitalist. . . . This is the really revolutionary way. Or else, the merchant establishes direct sway over production. However much this serves historically as a stepping stone . . . it cannot by itself contribute to the overthrow of the old mode of production, but tends rather to preserve and retain it as its precondition. (*Capital* III, ch. 20: 329)

The dominance of merchant capital, therefore, tended to undermine the feudal mode of production to some extent while at the same time hampering the rise of industrial capital and of truly capitalist production. This point is not merely of historical importance. This stage of development persists even now in many rural areas in the Third World, and some recent writers have stressed the dominance of merchant capital as an important factor delaying capitalist development in underdeveloped areas.

To start with, capitalist production was still based on older techniques of production, and the cost advantages of capitalist producers must have been pretty small, at least in comparison to later periods, especially after allowing for high transport costs and the high profit margins demanded by merchant middlemen. The process by which pre-capitalist modes of production are undermined by undercutting their prices therefore went on very slowly. The mechanisms of primitive accumulation were still going on, and were still the dominant factor in the growth of capitalism.

The situation was transformed by the rise of modern industry, in which the tools are taken out of the worker's hands and moved and regulated directly by a machine. Since machines are not limited by the physiology of the human body, productivity could rise dramatically. Genuine mass production appeared, with very large savings in costs. The dominance of merchant capital, dependent on monopolistic restrictions in trade, had to be swept aside, and the destruction of pre-capitalist production could accelerate, since capitalist producers had a decisive cost advantage. It is thus the emergence of modern industry that is the real turning point in the history of capitalism and of capitalist expansion throughout the world.

Modern industry did not come into being simultaneously in all branches of production. When one branch of industry is revolutionized, it places greatly increased demands on branches connected with it, and thus creates strong pressures for further innovations. As Marx argued:

> A radical change in the mode of production in one sphere of industry involves a similar change in other spheres. . . . Thus spinning by machinery made weaving by machinery a necessity. . . . The revolution in the modes of production of industry and agriculture made necessary a revolution in the general conditions of the social process of

production, i.e., in the means of communication and transport. . . . Modern industry had therefore itself to take in hand the machine, its characteristic instrument of production, and to construct machines by machines. . . . It was only in the decade preceding 1866, that the construction of railways and ocean steamers on a stupendous scale called into existence the cyclopean machines now employed in the construction of prime movers. (*Capital* I, ch. 15: 383-4)

So, the process was hardly complete in the second half of the nineteenth century, although it had started in the late eighteenth century. Indeed, some branches of production are still not fully industrialized even now. The transition to modern industry, generating these great disproportions between different industries, lasted for a whole historical epoch; broadly, the whole nineteenth century.

This unevenness in the introduction of modern industrial methods is particularly important because, without it, it is difficult to see any basis for large-scale trade between industrial and non-industrial areas. Specifically, since cotton textiles were the first major product to be produced by industrial methods, and since England was the centre of this industrial revolution, England came to have a pressing need both for extended markets for cotton goods and for sources of supply of raw cotton. The consequences of this for India will be discussed in the next section. Modern industry is the highest stage of capitalist development that Marx discussed, since it was the highest stage reached in his time. He discussed the concentration and centralization of capital, and foresaw the development of monopoly as an inevitable consequence of the competitive process, but it was left to his successors to designate monopoly capital (or finance capital) as a stage beyond modern industry.

Capitalism, then, after a long, slow start in which it met the external world primarily through the mediation of merchant capital, came to life with the rise of modern industry, sweeping aside merchant capital and imposing a whole series of massive transformations on the world economy. At the same time, however, huge parts of the world remained in a pre-capitalist stage of development and resistant, because of their internal structure, to the impact of market forces. This is the context of Marx's writings on colonialism.

2.5 COLONIALISM

Marx did not discuss colonialism in general terms; his views must be deduced from scattered references in his major writings and from articles about special cases, notably about Ireland, about the British empire in India and (much more superficially) about western, particularly British, dealings with China.

Marx wrote a considerable amount about Ireland (Marx and Engels 1971), mainly in the form of speeches, passing references in correspondence and the like. He argued that Ireland's poverty and misery, compared with England's status as the leading capitalist centre, were not caused primarily by any internal difference in the prior mode of production, but by external (English) oppression and exploitation. The expulsion of the peasantry and the creation of capitalist farms under the aegis (and to the benefit) of the (English) landed aristocracy followed essentially the same course as in England, though it was carried out with even greater brutality, but: 'every time Ireland was about to develop industrially, she was crushed and reconverted into a purely agricultural land. . . . The people had now before them the choice between occupation of land *at any rent*, or starvation' (Marx and Engels 1971: 132). The main cause of industrial failure in Ireland was the absence of protective tariffs: Irish industry could not survive English competition. In this, Ireland's fate does not seem very different from that of various country districts of England, except for the absence of political constraints on exploitation. Like workers from rural areas of England, the Irish were forced to migrate to seek work in the industrial cities of England. The difference was the existence of a revolutionary (though not socialist) nationalist movement.

Marx was especially concerned to see a nationalist revolution against the aristocracy in Ireland, since this would undermine their hold in England, reduce divisions between Irish and English workers in England, and thus advance the socialist revolution in England, which 'being the metropolis of capital . . . is for the present the most important country for the workers revolution, and moreover the *only* country in which the material conditions for this revolution have developed up to a certain degree of maturity' (Marx and Engels 1971: 294). Neither Marx nor Engels thought that revolution in Ireland could be socialist. Engels, after Marx's death, argued that the Irish wanted land, to become independent peasants and 'after that, mortgages will appear on the scene and they will be ruined once more'. They should, however, be encouraged to 'pass from semi-feudal conditions to capitalist conditions' (p. 343). This view of the regressive effect of British rule in Ireland contrasts with Marx's view of its effects in India.

The articles about India and China (Marx 1969; Marx and Engels n.d.) were written for the *New York Daily Tribune*. The main series was published during 1853, and includes both commentary on issues of current interest and a number of articles in which Marx set out his considered view on India; these few 'set piece' articles are the main source. In 1853, five years after the writing of the *Communist Manifesto*, Marx had arrived substantially at his mature position, but the economic analysis which culminated in *Capital* was not yet worked out in detail. Where he returned to the same topics in *Capital*, however, there is little sign of any change in his thinking.

How much did Marx know about India? It is obvious, both from the articles and from the 'Notes on Indian History' which he compiled, that he had read virtually everything available to him on India and was exceedingly well informed on the political and military history of the sub-continent. There was, however, much that he did not know, probably because no one at that time (or perhaps since) knew it. Thus, in an article of 7 June 1858 (Marx 1969: 313) he discussed debates then going on in England about the real nature of land tenure in India, without firmly coming down in favour of any one interpretation, and in an article of 23 July 1858 (Marx 1969: 330) he discussed contemporary debates about the burden of taxation in India without being able to settle the question of whether or not Indian cultivators are 'overtaxed', in the sense that taxation threatens the resources needed for reproduction. These two issues (land tenure or the relations of production, and the extent of exploitation and the size of the potential surplus product) should presumably be crucial to a Marxist analysis of Indian society, but the information was simply not available.

Marx examined the origins and development of the East India Company, arguing that it had, from an early date, two objects: to develop trade, and also to 'make territorial revenue one of [its] sources of emolument'. As the company's territories expanded from the middle of the eighteenth century to the middle of the nineteenth, the time when Marx was writing, it came more and more under the control of the British state, creating a peculiar hybrid of public and private power typical of the oligarchic British state of that epoch.

The whole character of the British relationship with India was transformed in the early nineteenth century by the rise of industrial capital. Before then, Indian textiles were among products exported to Britain, with a drain of precious metals to India to pay for them. In 1813 trade with India was thrown open to competition, the balance of trade soon turned the other way, and India was flooded with British textiles. By the mid-nineteenth century, the coalition of interests that lay behind the original British drive into India was breaking up.

> Till then the interests of the moneyocracy which had converted India into its landed estates, of the oligarchy who had conquered it by their armies, and of the millocracy who had inundated it with their fabrics had gone hand in hand. But the more the industrial interest became dependent on the Indian market, the more it felt the necessity of creating fresh productive powers in India, after having ruined her native industry. You cannot continue to inundate a country with your manufactures, unless you enable it to give some produce in return. . . . The manufacturers, conscious of their ascendancy in England, ask now for the annihilation of these antagonistic powers in India, for the destruction of the whole ancient fabric of Indian Government, and for the final eclipse of the East India Company. (Marx 1969: 107)

Here is the key to Marx's arguments. While merchant capital and its allies exploit and destroy without transforming, industrial capital destroys but at the same time transforms.

What were British motives in India? Who were the beneficiaries of empire? Once it became a territorial power, the

East India Company ceased to be profitable, as the proceeds of taxation were eaten up by the administrative and military costs of occupation; the need for financial support was a vital lever driving the East India Company into the hands of the British government. On the other hand, private citizens, principally the employees of the Company, did very well, with inflated salaries and many opportunities for private corruption, looting and perquisites of one sort or another. This is characteristic of the rise of capitalism, a period in which the state and the privileges it could grant were a major source of support for the 'moneyocracy' and the 'oligarchy'.

The other principal beneficiaries were the industrial bourgeoisie. I have already discussed the ambiguities in Marx's discussion of the need for markets. Here it is clear that it is not markets in general that are needed, but markets for cotton textiles. 'At the same rate at which the cotton manufactures become of vital interest for the whole social frame of Great Britain, East India became of vital interest for the British cotton manufacturer' (Marx 1969: 107). This links up with the statement quoted above: 'You cannot continue to inundate a country with your manufactures unless you enable it to give you some produce in return.'

Marx presented a theory of capitalism in the abstract, but he knew that the real world was far from reducible to the play of pure economic abstractions. He did not argue that capitalism in Britain had to have colonies, but that once history had taken that turn, there was no going back. India became necessary, not to capitalism in general, but to capitalism as it had in fact developed. England had a trade surplus with India (as a result of cotton exports), which India financed from its surplus with China (the opium trade), while China in turn exported tea and other products both to England and to Australia and the USA, which had surpluses in trade with England, closing the circle. Marx analysed the way in which the opium trade was a linchpin of this system, and therefore had to be protected and expanded (by force), while at the same time the effects of the opium trade in China actually diminished China's capacity to import other goods from the west. The creative tension between theory and historical specificity in Marx's writings is one mark of his greatness.

There is no suggestion that the workers in England gained from the colonies, except in so far as the cotton industry in England expanded, and thus employed more, at the expense of Indian textile production. They were no more secure in their jobs, nor were they better paid as a result:

> As to the working classes, it is still a much debated question whether their condition has been ameliorated at all as a result of the so-called public wealth. ... But perhaps also, in speaking of amelioration, the economists may have wished to refer to the millions of workers condemned to perish, in the East Indies, in order to procure for the million and a half of work people employed in England in the same industry, three years of prosperity out of ten. (Marx, *Poverty of Philosophy*, 1847, cited in Marx 1969: 35)

The quotations from Engels (not Marx) which Lenin used to link the idea of a labour aristocracy to the possession of colonies (Lenin 1950: 545) mostly date from later, and are very ambiguous, referring to the bourgeois ideas of some English workers rather than to any material benefit to them.

Marx did not discuss, in any general way, why trade promotion should involve military conquest and direct administration of pre-capitalist areas. Two motives emerge from particular cases: first, to exclude other nations and to ensure unimpeded entry of the conquering power's own goods and, second, because Asiatic society is very resistant to penetration by trade alone, so direct use of state power is called for. Marx also stressed the inheritance both of colonial territory and of vested interests (such as the large and wealthy stratum of employees of the East India Company) from earlier stages of development.

What, then, was the effect of British rule in India? Marx set out his views in a famous pair of articles: 'British rule in India', and 'The future results of British rule in India' (Marx 1969: 88 ff.; 132 ff.).

Asiatic society, according to Marx, was based on a village economy, characterized by a union within the village of agriculture and handicrafts, a traditional, hereditary division of labour and an absence of private property in land. The first two characteristics are reminiscent of the feudal structure from which capitalism emerged. Feudalism was broken up primarily by the conversion of feudal into bourgeois property in land and the expulsion of the peasants from the land. In the absence of private landed property, this form of transformation was blocked in India. In the Asiatic mode of production, surplus was not creamed off by individual landlords, but by the state, as the highest representative of communal landownership, in the form of taxation. Marx quoted earlier writers saying that the village structure stands unaltered as states and empires come and go above it. The East India Company, in occupying India, had, in the first instance, simply replaced these previous states.

Marx argued that it was the combination of a need for large-scale public works (irrigation works, etc.) for climatic and geographical reasons, together with a 'low level of civilisation', which called into existence 'the interference of the centralising power of government'. Technical requirements alone did not create Asiatic despotism: Flanders and Italy also needed large-scale works but in Europe, in a different social context, private enterprise was driven to voluntary association. In a striking (and much quoted) phrase, Marx wrote:

> There have been in Asia, generally, from immemorial times, but three departments of Government: that of Finance, or the plunder of the interior; that of War, or the plunder of the exterior; and, finally the department of Public Works. . . . Now the British in East India accepted from their predecessors the department of finance and war, but they have neglected entirely that of public works. (Marx 1969: 90; the argument and the phrases come from a letter by Engels to Marx, *ibid*.: 451-2)

He added: 'in Asiatic empires we are quite accustomed to see agriculture deteriorating under one government and reviving again under some other government.' It seems, in fact, that the neglect of public works was a result of the breakup of the Mogul empire, before the British conquest, and that public works revived at around the time that Marx was writing, presumably because of the interest of industrial capital in expanding markets. The real devastation that British penetration into India brought with it was the destruction of

Indian handicraft textile production by competition from the mechanized textile industry of Lancashire.

Marx discussed the reasons why Asiatic production was so resistant to capitalist competition, with special reference to China (Marx 1969: 393ff.). The production of cloth was integrated with farm work and the time when agricultural work was slack could be used for handicrafts, so that the costs of actually producing the cloth were almost non-existent. The producers controlled their own means of subsistence, and thus could not be starved out by undercutting. It was only with the direct assistance of state power that the destruction of Indian textiles could occur, and even so it proceeded fairly slowly. In China, where direct European control was absent, Lancashire textiles made even less impact: this, according to Marx, was a major reason for British aggressiveness towards China. The exact mechanisms by which British textiles conquered the Indian market are rather unclear in Marx's writings.

Between the neglect of public works and the destruction of the textile industry, British rule produced widespread misery in India. It did, however, have its progressive side as well. English industrial capitalism, according to Marx, had an interest in the development of the Indian economy. This meant, above all, the building of railways, which Marx expected to initiate further industrial development, and to break down the isolation of Indian rural life. He gave an impressive list of the modernizing and integrating effects of British rule:

> [Political] unity, imposed by the British sword, will now be strengthened and perpetuated by the electric telegraph. The native army, organised and trained by the British drill-sergeant was the *sine qua non* of Indian self-emancipation. . . . The free press is a new and powerful agent of reconstruction . . . private property in land – the great desideratum of Asiatic society. From the Indian natives . . . a fresh class is springing up, endowed with the requirements for government, and imbued with European science. (Marx 1969: 133)

In short, British rule was destroying the static Asiatic society and creating the pre-conditions both for industrial capitalism and for the creation of a modern Indian nation state, but not automatically or painlessly:

> All the English bourgeoisie may be forced to do will neither emancipate nor materially mend the social condition of the mass of the people, depending not only on the development of the productive powers, but on their appropriation by the people. But what they will not fail to do is to lay down the material premises for both. Has the bourgeoisie ever done more? Has it ever effected a progress without dragging individuals and peoples through blood and dirt, through misery and degradation? The Indians will not reap the fruits of the new elements of society scattered among them by the British bourgeoisie till in Great Britain itself the now ruling classes shall have been supplanted by the industrial proletariat, or till the Hindoos themselves shall have grown strong enough to throw off the English yoke altogether. (Marx 1969: 137)

Marx's argument, then, can be summarized: British rule in India (a) causes massive misery, (b) creates the preconditions for massive advance and (c) must be overthrown before the benefits can be enjoyed. This argument has frequently been regarded as surprising and paradoxical. I cannot see why it should seem so to a Marxist; replace the words 'British rule' with 'capitalism' and it is exactly the argument of the *Communist Manifesto*. Even the tone, the style is the same: the deliberate juxtaposition of the most exalted praise for material achievements and the shocking images used to bring home the concomitant human misery. The article was, after all, written only five years after the *Manifesto*.

There are, I think, two reasons why Marx's arguments have been regarded as an embarrassing lapse on his part. First, Marxists have often (rightly) aligned themselves with broadly based movements of national liberation, and have wanted, for propaganda reasons, to ascribe all social evils to the foreign oppressors and to see the oppressed nation as inherently progressive and morally superior. Whether it is wise to cover up the evils of the past and of the indigenous social structure is another matter; Marx did not think so. Second, Marx's predictions seemed to fail. India did not, under British rule, develop into a major industrial country.

The assessment here must depend on what time scale Marx expected for the developments he predicted; there is no clear indication in his articles. Other passages make it clear that the village organization remained and was very resistant to change. The factors Marx listed as Britain's bequest to a future independent India (unity, the native army, the free press, an educated middle class) are surely exactly the factors that have given modern India its distinctive character. I shall not pursue these arguments here, since the reasons for the slowness of development in the Third World since Marx's time will be discussed in later chapters.

Is Marx's analysis of India inconsistent with his opinions on Ireland? Since Marx's writings on Ireland generally date from later (though he was writing in support of Irish nationalism as early as 1848), is there evidence of a change in Marx's view on colonialism? I think not. Marx wrote with detachment about the Indian mutiny of 1857, expressing no support for the rebels and cataloguing the atrocities of both sides. The reason is clear: he regarded Indian independence at that date as unattainable since its material and social foundations did not yet exist. This is even clearer in his description of the Taiping rebels in China:

> It seems that their vocation is nothing else than to set against the conservative disintegration [of China] its destruction, in grotesque horrifying form, without any seeds for a renaissance. . . . Only in China was such a sort of devil possible. It is the consequence of a fossil form of life. (Marx 1969: 442, 444)

In Ireland, by contrast, a modern democratic nationalist movement existed, since Ireland had a different mode of production and was at a different stage of development. Marx's political analysis was always based on analysis of particular situations.

2.6 SUMMARY

Marx defined capitalism in terms of the relation between a class of free wage labourers and a class of capitalists. Competition compels accumulation and technical progress.

Capitalism does not need a subordinated hinterland or periphery, though it will use and profit from one if it exists. Up to the industrial revolution, capitalism's external relations were mediated through merchant capital, and did not necessarily transform the other societies which were drawn into the world market. Once industrial capital had taken charge, capitalist conquest could play a progressive (though brutal) role by initiating capitalist industrialization. The origins and rapid development of capitalism in Europe and its slow penetration in Asia were the result of differences in the preceding modes of production in these areas; European domination was a consequence, not a primary cause, of this difference.

3

Luxemburg

After Marx's death in 1883, there was something of a lacuna in the development of Marxist thought until the early twentieth century, when there was an explosion of Marxist writing. I shall deal first with the work of Rosa Luxemburg, before describing the creation of what I shall call the 'classical' Marxist theory of imperialism, by Hilferding, Bukharin and Lenin. Luxemburg followed Marx much more closely than the other writers mentioned, who developed a distinctly new set of ideas.

Her main work was *The Accumulation of Capital*, published in 1913 (Luxemburg 1951, cited below as *Accumulation*). It was heavily criticized, and in 1915 she wrote a reply (Luxemburg 1972, cited below as *Anti-Critique*), eventually published in 1921. A number of her arguments emerge much more clearly in the *Anti-Critique* than in the original presentation, so I shall use it extensively. (Readers of *Accumulation* may find it helpful to regard sections one and two of that book as a sort of enormously extended prologue, with the main argument starting on page 329 of the edition that I have cited.) Some of my arguments derive from a particularly thorough, though in parts sharply polemical, critique of both these works by Bukharin (1972b).

Luxemburg put forward two distinct arguments. First, she thought that she had detected a logical flaw in Marx's analysis of expanded reproduction which made it impossible to realize (i.e. to sell) goods corresponding to that part of surplus value destined to be reinvested, without having 'outside' (non-capitalist) buyers. For this reason, she argued, capitalism cannot exist in a pure form, but only in conjunction with non-capitalist systems. I shall argue that she was simply wrong on this point. Second, she followed Marx in arguing that capitalism was, in fact, surrounded by pre-capitalist economic formations, and that competitive pressures drive capitalist firms and capitalist states to trade with these 'outside' economies and ultimately to break them up. *Accumulation* contains a fair amount about the impact of capitalism on pre-capitalist societies which remains relevant despite the failure of her first argument, since its inclusion is justified by the second.

She insisted on an important conceptual point. The distinction between 'inside' and 'outside' from the point of view of capitalism (e.g. 'outside buyers') means inside or outside *capitalist relations of production*. The world is divided into nation states, colonies, and the like, but it is also divided into a capitalist sector and a non-capitalist sector, and it is the latter division that is relevant for her purposes. Marx also drew this distinction, but it is to Luxemburg's credit that she maintained it consistently throughout her work.

In her picture of the world, capitalism exists alongside other modes of production, but remorselessly expands into its non-capitalist environment, ultimately swallowing it all up. Since she argued that capitalism needs this non-capitalist environment to survive, it follows that capitalism's triumph, the replacement of all pre-capitalist systems, must also be the signal for its collapse:

> Capitalism is the first mode of economy with the weapon of propaganda, a mode which tends to engulf the whole globe and to stamp out all other economies, tolerating no rival at its side. Yet at the same time it is also the first mode of economy which is unable to exist by itself, which needs other economic systems as a medium and soil. Although it strives to become universal and, indeed, on account of this tendency, it must break down – because it is immanently incapable of becoming a universal form of production. (*Accumulation*: 467)

3.1 THE REALIZATION OF SURPLUS VALUE

In Marxist theory, surplus value originates in production, where the value produced by a worker exceeds the value of his labour-power. The value created is embodied in a product, which must be sold to 'realize' the value in money terms, before the capitalist can buy fresh means of production and labour-power to start the process again. Marx analysed the realization of the product, and the reproduction of the system as a whole, in a purely capitalist economy, containing only workers and capitalists, plus hangers on (priests, prostitutes, etc.) who derive their incomes from the capitalists. Luxemburg argued that expanded reproduction is impossible in this context.

I have already outlined Marx's analysis of reproduction, but I shall restate it here in order to see Luxemburg's objections. For reproduction to continue smoothly, the entire product at the end of a period of production must be realized, i.e. sold to someone. This requires two conditions: the total value of demand, of spending, must equal the value of the product, and the particular goods which make up the total product must match up with the wants of the purchasers. Luxemburg's main concern is with the first of these. How did Marx deal with it? The product is in the hands of the capitalists. Where does demand come from? Some comes from capitalists themselves; they must replace used up means of production, and also buy extra means of production (in the case of expanded reproduction). They also buy goods for their personal use. Another part of total demand comes from workers who spend their wages on consumption goods. Since wages are paid by capitalists, we can think of workers' demand for goods as being an indirect form of spending by capitalists. Finally we have the hangers on. Their spending again derives from a redivision of capitalists' incomes, so this again we can think of as indirect spending by capitalists.

It seems, then, that goods belong to capitalists and they are bought, directly or indirectly, out of the spending of capitalists. It seems strange, at first sight, that capitalists should buy their own products, and it is probably this apparent difficulty that lies behind Rosa Luxemburg's unwillingness to accept the argument. It is not, however, a problem at all when we realize that capitalism, by definition, consists of many independent units which exchange their products on the market. Money is purely an intermediary in the redistribution of products from their sector of origin to the sector where they are to be used. The condition for surplus value to be realized is that it must be spent. Capitalists get surplus value by paying less to workers than the value created, but they must (collectively) spend the surplus (on consumption, on buying extra means of production, or on advancing wages to extra workers) in order to realize it. This will not necessarily happen: if the prospects of profit are poor, capitalists may hold back from investment and make the situation worse.

Luxemburg's approach is not easy to pick out in the *Accumulation* (though it emerges fairly clearly in chapter 25) but in the *Anti-Critique* the problem is set out very clearly, and we can best understand her difficulty by extracting a series of quotations from that work.

> Let us imagine that all the goods produced in capitalist society were stored up in a big pile at some place, to be used by society as a whole. We will then see how this mass of goods is naturally divided into several big portions of different kinds and destinations. (*Anti-Critique*: 51)

Consumption by workers and capitalists, together with replacement of means of production, account for parts of this 'pile', and pose no serious problems of analysis; they are exchanged in the fashion described in Marx's analysis of simple reproduction. But in addition there must be

> a portion of commodities which contains that invaluable part of surplus value that forms capital's real purpose of existence: the profit designed for capitalisation and accumulation. What sort of commodities are they, and who needs them? (*Anti-Critique*: 55)

As Luxemburg herself said, 'here we have come to the nucleus of the problem of accumulation, and we must investigate all attempts at a solution'. The buyers cannot be workers (their spending is accounted for) nor intermediate strata ('like civil servants, military, clerics, academics and artists'), since their income is derived from diverted profit or from taxes on wages and their spending should be included among the forms of consumption already considered, nor can the buyers be capitalists as consumers (since this spending is at the expense of accumulation, and cannot bring accumulation about).

This is the crux: 'Perhaps the capitalists are mutual customers for the remainder of the commodities – not to use them carelessly, but to use them for the extension of production, for accumulation' (*Anti-Critique*: 56-7). This is in line with Marx, the orthodox Marxist tradition, and with modern economics, but she rejected the possibility:

> All right, but such a solution only pushes the problem from this moment to the next . . . the increased production throws an even bigger amount of commodities onto the market the following year . . . [will] this growing amount of goods again be exchanged among the capitalists to extend production again, and so forth, year after year? Then we have the roundabout that revolves around itself in empty space. That is not capitalist accumulation i.e. the amassing of money capital, but its contrary: producing commodities for the sake of it; from the standpoint of capital an utter absurdity. (*Anti-Critique*: 57)

From this she drew the conclusion that there must be buyers outside capitalist relations of production.

What are we to make of this argument? First, there is an implicit appeal to a teleological interpretation of capitalism which runs right through Luxemburg's treatment of accumulation. Production must have a purpose. We cannot have production for its own sake. This line of argument (closely related to several versions of under-consumptionism, for example Hobson's) is surely misconceived. The essence of capitalism is that it is a decentralized (or anarchic) system. As a system it does not have, nor does it need, a purpose. Individual capitalists, workers, organizations of various sorts, may have purposes, but the system as a whole cannot. Individual capitalists accumulate (under favourable conditions) because they are forced to by competition, something she understood well enough in other contexts.

Second, she seems to have thought that if the surplus product is exchanged among capitalists for accumulation, it must imply a continuous increase in the production of means of production somehow disconnected from consumption. This is incorrect; if productivity, the real wage rate, and the proportion of surplus value accumulated all remain constant, then both workers' and capitalists' consumption will expand in line with total output. As capital accumulates, more workers are employed, so there is more spending on wage goods. At the same time, the amount of profit (surplus value) expands and, if a constant proportion is spent by the capitalists on consumption (or passed on to servants, charities, etc., to spend), capitalists' spending expands in line with accumulation. The whole system expands together.

Third, what of the need to accumulate money capital? Accumulation by capitalists must clearly be distinguished from hoarding by misers. Capitalists only accumulate money capital temporarily, in order to set it in motion as a functioning, profit-making capital. (This is what distinguishes money capital from idle hoards of money.) The conversion of surplus value into money is an essential intermediate stage in converting it into additional capital, but it is only a temporary stage, and there is no reason why all capitalists should seek to pass though this stage simultaneously. Provided some capitalists have funds in hand, they can buy additional means of production and advance additional wages to new employees, to be spent on the products of consumer goods industries, thus providing a further group of capitalists with money capital to spend on new investment, and so on.

Her difficulty seems to arise from a confusion of levels of abstraction akin to her search for a 'purpose' of production. She insisted that the problem of realization must be examined on the level of the aggregate social capital, but she treated the aggregate capital as though it were an individual capital which has to sell to others, and buy from others. She seems to have been unwilling to recognize the difference between a system and a component element within a system.

She also asked: if surplus value can be realized within the system why should crises occur in which commodities cannot be sold? The answer is surely obvious: what has been shown is that it is *possible* for surplus value to be realized in this way, not that it necessarily *will* be. If new investment is expected to be profitable, it will be undertaken. If not, investment will not take place, and the process breaks down. Again, she overlooked the anarchy of capitalist production; individual capitalists do not necessarily act in the interests of the system. Joan Robinson, in her introduction to the *Accumulation*, has suggested that Luxemburg could be read in terms of the possibility of deficient aggregate demand. Large parts of Luxemburg's writings can be interpreted in this way, but it is clear that her primary emphasis was not on the *possibility* that capitalists might not choose to buy each other's products and thus sustain demand, but on the absurdity (in her eyes) of supposing that they could *ever* do so.

Finally, we can ask what use non-capitalist buyers would be in solving what I have already argued is a non-problem. Once capitalists have converted surplus value into money capital, they exchange it for the elements of productive capital by buying additional means of production and employing additional workers who, in turn, spend their wages on means of subsistence. Where are they to obtain these commodities from? If, following Luxemburg, we say that they cannot get them by exchange within the system, then they must buy from non-capitalist sources. Either there must be pre-capitalist sellers of machine tools, integrated circuits, computers, and so on, or (following Bukharin's ironic suggestion) capitalists must first sell these goods to non-capitalist buyers, and then buy them back again. This is clearly absurd.

In saying this, I do not deny that capitalism in fact trades with non-capitalist sections of the world economy. Trade outside the capitalist world is easily incorporated into the analysis of exchange as a redistribution of the product between different branches of the economy. Where there is external trade, products are exported and goods equivalent in value take their place by being imported. So, for example, Britain in the nineteenth century produced more cotton textiles than it consumed domestically, but did not produce raw cotton. The one was exchanged for the other. Trade alters the commodity mix of the 'pile' of products (using Luxemburg's own metaphor) but not its value (abstracting from any inequality of exchange, which is a different issue).

In a similar vein, Luxemburg argued (in *The Accumulation of Capital*) that Marx's schemes of expanded reproduction cannot incorporate an increasing organic composition of capital. She concluded that there will be a shortage of means of production, and hence that non-capitalist suppliers of means of production are needed. Against this we can argue that the problem arises only because Marx had picked the figures he used specifically to illustrate the case of a constant organic composition. Critics of Luxemburg immediately produced examples in which the difficulty did not arise, and she effectively conceded their point (*Anti-Critique*: 48) by rejecting, as irrelevant, numerical or mathematical examples of the sort she herself had relied on in *Accumulation*. Luxemburg (like Marx himself) got into some difficulties in constructing numerical schemes of expanded reproduction, by insisting that the surplus value of each sector of the economy must be reinvested in the same sector. There is a long and vitriolic attack on Bauer (in the *Anti-Critique*), for assuming a transfer of capital (which she interpreted as a 'gift') from one department to another. It is, however, clear that the equalization of profit rates requires free mobility of capital throughout the economy.

She did raise some real problems about the commodity mix of output. Not only does the value of the product have to be matched by a corresponding value of spending, but the composition of output (the proportion of means of production, consumer goods and so on) has to be right. So long as the proportions are right to start with and the system expands steadily, one can show that the proportions will remain right, even, as noted above, with an increasing organic composition of capital. This does not, of course, solve the problem in practice. Luxemburg was right to stress that capitalist production does not expand evenly and predictably, and it is also true that in some circumstances relatively small initial disproportions can grow, and disrupt reproduction, if we insist on all of the product being used (see Morishima 1973, ch. 10, for an example). Here again we step outside the orderly world of the schemes of reproduction. Capitalist firms normally carry stocks and retain some spare capacity, thus providing an elasticity that the abstract schemes of reproduction do not allow for. In the real world there are recurrent crises which offer the opportunity of restructuring production. In any case, trade with non-capitalist sectors may sometimes help (if there is, say, a shortage of raw cotton) and sometimes not (if the shortage is of electronic equipment).

3.2 THE PROCESS OF CAPITALIST EXPANSION

If Luxemburg was wrong to argue that capitalism *needs* a non-capitalist environment, she was surely right to stress that it did in fact appear and grow in such an environment.

> Capitalism arises and develops historically amidst a non-capitalist society. In Western Europe it is found at first in a feudal environment from which it in fact sprang . . . and later, after having swallowed up the feudal system, it exists mainly in an environment of peasants and artisans. . . . European capitalism is further surrounded by vast territories of non-European civilisation ranging over all levels of development. . . . This is the setting for the accumulation of capital. (*Accumulation*: 368)

The two sectors of the world economy, capitalist and non-capitalist, do not live side by side in a state of peaceful co-existence. Luxemburg saw non-capitalist modes of production as essentially static: the equilibrium is not disturbed from that side. Capitalism, by contrast, is driven into constant expansion:

> Moreover, capitalist production, by its very nature, cannot be restricted to such means of production as are produced by capitalist methods. Cheap elements of constant capital are essential to the individual capitalist who strives to increase his rate of profit. . . . From the very beginning, the forms and laws of capitalist production aim to comprise the entire globe as a store of productive forces. Capital, impelled to appropriate productive forces for purposes of exploitation, ransacks the whole world, it procures its means of production from all corners of the earth, seizing them, if necessary by force, from all levels of civilisation and from all forms of society. (*Accumulation*: 358)

As well as seizing means of production wherever they are to be found, capital is always on the lookout for cheap labour. In pre-capitalist societies, labour is usually 'rigidly bound' by the traditional organization of production, and it has to be 'set free' to become useful to capital (*Accumulation*: 362). Unfortunately, in the *Anti-Critique*, she went back on this perfectly good line of argument when she vigorously rejected Bauer's explanation of imperialism as a search for labour-power, on the grounds that capitalism necessarily produces unemployment of labour in its homelands.

She also argued that capital can do things in the colonies that it could not get away with at home, giving it an elasticity and capacity to respond to events that it would not otherwise possess. Her example is the creation of 'immense' cotton plantations in Egypt during the American civil war:

> Only capital with its technical resources can affect such miraculous change in so short a time – but only on the pre-capitalist soil of more primitive social conditions can it develop the ascendancy necessary to achieve such miracles. (*Accumulation*: 358)

Here there is clearly some conception of the political and ideological conditions necessary for accumulation, but they are not spelt out in any systematic way.

The arguments set out above are not, of course, wholly new. The world-wide expansion of capitalism was a constant theme in Marx's writings, but it was to some degree pushed into the background in *Capital* by the theoretical task of analysing a pure capitalist mode of production. Luxemburg brought this aspect of Marx's thinking back into the limelight. She was surely right to argue that, in the real history of capitalism, the expansion of capitalist relations of production is one of the most important, perhaps the most important, process at work.

The conceptual framework of her analysis was, however, rather crude. She dealt, as many Marxists have done, in a single and undifferentiated concept of 'capital', without any clear specification of the stages of development which capitalism goes through, of the possible divergent interests of particular sectors, or of the political mechanisms by which the interests of 'capital' are translated into the policies of particular national states. In her description of the pre-capitalist societies into which capitalism expands, there is a similar lack of distinctions, and a lack of analysis of the internal workings of these societies. She simply treated all pre-capitalist societies as 'natural economies', that is, systems of local self-sufficiency, of production for direct use rather than for commodity exchange. I have already discussed Marx's analysis of the resistance of such forms of economy to penetration by commodity trade. Luxemburg put forward similar arguments:

> In all social organisations where natural economy prevails . . . economic organisation is essentially in response to the internal demand; and therefore there is no demand, or very little for foreign goods, and also, as a rule, no surplus production, or at least no urgent need to dispose of surplus products. What is more important, however, is that, in any natural economy, production only goes on because both means of production and labour power are bound in one form or another. . . . A natural economy thus confronts the requirements of capitalism at every turn with rigid barriers. Capitalism must therefore always and everywhere fight a battle of annihilation against every historical form of natural economy. (*Accumulation*: 368-9)

In this passage, and elsewhere, there is a direct identification of natural economy with pre-capitalist organization, with only simple commodity production as an intermediate stage. Everything is subordinated to her vision of a world divided between the ever-expanding domain of capital and the surrounding 'medium and soil' of static, closed natural economies, with a fringe of pre-capitalist societies in the process of dissolution marking the boundaries. This is surely too simple. As she recognized herself, capitalism in its expansion incorporates other forms of organization into its own world economy (slavery, bondage of various forms), while at the same time, pre-capitalist forms of organization (the feudal *corvée* farm, to quote her own example) have, at various stages, traded their surplus product on a large scale (*Accumulation*: 357). I shall discuss these issues in later chapters, simply noting here that to a certain extent Luxemburg's own grasp of the real historical process came into conflict with her attempts to reduce it to a single driving force, the accumulation of capital.

How is the 'struggle against natural economy' carried out? She listed four ends pursued by capital:

(1) To gain immediate possession of important sources of productive forces such as land, game in primeval forests, minerals, precious stones, and ores, products of exotic flora such as rubber, etc. (2) To 'liberate' labour power and to coerce it into service. (3) To introduce a commodity economy. (4) To separate trade and agriculture. (*Accumulation*: 369)

These fall into two groups. The first two represent ways in which a natural economy can be forced directly into capitalist production (cf. Marx on primitive accumulation). The third and fourth represent a more indirect route in which simple commodity production is installed and then undermined either directly or by competition with the cheap products of capitalist industry.

Throughout, she emphasized the use of force, state power and fraud, as Marx did in his treatment of primitive accumulation. She wrote:

At the time of primitive accumulation, i.e. at the end of the Middle Ages ... right into the nineteenth century, dis- possessing the peasants ... was the most striking weapon. ... Yet capital in power performs the same task even today, and on an even more important scale – by modern colonial policy.... Accumulation can no more wait for and be content with, a natural internal disintegration of non-capitalist formations ... than it can wait for the natural increase of the working population. Force is the only solution open to capital: the accumulation of capital, seen as an historical process, employs force as a permanent weapon, not only as its genesis, but further on down to the present day. (*Accumulation*: 369-71)

These themes are developed through examples, which I shall survey very briefly. Her discussion of India is vague on critical points; the story seems to be that the British first set out to transform land into private property, and then to ruin the producers by overtaxation, neglect of public works, and so on, in order to force them into debt and take over their lands. This process recurs in other cases, and is a major route by which pre-capitalist formations are undermined. (She seems, incidentally, to have been unaware of Marx's writings on India, which present a rather more complex picture.) Her chapter on 'the introduction of commodity economy' is rather disappointing; the only real example is the introduction by force of the opium trade into China. This is a very special case, since it was the addictive nature of the commodity, not force, that ensured it a market, while the force was directed at the Chinese state, and not at the 'natural economy' of the Chinese villagers.

She then discussed the separation of industry from agriculture under the title of 'the struggle against peasant economy', giving a very interesting description of the evolution of American agriculture from the self-sufficient peasant agriculture of the pioneer settlers on the frontier. 'It is a recurrent phenomenon in the development of capitalist production that one branch of industry after the other is singled out, isolated from agriculture, and concentrated in factories for mass production' (*Accumulation*: 395). The analysis of this process turns out, however, to be rather difficult to fit in to her general framework. The problem is that if a peasant household chooses to remain self-sufficient, producing the goods it consumes itself, there are really only two options: either they must be left alone, or they must be expelled altogether. Direct legal compulsion to produce only a limited range of cash crops, though it has been used in some colonies, was not of significance in the American case.

What, in fact, brings about the separation of agriculture from industry while still leaving behind an agricultural peasant class is the availability of cheap industrial products which make it worth the peasants' while to specialize, rather than forcing specialization on them. She was generally reluctant to admit to the material superiority of capitalist methods of production, in contrast to Marx who always stressed the dual character of capitalism, at once brutal and progressive. She did, of course, describe the cheapness of the products of capitalist industry, the massive scale of its works, the enormous transformations that it has made, but always in such a way as to stress the brutality behind it rather than the technical achievements, where Marx always stressed both. This characteristic of her thought reflects the general opinion among Marxists at the time that capitalism was coming to an end and had become a fetter on the development of the forces of production. The enormous development of production since then suggests that this was an over-simple view.

She also discussed the use of money taxes to force peasants to sell products. This is certainly an important method, but it forces the peasant to sell, not buy (it is the recipients of tax revenue who do the buying), and it does not, therefore, explain how markets are created among the peasantry. At the same time she described how overtaxation, indebtedness, foreclosure of mortgages, and so on, were used to separate the American peasant from the land. This process leads, of course, to capitalist agriculture rather than to the separation of industry from a peasant agriculture.

Luxemburg's analysis focused on the distinction between capitalist and non-capitalist modes of production and not on differences or conflicts between nation states. This gives her analysis its distinctive character and constitutes a large part of its importance. To deal with the developments of her own time (the run-up to the First World War), she clearly had to link her work to the system of national states. I shall not spend long on this, since there is less of interest in it, and much of it depends on arguments about realization of surplus value that I have already dismissed as false.

The main ways in which the state intervenes, apart from those described already, are through international loans, protective tariffs and armaments expenditure. Her basic argument was that non-capitalist markets are necessary to the existence of capitalism, and are becoming scarce, so there is a struggle between capitalist states to establish spheres of interest and to bind them to the 'mother country' with protective tariffs, to ensure a sufficiency of markets for the capitalists of the state concerned. This argument loses most of its force if, as I have argued, the need for external markets is illusory. Her second line of argument remains; the struggle for cheap labour and raw materials can explain inter-imperialist rivalry. This is, in fact, a component of the arguments of Bukharin and Lenin (chapter 6). Her analysis was still rather weak, because the links between competing capitals and competing states were not spelled out.

International loans, she argued, serve to reduce backward but nominally independent states (for example Turkey) to servitude, though they can also serve to finance the initial development of young capitalist states. They can finance the infrastructure (railways and the like) needed to incorporate new areas into the capitalist sphere, and simultaneously allow the old centres of capitalism to participate in the exploitation of new areas. For example, tax revenue from pre-capitalist agriculture in Turkey was paid as interest to German capitalists who had made loans to build railways. This emphasis on the interlinking of capitalist and non-capitalist forms of exploitation is valuable, and has been developed by more recent writers.

3.3 SUMMARY

Rosa Luxemburg's work remains of seminal importance, despite its analytical failings. At a time when there was a danger that Marxist thought would focus exclusively on the advanced sectors of industry in the advanced countries, she forced Marxists to pay attention to the masses of people who were being incorporated into the capitalist mode of production, or who still remained outside it. In this her work parallelled that of Lenin (in *The Development of Capitalism in Russia*, not *Imperialism*), in many respects her opponent.

Whatever its analytical failings, her real contribution was to insist that the mechanisms of primitive accumulation, using force, fraud and state power, were not simply a regrettable aspect of capitalism's past, but persist throughout the history of capitalism at the margin where capitalist and pre-capitalist economic systems meet. This margin is not geographical but social, it exists within countries rather than between them, and if the capitalist form of organization had triumphed completely in a few places (England, for example), the unequal struggle still continued in vast areas of the world.

4

Hobson

J. A. Hobson was not a Marxist, but his influence on later Marxist writers was so great that he cannot be ignored in a study of Marxist theories. Lenin drew on Hobson's ideas, and some writers even talk of a 'Hobson–Lenin' theory of imperialism, though that overstates the similarity between them. Baran and Sweezy followed Hobson much more closely than Lenin did, though the similarity between their work and Hobson's has not been noted as frequently.

. Hobson's theory of imperialism is set out in his *Imperialism* (Hobson 1938; first edition 1902); the under-consumption theory it is based on appeared in his first book, written jointly with A. F. Mummery (Mummery and Hobson 1889), and remained a constant theme for the rest of his life. He introduced a line of argument in which the emergence of widespread monopoly is said to lead to under-consumption (or over-saving), growing foreign investment, and imperialist expansion. A simple version would run something like this: (1) monopoly increases the share of profit, and concentrates it into fewer hands; (2) a large fraction of monopoly profit is saved, so saving tends to increase; (3) domestic investment opportunities are limited (it is sometimes also argued that monopoly reduces investment), so saving tends to outrun investment; (4) excess saving produces a chronic lack of demand, unless some outlet is found; (5) capital export can provide an outlet for excess saving; (6) a pressure for annexation of territory emerges, to safeguard existing investments or to open the way for new investment. A second, related, line of argument links demand deficiency to a search for external markets, and hence to annexation.

Hobson's *Imperialism* was primarily a polemic. He based his case against imperialism on a cost-benefit analysis, arguing that the costs were high, and the alleged benefits either small or altogether illusory. Imperialism, he said, is bad business, a line of argument which goes back to the classical economists (at least). He backed the case up with other arguments; imperialism was bad for democracy (because of the side effects of militarism), bad for the peoples subjected to foreign rule (whatever the claims of the imperialists), bad for Britain's reputation, and so on. On Hobson's case against imperialism, see Allett (1981) and Porter (1968). His explanation of imperialism was a by-product, which has to be disentangled from the anti-imperialist polemic. The key chapter, 'the economic taproot of imperialism', is constructed as a reply to the argument that imperialism is necessary, or at least desirable, to provide an outlet for surplus capital or for surplus products. This idea, which was widely held at the time, has been called 'the capitalist theory of capitalist imperialism' (Etherington 1984). It presented a particularly difficult challenge, because it had so much in common with Hobson's own views.

He was committed to a theory of under-consumption in which excess saving leads to a chronic lack of demand. The idea that foreign investment can provide an outlet for surplus saving is a natural extension of this under-consumptionist theory. If no other solution were possible, imperialism would presumably be in the interest of all classes (in the imperialist country), in order to stave off depression and unemployment. Hobson's reply was that income redistribution ('social reform') would remove excess saving and eliminate the need to invest abroad. The analysis of under-consumption and its causes was therefore a vital step in his case against imperialism, as well as in his positive theory. His case for social reform obviously falls far short of a Marxist case for socialist revolution, but that has not stopped Marxists drawing on his theoretical ideas.

The other half of Hobson's positive theory emerges as an answer to the question: if imperialism was 'bad business', how had Britain been led into adopting it? (Hobson 1938: 46). His answer contains several elements. First, there are a number of interest groups who stand to gain from imperialism. Since imperialism is bad for the nation as a whole, they are a minority, but they occupy positions of influence. Second, many support imperialism for misguided reasons, in the belief that it is needed to provide markets, out of an ill-informed nationalism, a desire to spread the supposed benefits of 'civilization', and so on. Taken together, these explanations might be regarded as sufficient, though if this were all Hobson offered one could hardly regard it as a distinctive theory. He did not, however, leave it at that. What unifies his account of the politics of imperialism is his insistence that this motley collection of forces is directed and channelled by a relatively small group of financiers.

Hobson's theory, then, can be divided into two distinct elements, introduced for rather different reasons. First, there is an economic theory intended to explain high levels of foreign investment, and to show that it would be unnecessary if income were redistributed. Second, there is a political theory linking foreign investment to imperialist policies. It is worth noting that these two aspects of the theory need not stand or fall together. It could be that Hobson was right in his explanation of foreign investment but wrongly believed that it accounted for imperialism, or that he was right to link imperialism to foreign investment but wrong in explaining the causes of capital export.

4.1 UNDER-CONSUMPTION

Hobson argued that excessive saving can cause slumps. Investment is needed to provide for (future) consumption, so if saving is too high, and consumption correspondingly low, saving may exceed the available opportunities to invest.

> The object of production is to provide 'utilities and conveniences' for consumers. . . . The only use of Capital being to aid the production of these utilities and conveniences, the total used will necessarily vary with the total of utilities or conveniences . . . consumed. Now saving, while it increases . . . Capital, simultaneously reduces the quantity of utilities and conveniences consumed; any undue exercise of this habit must, therefore, cause an accumulation of capital in excess of

that which is required for use. (Mummery and Hobson 1889: v)

The argument is quite general; it does not matter whether saving is high because of monopoly or simply because people happen to want to save a great deal.

The notion of 'under-consumption' or 'over-saving' has been severely criticized, since investment constitutes a demand for goods (machinery, and so on) on a par with consumption demand.

Once we accept the importance of the investment goods industries, [Mummery and Hobson's] argument falls to the ground. The demand for investment goods has nothing to do with the expenditure of consumers, but depends on the profitability expectations of capitalists. (Bleaney 1976: 157)

Bleaney's criticism, as it stands, goes too far. Mummery and Hobson did not ignore the demand for investment goods; they argued that it depends on the immediate future demand for consumer goods (e.g. 1889: 27-8). They also admit that investment can run ahead of this level, but they argue that excessive stocks of capital have no economic value (1889: 35). Unused capital cannot be piled up indefinitely.

The core of truth in the criticism is that Mummery and Hobson often argue as though future consumption were fixed, and investment possibilities fixed with it. Suppose, for example, that an economy is growing steadily with no problems, and that saving increases. According to Mummery and Hobson, it seems that excess saving would necessarily emerge. Against that, one could argue that increased saving would lead to an increased rate of growth of output, and hence of incomes and of consumption. Any rate of saving can be accommodated by an appropriate rate of growth. Mummery and Hobson could reasonably reply that growth is limited by the availability of labour and natural resources. That is indeed what they assumed (e.g. 1889: 29). They did not stress the point, and it is not clear to me that they appreciated its significance, but it saves their case. If the amount of capital that can be used is constrained by the supply of labour, or of other essential inputs, then extra saving cannot necessarily be absorbed by an accelerated growth rate, and the over-saving problem returns.

The under-consumptionist case is still not established. A mainstream economist can argue that excess supply of investment funds will drive down the interest rate, and eliminate the problem. Mummery and Hobson discussed this objection, but not very convincingly (1889: 130-1), because they thought that an increase in consumption is needed to eliminate the excess saving. A fall in the interest rate certainly could eliminate an excess supply of investment funds by reducing savings. The evidence suggests that individual savings do not respond much to a fall in interest rates, though the resulting shift of income away from rentiers may reduce aggregate savings. So far, so good, for the under-consumptionists. Lower interest rates, however, could also help to absorb additional saving by encouraging the use of more capital-intensive methods of production (because capital is relatively cheaper), so a given labour force uses more capital. High savings could lead to a progressive increase in the capital-labour ratio, with a falling interest rate, until the capital-labour ratio is high enough for saving to be absorbed in maintaining the new, higher level of capital intensity. Growth and capital models of this sort are now commonplace: for example, Solow (1956). Mummery and Hobson seem to have been so committed to the notion of fixed relations between capital and output (e.g. 1889: 23-8) that they never considered substitution of capital for labour as a possibility.

To summarize, if the labour force is limited, if saving is unresponsive to interest rate changes, and if production methods are fixed (or possibilities of substitution limited), it is possible for excessive saving to cause depression. The first two conditions are quite plausible, the third is more doubtful.

4.2 MONOPOLY AND CAPITAL EXPORT

In his later work, Hobson blamed excessive saving on inequality in the distribution of income, with monopoly as one possible cause of inequality. (The first time around, with Mummery, he argued that excess saving might be a problem, without saying much about the reasons for high savings.)

> If a tendency to distribute income ... according to needs were operative, it is evident that consumption would rise with every rise of producing power, for human needs are illimitable, and there could be no excess of saving. But it is quite otherwise [when some have] a consuming power vastly in excess of needs or possible uses. (Hobson 1938: 83)

The inconsistency in the quotation is characteristic of Hobson's rather casual style (if needs are illimitable how can income exceed needs?), but the message is clear enough; excess saving may occur when some have high incomes and save a lot, while others would like to spend more but do not have any income to spend.

Monopolies ('trusts') appear as a rather secondary factor: any cause of inequality would do as well. They matter because they represent a plausible explanation for an increase in inequality, particularly in the USA, in the late nineteenth century (Hobson had no direct measures of inequality), and may thus help to explain the emergence of inter-imperialist rivalry. Monopolies may increase prices, and hence profits and inequality, and they might also reduce wastage of capital, reducing costs, increasing profit, and simultaneously reducing the amount of capital required (Hobson 1938: 75-6). Subsequent discussion has mostly concentrated on the increase in profits. A reduction in the capital used to produce a given output is a possible, but not inevitable, outcome of the formation of a trust. It depends on the market structure before and after the change. In some market structures firms may be uneconomically small (monopolistic competition), in others they may deliberately hold excess capacity, and hence excess capital, in order to be able to threaten competitors with a price-cutting war. Hobson did not make it clear exactly what he had in mind. In any case, the result is similar to a profit increase, so I shall concentrate on that case.

When saving exceeds the scope for domestic investment, owners of capital look for investment opportunities abroad (Hobson 1938: 77-8). I have argued above that Hobson's argument is only valid if output and investment are constrained by a limited supply of labour. If his case is to make any sense, it must therefore be reformulated in those terms. The question then is: what happens when monopoly becomes more widespread, if labour scarcity prevents the economy from growing any faster, and a large fraction of monopoly profit is saved?

Consider first the effects of increased monopoly in the absence of foreign trade and investment. If a monopoly replaces competitive firms in a single industry, it produces less, and sells at a higher price. It therefore employs less labour and less capital. If the shift to monopoly is widespread, the demand for labour falls, so wages fall, and the demand for investment funds falls, bringing down the interest rate. Monopoly profit accounts for an increased share of total income, while the shares of wages and interest are reduced. It is important to distinguish between monopoly profit and interest; Hobson did not make a clear distinction. The share of profit (interest plus monopoly profit) rises initially, so saving rises (recall that saving out of profit is assumed to be high). There is a minor complication to deal with here, for completeness. As more capital is accumulated, the demand for labour rises, and the wage will rise back towards its initial level. Hobson does not seem to have recognized this, but it is a necessary consequence of assuming that labour is scarce (as it must be, for his argument) and that wages are determined by supply and demand. As wages rise, the return to investment falls, and the interest rate will be forced down even further. Over time, then, the burden of monopoly profit must be, at least partially, shifted from wages to interest. To the extent that more capital-intensive techniques are adopted in response to lower interest and growing wages, the fall in interest will be slowed down, and wages will remain below their level in a competitive system.

The main conclusion so far is that increased monopoly will tend to force down interest rates; this is simply the reflection of an increase in the supply of capital, as a result of increased saving, relative to the demand for capital. If interest rates are flexible enough, a closed economy may be able to absorb the effects without chronic depression, but it is quite easy to justify Hobson's conclusion that monopoly leads to over-saving and to a slump.

In a theory of imperialism, it is the effect of monopoly in an open economy that counts. Consider trade in goods, without export or import of capital. By definition, trade must be balanced (unbalanced trade corresponds to capital inflows or

79

outflows), so exports cannot make up for deficient home markets across the board. This does not necessarily nullify Hobson's claim that imperialism is motivated by the search for export markets, because each business may think, rightly, that enlarged export markets for its own product would be good for it, without taking account of the indirect effects. Balanced trade may help to alleviate the effects of over-saving indirectly, since a low interest rate means relatively low prices for capital-intensive goods, and a shift of exports towards capital-intensive industries is equivalent to substitution of capital for labour. It should also be noted that increased monopoly in some, but not all, industries would tend to change the pattern of trade; one cannot say much in general about the likely results.

In any case, it is capital export that is important for the theory. If the interest rate falls, because of increased saving, while the returns on investment (or lending) abroad do not, capital will flow out to the relatively more attractive invest-ment opportunities abroad. Hobson's conclusions on this essential point survive. Note that it is not necessary to assume that the capital–labour ratio is fixed to conclude that monopoly will encourage capital export, since a falling interest rate can cause both capital–labour substitution at home and export of capital. It is true that the scope for foreign investment may itself be limited, in the end, by the same factors that limit home investment. However, if scarcity of labour matters, as I have argued, surplus labour in underdeveloped areas can help. Large investments may be needed to open up new areas, and, in any case, imperialism can be explained by a struggle for control of limited opportunities. (See Allett 1981: 145-6.)

Hobson may have tried to prove too much. He did not need to argue that there is excess saving to explain a search for export markets and for investment opportunities abroad. First, it is always true that owners of capital will search for better investment opportunities, even if it is quite possible to obtain a modest return at home. Second, and more to the point here, wherever competition is less than perfect (i.e. almost everywhere), firms find that their sales are limited by the extent of the market for their particular product. They are always anxious to expand their sales, by exporting or by setting up production abroad, whether there is any overall deficiency of demand or not. Even if the stronger forms of under-consumption are rejected, for example if additional saving could always be absorbed through a fall in the interest rate, the explanation of foreign investment survives.

It may be, however, that Hobson's theory misses the real reasons for the upsurge of capital export from the main capitalist countries towards the end of the nineteenth century. Consider Britain. The theory says that excess saving is the result of inequality in incomes; to explain the rapid growth of capital export in the late nineteenth century as a result of over-saving, as Hobson did, would require growing inequality in that period. The available evidence suggests the reverse; the share of wages and salaries in national income was growing, albeit slowly. It has been argued that large capital exports from Britain were the result not of high savings, but of an unusually low rate of domestic investment (Foreman-Peck 1983: 130). In any case, few would argue that monopoly was an important factor in Britain at that date.

One might try to save the theory by arguing that British expansionism was a response to increasing threats from rival powers, where monopoly and inequality were increasing. That seems to have been Hobson's line of argument; he stressed the entry of the USA into the race for colonies (Hobson 1938: 72-9). The USA did switch from being a net importer of capital to a position of near balance, but the main switchover seems to have been completed around 1870, earlier than Hobson suggested, and rather early to be described as a result of monopoly. From about 1880 to 1910, little trend is visible (Foreman-Peck 1983: 129, fig. 5.1).

The main problem in applying Hobson's theory to the facts of history is that it describes what would happen if monopoly grew, or, more generally, if inequality increased, *while other factors remained constant*, which they did not. Capital export may have increased because of a push of falling interest rates and lack of investment opportunities at home, but it could equally well have increased because of the pull of improved profit opportunities or reduced risks elsewhere. Even if the push explanation is preferred (as it is by Edelstein 1982), the push might be explained by factors outside Hobson's theory.

4.3 THE POLITICS OF IMPERIALISM

Hobson's main concern was with the expansion of the British empire in the period from 1870 to the turn of the century (when he was writing). The bulk of the territories acquired during this period were in tropical Africa and Asia, and were already well populated; they were not likely to prove suitable for large-scale European settlement. He noted the growing inter-imperialist rivalry of the period, which he regarded as dangerous, and as relatively new. The United States had entered the race particularly suddenly, but so had others. He enumerated the financial costs, mainly in terms of military spending, attributing nearly all of military spending to imperialism, on the grounds that inter-imperialist rivalry was the main source of international tension. He also argued that militarism and similar developments are more generally harmful. These costs could not be justified by the benefits of trade with subject territories, since trade with the tropical empire was small, growing slowly, and not dependent to any very large extent on political control.

To assess the costs and benefits of imperialism, it is necessary to have some alternative in mind. Hobson was in a difficult position, because he held that there is a chronic tendency to over-saving. Empire may provide investment opportunities and preserve employment, benefiting a large part of the population. If so, it could be rational, from a national point of view, to support imperialism; this is the 'capitalist theory of capitalist imperialism'. Hobson avoided this conclusion by suggesting a better alternative for the majority of the population; if income were more equally distributed, saving would fall, and a shortage of investment opportunities would cease to be a problem. The costs of imperialism could be avoided.

If imperialism is bad business, why does it happen?

> The only possible answer is that the business interests of the nation as a whole are subordinated to those of certain sectional interests. . . . This . . . is the commonest disease of all forms of government. (Hobson 1938: 46)

He listed the interests involved, including the armaments trade, export and shipping trades, the armed forces, those who find jobs in the apparatus of empire, and so on. There is nothing very original about this; it is in a direct line of descent from Adam Smith's attack on mercantilism as the creature of special interests.

What makes Hobson's story distinctive is the central role he assigned to the financiers, who 'form the central ganglion of international capitalism'.

> United by the strongest bonds of organization, always in closest and quickest touch with one another, . . . they are in a unique position to manipulate the policy of nations. . . . Every great political act involving a new flow of capital, or a large fluctuation in the values of existing investments, must receive the sanction and practical aid of this little group of financial kings. (Hobson 1938: 56-7. I have omitted implicitly anti-semitic remarks; his earlier writings on the Boer war were virulently anti-semitic.)

The main gainers from imperialism are investors. British policy has been 'primarily a struggle for profitable markets of investment' (1938: 53), and 'the period of energetic Imperialism' was also the period in which income from foreign investments grew rapidly (1938: 52). Investors stand to gain from annexations which reduce political risks, especially if they have invested already on terms which take account of risks; as the risks are eliminated, the value of the investment increases. Financiers also gain from any source of turbulence in the values of investments, since their position as insiders allows them to speculate successfully. This may appear inconsistent (investors seek the elimination of risks, financiers thrive on them), but presumably the capital gains when risks are reduced are among the changes in value that offer good prospects for insiders.

To get their way, the financiers must build a pro-imperialist coalition. The interests already listed can all be recruited. Political support can be bought, and influence can be exerted indirectly, through pressures on newspapers, and so on.

> The controlling and directing agent . . . is the pressure of financial and industrial motives, operated for the direct, short-range, material interests of small, able, and well

> organized groups. . . . These groups secure the active co-
> operation of statesmen . . . partly by associating them
> directly in their business schemes, partly by appealing to
> the conservative instincts of . . . the possessing classes. . . .
> The acquiescence . . . of the body of a nation . . . is secured
> . . . by playing on the primitive instincts of the race.
> (Hobson 1938: 212)

Some have argued that Hobson had a psychological theory
of imperialism, because he stressed irrational or non-rational
motives (Mitchell 1965; see also Semmel 1970: 223). Irrational
motives are, it is true, among the (many) factors that Hobson
discussed ('the primitive instincts of the race') but he
repeatedly stressed that they are channelled and harnessed
by the financiers. In particular, psychological motives play no
role in determining the direction, timing, or character of
imperial expansion. They might perhaps be a necessary
condition, but beyond that they play no explanatory role.
Hobson himself was quite clear about their subordinate role:

> aggressive Imperialism . . . is not in the main the product
> of blind passions of races or of the mixed folly and
> ambition of politicians. It is far more rational than at first
> sight appears. . . . it is true that the motive power of
> Imperialism is not chiefly financial: finance is rather the
> governor of the imperial engine, directing the energy and
> determining its work. (Hobson 1938: 47, 59)

Etherington (1984: 70) described the section of the book on
financiers as 'so irrelevant to Hobson's other economic
arguments that one wonders why he included it in the book'.
Cain (1978: 568) accepted that Hobson did stress the role of
financiers, but regarded it as a passing aberration, a 'return to
the old radical obsession with the financier as demon king'.
He presented evidence that Hobson modified at least some of
his views later; maybe so, but he reprinted *Imperialism* as late
as 1938, after a long interval. The conspiracy theory element
in Hobson's argument distressed Cain (1985), as it did
Etherington; they are right to argue that the theory could be
reformulated without it, but the fact remains that it is
precisely the conspiracy of financiers that gives Hobson's
theory what explanatory force it has. Without their directing

intelligence, the theory loses its distinctive character, and becomes merely a list of pro-imperialist forces; it cannot offer any explanation of the pattern or timing of imperialist advance. (I shall argue that even with the special role of the financiers the theory does little better.)

A related issue is whether, as Cain (1985) argued, Hobson saw a conflict between the interests of industry and finance. He certainly saw a conflict between the interests of the financiers and the British people (which were best served by social reform), but whether he saw a conflict between the interests of industrial capitalists and of financiers (except in incidental matters) is more doubtful. A considerable range of industries are listed among the gainers from imperialism, while capitalists as a whole presumably have an interest in resisting redistribution of income. In the absence of social reform, overseas investment is better for the industrial capitalists than no investment at all; the real problem is under-consumption. Incidentally, there is some evidence that Hobson had a concept of 'finance capital', similar to that of Hilferding (discussed in the next chapter): a fusion of financial and industrial capital, with finance in the driving seat. In his discussion of America (1938: 75-7), for example, Hobson argued that imperialism emerged when financiers had taken control of major industries within the country: there could hardly be a conflict between industrial and financial capital in this case.

What holds the story together, and provides it with any explanatory power it has, is the directing role of the financiers. Unfortunately, Hobson did not define the interests of the financiers at all sharply. They are said to have an interest in controlling existing potential future destinations for investment. Since one of the aims is to reduce risks, those areas where risks are low, or where conquest is impracticable may be left alone; it is no refutation of the theory to point out that the USA was a major destination for British investment, but Britain did not attempt a (re)conquest. Nor would it refute the theory to argue that many of the territories annexed in the late nineteenth century turned out to be quite valueless, provided they could reasonably have been expected to yield a return (no-one claims that financiers could see into the future). By the nature of the theory, it is no refutation to argue that the costs (to the nation) exceeded the returns. Since the financiers are said to have had an interest in turbulence for its own sake, any adventure, however wild, could be accounted for.

The trouble is not that the theory fails to explain the facts, but that it explains them too easily; it could explain almost anything. A satisfactory theory of imperialism must offer some more specific explanation of the pattern and timing of imperial expansion. Hobson did suggest a variety of relevant factors, which is a useful step, but no more. His theory therefore falls at the last hurdle. It is not, however, clear that any of the other theories surveyed in this book does very much better, and later writers, Marxist and non-Marxist, have drawn on his ideas extensively.

4.4 SUMMARY

Under-consumption is an important element in many theories of imperialism, so it is worth bringing the case against it together. The basic idea is that consumption demand is special, because consumption is the real aim of economic activity, while investment is subordinate to it, because investment exists to provide for future consumption. This is where the confusion starts. For an individual (or a planned economy), consumption may be the ultimate aim. A market system, however, is not the sort of thing that has an ultimate aim; it is no more than a mechanism, and one kind of demand is just as good as another in generating profits.

If consumption is too low, it is said, there will be a lot of saving to be invested, and a lack of opportunities to invest (because low consumption means low demand and hence low investment). This is a very naive view of investment, which ignores both the scope for economic growth and the scope for capital-intensive methods of production. For an under-consumption theory to work, it must show why neither of these escape routes is possible. Luxemburg made no attempt to do so, and her under-consumption arguments cannot be taken seriously. Hobson got quite a way further, but his is still a rather special and rather unconvincing case. Other versions will be discussed in later chapters.

How much does the failure of under-consumption theories matter? If the aim is simply to explain foreign investment (which can be an important element in a theory of imperialism), then it does not matter much. Foreign investment can be explained without using strong forms of under-consumption. However, any claim that capitalism could not survive without external investment has to be abandoned.

5

Hilferding

Between 1900 and 1920, the concept of imperialism was introduced into Marxist theory, and a definite theory of imperialism was constructed, by three writers: Rudolf Hilferding, Nicolai Bukharin and Vladimir Ilych Lenin. I shall call their theories the 'classical Marxist theories of imperialism', since I use the term 'classical Marxist' to mean Marxist writers from Marx to Lenin and Trotsky; Marx himself did not have a theory of imperialism.

It is not easy to separate the contributions of these three writers. Hilferding came first, and his massive *Finance Capital* contains almost every major point made by the others. It could therefore be argued that he deserves the real credit. He did not, however, put his arguments together into a definite concept of imperialism. Bukharin, in his *Imperialism and World Economy* transformed Hilferding's picture of developments inside the advanced capitalist countries into a coherent theory of the transformation of the world economy. I shall argue that Lenin's contribution, in his *Imperialism, the Highest Stage of Capitalism*, was primarily to popularize the theories of Hilferding and Bukharin, and to introduce ideas taken from Hobson. These judgements are based solely on the published record. The period before the First World War was one of unprecedented creative ferment in Marxist circles, both in Vienna and Berlin, where Hilferding worked, and among Russian *emigrés*. Ideas were in the air, especially about imperialism, and their original sources may be hard to trace.

It is easy to misunderstand the classical Marxist theories of imperialism, since the very word has expanded and altered its meaning. Today, the word 'imperialism' generally refers to the dominance of more developed over less developed countries. For the classical Marxists it meant, primarily, rivalry between major capitalist countries, rivalry expressed in conflict over territory, taking political and military as well as economic forms, and tending, ultimately, to inter-imperialist war. The dominance of stronger countries over weaker is certainly implicit in this conception, but the focus is on the struggle for dominance, a struggle between the strongest in which the less developed countries figure mainly as passive battlegrounds, not as active participants.

The classical Marxists have often been accused of Euro-centrism, and the charge is, to a fair extent, justified. Their concentration on the most advanced countries reflected the political realities of the times. Hilferding wrote during the build up to the First World War, Bukharin and Lenin after the war had started. The socialist movement had to hammer out a policy towards the war. All three thought of socialist revolution in the advanced countries as the necessary route towards socialism and the precondition for advance in less developed areas.

All of the writers named saw themselves as up-dating Marx to take account of a development that had taken place since Marx's time (though Marx had predicted it), the rise of *monopoly*. The term 'monopoly' in mainstream economics is used to mean a single seller who has no rival within a given market. In the Marxist tradition, however, 'monopoly' is used more broadly to refer to any major departure from atomistic competition. Where there are relatively few producers we can speak of a growth of monopoly, without excluding very fierce competition. Competition, in this case, does not take the form of price competition in a relatively impersonal market, as it does for competitive capitalism, but is instead a direct rivalry which can take a great variety of forms.

5.1 FINANCE CAPITAL

Hilferding's major work, *Finance Capital* (Hilferding 1981, cited below as *FC*), was mostly written around 1905 in Vienna, but not completed and published until 1910, in Germany. It was mainly concerned with the internal develop-ment of advanced capitalist countries. I will have to examine this aspect of Hilferding's work, since it is basic to his treatment of imperialism as well as to much work by subsequent writers, but I cannot go into detail, since it falls somewhat outside the scope of this book.

He started with a lengthy, interesting, but rather eccentric, treatment of the theory of money, a topic which I will pass over entirely here, only remarking that the obscurity of this first part of the book may well be one reason why the work as a whole has been treated with a kind of respectful neglect.

The next major element in his argument was the rise of the joint stock company as a new form of organization for the capitalist firm. A joint stock company is, in effect, a coalition of capitalists who share the profits and control of the firm in proportion to their shareholdings. Hilferding's treatment of the joint stock company, although it has some points in common with Marx's very fragmentary comments on the subject (*Capital*: III, ch. 27: 427ff.), is really the first thorough Marxist discussion of this important topic.

The formation of joint stock companies (modern corporations) represents a modification of the function of the capitalist. The previous form of organization, the individual enterprise, was limited in size by its owner's wealth, and could only grow to the extent that the individual capitalist saved the profits and ploughed them back. The joint stock company can assemble capital from many small shareholders, allowing the amalgamation of many capitals into one. At the same time, personal wealth ownership may be concentrated into fewer hands by the opportunities for swindling and speculation in shares, and the manipulations which holders of controlling blocks of shares can carry out. Hilferding stressed the way owners of large blocks of capital could use the joint stock form of organization to gain control of the capital of many small shareholders. Whatever its effects on the concentration of personal wealth, the rise of the joint stock company represented a massive concentration of economic power as well as a concentration of production. This was a fairly common theme among left-wing writers of the time; it was, after all, the time when magnates like Rockefeller and Carnegie were demonstrating the potential of these financial manipulations in practical terms.

The context is the process of concentration and centralization of capital, in which larger capitals drive out small, generating a tendency to monopoly. This process was central to Marx's work and to virtually all subsequent Marxist thought, and was very visible in the main capitalist countries at the time, especially Germany and central Europe. The development of the joint stock company simply accelerated the tendency to concentration already at work. Hilferding discussed the different forms which the centralization of capital can take in considerable detail.

The rise of monopoly in one sector has consequences for other sectors which deal with it, creating 'relations of mutual dependence and dominance'. In a competitive system where each firm has many potential suppliers and customers, it can be relatively indifferent to the policies of any single firm. Where the firm has only a few customers or suppliers it cannot be indifferent: a relation of mutual dependence grows up. As long as the firms that deal with each other are independent, there will be a struggle for dominance, since there are direct conflicts of interest between them (over the price at which they trade, for example). Hilferding asserted that: 'In the relations of mutual dependence between capitalist enterprises it is the amount of capital that principally determines which enterprise shall become dependent upon the other' (FC: 223). In particular, where a relatively competitive industry deals with a monopoly or cartel, it will fall under the control of the monopoly. Competitive firms will be reduced to the status of mere agents, unless they react by forming their own cartel or amalgamating in self-defence. In either case the monopolized sector of the economy will be effectively expanded. Monopoly is thus, in a sense, contagious: beyond a certain stage it tends to spread very rapidly. Hilferding saw the rapid spread of monopoly, and the tight linking together of different sectors of the economy by direct relations of interdependence and dominance (in place of impersonal market links), as a fundamental transformation of capitalism.

For Hilferding, the central actors in the growth of monopoly were the banks. I have omitted all mention of banks from the preceding pages to show that the main lines of Hilferding's account of the emergence of monopoly capitalism do not depend on his theory of the role of the banks. Hilferding's emphasis on the role of banks is dubious, because it was based on Germany, where the banks did play a central role. In other countries, essentially the same results came about in rather different ways.

The main function of banks is to centralize money capital, gathering together idle funds (capitalists' reserves, depreciation funds, and the like, as well as the savings of other social strata). On the principle of 'pooled reserves' most of the money can then be re-lent for productive (profitable) use, with only a relatively small portion held in cash as reserves. In Germany, banks also carried out a wider range of functions (acting on behalf of their customers in the buying and selling of shares, for example, as well as holding shares themselves), so they effectively controlled all the sources of money capital and thus, as a group, had enormous potential power. As long as banking was relatively competitive this made little difference: if one bank refused a loan there were others to turn to. However, the banks were in the forefront of the tendency towards monopoly, and in Germany the number of major banks fell to nine and then to six. (See Bukharin 1972a: 71; Lenin 1950: 210ff. Hilferding only gave factual detail in passing: e.g. *FC*: 121 n18.)

Given the rapid development of monopoly in banks, together with the concentration of control over all major sources of finance, it is easy to see how banks came to play a dominant role in the tightly interconnected and hierarchical capitalist system that Hilferding described. The banks, in turn, have a strong interest in promoting cartelization among their clients, since this reduces the risk that the firms to whom they have lent money will go bankrupt, and in promoting mergers so that the weaker firms are absorbed by the stronger (safeguarding the bank's money) rather than being driven to the wall by competition.

Hilferding summed up these transformations in his concept of *finance capital*, undoubtedly his best-known contribution to the vocabulary of Marxism. Marx analysed the division of capital into three fractions: *industrial capital* (productive enterprises, including capitalist agricultural enterprises), *financial capital* (banks and similar capitalist enterprises dealing in money capital), and *commercial capital* (merchant's capital; buying and selling goods rather than producing them). Hilferding argued that the separation of industrial and financial capital, which was characteristic of the era of competitive capitalism, disappears in the epoch of monopoly capitalism. *Finance capital is the product of the fusion of industrial and financial capital.* It is therefore vital not to confuse finance capital with financial capital.

Hilferding argued that as bank deposits grew, and opportunities for investment in commerce declined (because monopolies take direct control of buying and selling), the banks were effectively forced into investing directly in production.

> An ever-increasing part of the capital of industry does not belong to the industrialists who use it. They are able to dispose over capital only through the banks, which represent the owners. On the other side, the banks have to invest an ever-increasing part of their capital in industry, and in this way they become to a greater and greater extent industrial capitalists. *I call bank capital, that is, capital in money form which is actually transformed in this way into industrial capital, finance capital.* (FC: 225, emphasis added)

The concept of finance capital, as Hilferding presented it, is not entirely unambiguous. At a very simple level it is a label for that part of the total capital which comes into the hands of industrial capital via the banks or, more generally, via the financial system. Hilferding frequently used it, however, to indicate a unit of control: that part of a (capitalist) economy which is under the control of the banks. Perhaps the way of looking at it which best covers the way Hilferding and his successors have used the term, is to understand 'finance capital' as that fraction of capital in which the functions of financial capital and industrial capital are effectively united, in which the assembly of funds from a variety of sources is carried out by the same enterprise that effectively controls the productive use of the funds.

If this generalization of the concept is accepted, it opens the way to regarding the large multinational companies of today as part of finance capital. These companies are certainly not under the control of banks, but their head offices do perform many of the functions of financial capital in raising money from many sources (including small shareholders, by share issues), and also channel flows of capital from one subsidiary enterprise to another. Hilferding recognized the analogy between joint stock companies and banks, in that both can assemble capital from many sources (*FC*: 122). If we are to speak of an epoch dominated by finance capital it is essential to widen the concept and free it of its association with the dominance of banks, which was not found in all advanced capitalist countries.

Hilferding recognized that the role of the banks was rather different in England, where banks only gave credit for circulation and did not finance long-term capital investments. The result was a low interest rate on bank deposits, with the public buying shares via the stock exchange. Industry was therefore less dependent on the banks (*FC*: 225). He explained the greater dominance of the banking system in Germany, probably correctly, by the later and more rapid development of capitalism in Germany. In England, wealth became concentrated into the hands of industrial capitalists over a long period of time. German industrialists, to catch up, had to draw on the savings of other classes through the banks and through the formation of joint stock companies (*FC*: 306). This explanation should, perhaps, be taken a step further; the slower pace of development in England, together with the development of parts of the financial structure during the period dominated by merchant's capital, led to the emergence of a more varied financial system in which various financial functions, united in the banks in Germany, were carried out by different parts of financial capital (stockbrokers, merchant banks, clearing banks, etc.). There is no doubt that the whole process of concentration and centralization was somewhat retarded in Britain. This has substantial implications (since Britain, the least monopolized of the great powers, had the largest empire), but the explanation is probably fairly simple. The competitive struggle enforces the centralization of capital and, given Britain's relative lead in industry, the pressure of competition was felt less than in slightly less developed countries.

This section is best summed up in Hilferding's words:

> Finance capital signifies the unification of capital. The previously separate spheres of industrial, commercial and bank capital are now brought under the direction of high finance, in which the masters of industry and of the banks are united in a close personal association. The basis of this association is the elimination of free competition among

individual capitalists by the large monopolistic combines. This naturally involves at the same time a change in the relation of the capitalist class to state power. (*FC*: 301)

5.2 PROTECTIONISM AND ECONOMIC TERRITORY

Protective tariffs, that is taxes on goods imported into a territory, placing them at a disadvantage relative to locally produced goods, play a crucial role in Hilferding's arguments. This may seem surprising, since tariffs are often regarded as rather trivial and boring things best left for specialists to debate. We have to remind ourselves that the triumph of industrial capital in England was marked by the abolition of the Corn Laws (a form of protection of agriculture) and that protectionism versus free trade was the major issue of economic policy in all the advanced capitalist countries at the time Hilferding was writing. It is interesting to note, in passing, Hilferding's almost naive faith in the efficiency of free trade. Free trade 'would ensure the highest possible labour productivity and the most rational international division of labour' (*FC*: 311). This typically classical Marxist belief in the efficiency of capitalism in developing the forces of production would not be shared by many Marxists today.

Hilferding, like Luxemburg, stressed the competitive pressure to make the maximum possible use of the different natural conditions and resources to be found in different parts of the world, and the importance of large-scale operations in reducing costs. Capitalists must always seek, therefore, to maximize the territory open to them for their operations. The importance of tariffs is that they define a distinct national territory. With free trade, the advantages of a base in a large, rather than small, national territory would be minimal, but once protective tariffs are established and the scope for international trade shrinks, the size of the national territory is much more important. Small countries (he cited Belgium) are generally in favour of free trade.

Why then should tariffs be imposed? In the epoch of competitive industrial capital, 'infant industries' sought protection from foreign competition to enable themselves to get started. England, as the first industrial nation, did not need tariffs to the same extent, and was the protagonist of free trade, but as other countries embarked on industrial development, they felt the need for infant industry tariffs. Hilferding argued that these infant industry tariffs, if successful, were self-liquidating in competitive capitalism. Once the industry reaches the stage at which it starts to export, the exported goods have to be sold at the world market price and competition ensures that the price on the home market matches the export price. If the home market price were above the export price, firms would switch production to the more profitable home market until the differential was eliminated. Once home and foreign prices are equalized, the tariff is ineffective.

The rise of monopoly transforms the role of tariffs. Hilferding's arguments rely critically on the idea that it is much easier to monopolize a national market for a particular product than it is to monopolize the world market. He argued this mainly on the grounds that a much higher degree of concentration of capital than that yet achieved would be needed for cartelization to be possible on a world scale, as well as that 'cartels do not become as firmly established' on an international basis (but why?) and that there would be resistance to foreign-based cartels. These are not very strong arguments, at least as Hilferding put them (FC: 312), and it seems that he did not realize how crucial they are to his whole argument. He simply took it for granted that cartels must form on a national basis, and it was Bukharin, for whom the subject of study was the world economy, who really saw that this was a problem. Both Bukharin and Lenin devoted more attention to the possibility of cartelization on a world scale because they wished to refute Kautsky's theory of 'ultra-imperialism', a topic I will take up in the next chapter.

Given the impossibility of monopolizing the world market, tariff protection is necessary for trusts or cartels formed on a national basis to get any advantage from their monopoly position. Without protection, imports would pour in and undercut the monopoly as soon as the price was pushed above the world market level. The extent to which a national monopoly can raise the price above the world market price is directly determined by the tariff, up to the monopoly price level which they would set if the market were completely isolated. Thus monopolies and finance capital have a direct interest in increasing the level of protection. The later nineteenth and early twentieth centuries, the period of the rise of monopoly, also saw protectionism become much more widespread, after a period in the mid-nineteenth century when the tendency was, rather hesitantly, towards free trade. This analysis of tariffs was not original to Hilferding. It was hinted at by Engels, and widely discussed in the economic literature of Hilferding's time. Hilferding's contribution was to build it into a Marxist analysis of the rise of finance capital. (See the references in Bukharin 1972a: 75 n2.)

Hilferding's argument that monopolies seek tariff protection only applies to particular sectors. If a tariff is imposed on all goods, and if their prices rise correspondingly (prices of imported goods rise because the tariff is actually paid, home market prices of exported goods rise because of the scope for monopoly price fixing created by the tariff), then wages will, in a Marxist framework, have to rise in money terms to keep real wages (the value of labour-power) the same. Monopoly profits, in Hilferding's framework, should be seen as a redivision of surplus value, increasing the profit of the monopolies at the expense of remaining competitive sectors. He was not very consistent on this point, since he described monopoly prices as 'a tribute' imposed on consumers as a whole and not 'a deduction from the profit of the other non-cartelized industries' (FC: 308). He also argued that heavy industry was not very concerned about increases in the cost of living because labour costs are relatively unimportant given the high organic composition of capital (FC: 309). This will not really do, since wage increases will affect the price of the means of production used by heavy industry as well as their direct labour costs, and protection would presumably push up the prices of means of production anyway. He did, on the other hand, consider the possibility that protectionism may reduce the overall rate of profit through the reduction in efficiency which follows from a reduction in the international division of labour. The fact is that he did not have a complete theory of wages, or of prices and profits, in an economy where prices are affected both by monopoly and by external prices modified by tariffs. This cannot really be held against him, since I know of no one else who has such a theory.

We have seen that tariffs on exported (or potentially exported) goods are ineffective in a competitive industry. For a monopolized industry, however, they are not ineffective, because a monopoly can sell at different prices in different markets. Where there are many firms, they will each divert supplies into the high-price market, because each reckons its own effect on the price to be negligible. A monopoly, on the other hand, can deliberately hold up the price on the home market. Prices are no longer determined by impersonal market forces, but are, within limits, under the deliberate control of monopolies. To keep up the price in the home market, the monopoly must restrict the amount sold, since consumers buy less when the price is raised. The surplus can be sold on the world market at whatever price it will fetch, provided the price is enough to cover costs; if costs fall with increasing output, what is relevant is that the price should be enough to cover the extra cost of producing the extra output, which will be lower than the average cost of producing the whole output. (See any economics textbook on average and marginal cost, and on discriminating monopoly.)

It may, therefore, pay a monopoly to sell in the world market at a price below the average cost of production, not just to get rid of a temporary surplus, but as a regular practice. An example may make this clear. Suppose that the cost of producing 100 units is $100, and of producing 200 units, $150. The average cost of 100 units is thus £1 per unit, and of 200 units is $0.75 per unit. Now consider the pattern of sales set out below

Home market sales: 100 units; price: $1.50; revenue: $150.
Export market sales: 100 units; price: $0.60; revenue: $60.
Total sales: 200 units; total revenue: $210.

Selling on the home market alone would bring a profit of $50 (revenue of $150, cost $100). The export of 100 units has brought in extra revenue of $60 and increased costs by $50, increasing profit to $60 ($210 – $150), despite the fact that the 100 exported units have been sold at below the average cost of producing all 200 units ($0.60 compared with average cost of $0.75). In the same example, consider an enterprise without a protected home market which has to sell all of its output at the world market price. If it too had an output of 200 units, then it would be operating at a loss: receipts of $120 and costs of $150; loss of $30. It is true that a sufficiently large enterprise might be able to overcome this disadvantage (say: output 600, cost $300), but it is clear that enterprises with monopoly control over a protected home market are at an advantage in the struggle for survival in the world market.

It may be asked: if all countries were to protect their markets, where could this 'world market' or 'external market' be found? Hilferding did not give a clear answer. He seems to have assumed an incomplete development of protection, leaving large sections of the world unprotected. It could also be pointed out that if monopolies take full advantage of the tariff to raise their price, foreign goods can still penetrate the protected home market. To continue the example given above, if the world market price is $0.60 and the tariff, per unit, $0.90, then a domestic monopolist can sell at $1.50, but a foreign supplier could also sell at $1.50, pay the $0.90 in customs duty and receive a net revenue of $0.60, the same as in a unprotected part of the world market.

Note that Hilferding argued that monopolies exploit all consumers within their protected territory, whether they live in the metropolitan areas or the colonies; it is not a question of an imperialist country exploiting its subject territories, but of monopolies exploiting everyone else. Protection, by supporting monopoly, serves the interests of a ruling class, and specifically of a section of that class, finance capital.

Hilferding therefore argued that the function of protectionism had been completely transformed. 'From being a means of defence against the conquest of the domestic market by foreign industries it has become a means for the conquest of foreign markets by domestic industry' (FC: 310).

> As we have seen, the protective tariff brings the capitalist monopoly an extra profit on its sales in the domestic market. The larger the economic territory, the greater the volume of domestic sales ... and the larger therefore the cartel's profits. The greater this profit, the higher the export subsidies can be, and the stronger therefore is the cartel's competitive position on the world market. (FC: 313)

Protectionism divides the world into distinct national economic territories, and the rise of monopoly impels protectionism to new heights. This is the basis of a theory of imperialism (though Hilferding adduced further arguments, which I will discuss in the next section). To quote him:

> The policy of finance capital has three objectives: (1) to establish the largest possible economic territory; (2) to close this territory to foreign competition by a wall of protective tariffs, and consequently (3) to reserve it as an area of exploitation for the national monopolistic combines. (FC: 326)

5.3 CAPITAL EXPORT

The international movement of capital on a really large scale started around the 1870s, and reached a peak in the years immediately before the First World War. It was never again to reach such levels, relative to the scale of total investment, but Marxists of the time could not, of course, see into the future. The export of capital was therefore an important topic in their writings. It had become almost a truism to say that 'the export of capital tends to replace the export of commodities'; it had to be incorporated into the analysis.

It is clear that Hilferding thought of the movement of capital from one geographical area or industrial sector to another as an entirely normal part of capitalism. Capital seeks out the cheapest locations for production, the most favourable natural conditions and the richest natural resources. There are, however, distinctions which Hilferding did not draw but which are important to his arguments. Starting with his concept of a 'national economic territory' (which may be larger than the 'nation' narrowly defined, because it includes colonies, spheres of influence, and so on), we can distinguish three forms of capital export. First, there is the movement of capital to underdeveloped parts of the economic territory. There is, according to Hilferding, a motive to expand territory in order to gain these fields for investment. Second, there is investment in 'unclaimed', or independent but backward, parts of the world. This investment may serve as a means of incorporating the area concerned into the national territory (preferential treatment may be a condition of granting a loan), or it may create a motive for its subsequent incorporation in order to safeguard the investment. Third, there is investment in the territory of another nation. This would tend to decrease the importance of the division of the world market into different territories, rather than creating a motive for territorial expansion.

What are the reasons for capital export? Hilferding treated the constant movement of capital in search of maximum returns as normal, but there are some additional arguments that apply specifically to capital export. One is the desire to overcome other countries' protective tariffs by producing within their tariff walls, taking advantage of the tariffs that are designed to shut you out. In the case where the tariffs are imposed by a weak state, this falls into my second category, and may be a prelude to the incorporation of the capital importing country into the sphere of influence of the capital exporter. Where the capital importing country is a major power, however, it falls into my third category, and tends to undermine the effect of protective tariffs in reserving the 'national territory' for the national capital.

Hilferding did mention the 'falling rate of profit' (FC: 315), but immediately, and rightly, qualified the argument by pointing out that the price of internationally traded goods is not determined by conditions in the most advanced countries alone; both advanced and underdeveloped countries have to sell their goods on the world market at a single price. If advanced countries have a higher organic composition of capital, it is because capital-intensive methods are more profitable at the existing prices. Underdeveloped areas producing the same goods by less advanced methods must have higher costs and a lower profit rate (unless they have other advantages such as low wages, which are in themselves sufficient explanation for the movement of capital).

Hilferding did, however, regard differences in interest (and profit) rates as an important motor of capital exports. The highly developed financial systems of the advanced countries lead to lower interest rates and greater availability of (money) capital, hence they are the main centres for raising loans and floating new enterprises. Underdeveloped countries also attract investment because wages are low, the low quality of labour being compensated by long working hours, and also because rent on land is low. These reasons need no discussion, since they are so obvious. He also discussed the creation of markets for capital goods by the export of capital, but he treated these mainly as effects of capital export rather than causes of it. The export of capital stimulates the development of the capital goods industries, creates supplies of cheap goods, and raises the rate of profit. It therefore generates a period of accelerated growth for capitalism.

What is the connection between the rise of finance capital and the growth of capital export? This was clearly a vital question for Hilferding, since he hoped to show that the main developments of capitalism in his time were linked to the rise of finance capital. His answer ran in terms of institutional changes, such as the adoption of the joint stock form of organization and the linking of banks and industrial firms. Opportunities for capital export had been there all along, but had been left unclaimed for lack of adequate organizational forms to take advantage of them. The joint stock form made it possible for subsidiaries to be established abroad without the emigration of the capitalist. The link between the banks and industrial companies made for easier access to funds, often through a foreign subsidiary of the bank. A large company has a great advantage in setting up a new installation from scratch in a new location, because of its size alone.

The development of finance capital also changed the form of capital export. Countries in which finance capital had not developed far (Britain, France) exported capital by portfolio investment, the granting of loans and the purchase of shares in foreign enterprises. Where finance capital was more developed (Germany, USA), capital export tended to take the form of direct investment in productive enterprises controlled from the capital exporting country, ensuring that the capital exporter had far tighter control. The greater efficiency of finance capital in investment abroad is a competitive advantage which hastens the transformation of capital into finance capital.

I have already touched on some of the connections between the export of capital and the creation and expansion of a 'national economic territory'. Territorial expansion opens up new opportunities for investment, while investors may call on the 'home' state to create a political and juridical environment suitable for their activities. Trade can go on between various different social organizations, but capital investment requires the creation of capitalist relations of production. Where these are not already well established, colonial control may be a way of creating them. All of this is in line with Marx, Luxemburg and Hobson.

The emphasis in Hilferding's book is on the most advanced countries, the centres of finance capital, but he did have something to say about the impact of these developments on less developed areas. The establishment of capitalist relations of production in new areas is carried though, where necessary, by force. Hilferding's comments could have been taken direct from Rosa Luxemburg (or vice versa); they do not differ on the methods of capitalist expansion, and there is, as we have seen, a fair measure of agreement on the reasons.

> Violent methods are of the essence of colonial policy, without which it would lose its capitalist rationale. They are just as much an integral part of it as the existence of a propertyless proletariat is a *conditio sine qua non* of capitalism in general. The idea of pursuing a colonial policy without having to resort to its violent methods is an illusion to be taken no more seriously than that of abolishing the proletariat while maintaining capitalism in existence. (*FC:* 319)

The export of capital is the primary driving force behind this violent breakup of pre-capitalist societies.

> The export of capital, especially since it has assumed the form of industrial and finance capital, has enormously accelerated the overthrow of all the old social relations, and the involvement of all the world in capitalism. Capitalist development did not take place independently in each individual country, but instead capitalist relations of production and exploitation were imported along with capital from abroad, and indeed imported at the level already attained in the most advanced country. (*FC:* 322)

The import of capital could have favourable effects on the development of capitalism in less developed areas, especially in the early stages, when capital was imported to build railways and build up industries serving the local market. Even in this case, there are disadvantages of capital import in the drain of profit abroad, though a large enough territory may be able to 'naturalize' foreign capital (Hilferding's example is the absorption of French and Belgian capital in Germany). However, the export of capital is increasingly directed to the production of raw materials for export. This leads to economic and political dependence (*FC*: 330). Hilferding thus anticipated themes developed by later writers, but he soon turned away from these issues to discuss the way in which small countries became the battlefield for the struggles of the major powers, and hence gets back to the subject of the advanced countries, his main interest.

5.4 IMPERIALISM

The rise of finance capital brought about a fundamental transformation in class structure, in the role of the state, and in the ideological sphere. In the epoch of competitive capitalism, capital was divided into three distinct fractions: industrial, commercial and financial. The dominant ideology of industrial capital was liberalism, both economic liberalism or *laissez-faire*, and the more radical political liberalism in which the claim to independence of individual capitalists and commodity producers was translated into a doctrine of the rights of the individual citizen. This ideology never became dominant in a pure form. Hilferding drew an interesting contrast between England, on the one hand, and continental Europe on the other. In England, the victory of capitalism was won at a very early stage, before liberalism had achieved its classical political form, and as a result English ideology was dominated by the narrowly economic doctrines of *laissez-faire*. Political liberalism never took root in its stronger forms. Free trade, on the other hand, perfectly expressed the interests of industrial capital in England when England was the dominant industrial nation and had nothing to fear from international competition. The dominance of the ideology of competition proved difficult to shake off when it became outdated, with the rise of finance capital in other nations. In continental Europe, industrial capital needed protection and state assistance from the beginning, being weaker initially as a result of a later start. *Laissez-faire* ideology never took so firm a hold, and the classical liberal hostility to the state was very much weakened. The protagonists of free trade, for a long time, were the agricultural interests, since northern Europe was a grain exporting region. The struggles in Germany, Italy and Austria to create modern nation states out of pre-capitalist political structures also generated support for the state. There were, therefore, considerable elements of statist ideology for finance capital to build on. Pre-capitalist ideologies were never wholly eliminated, and could be incorporated into the ideology of finance capital.

The rise of finance capital unified industrial and financial capital, while commercial capital was reduced to a totally subordinate status. The primary justification for the separate role of commercial capital had been the need to collect together the output of many small firms, to gain the economies of trading on a large scale. Once production was concentrated into large units, this justification vanished, especially in exchanges between one sector of production and another, where large firms prefer to deal directly with each other. Where commercial capital survived at all, it was reduced to the status of an agent for finance capital.

The integration of capital by finance capital was cemented, according to Hilferding, by a 'personal union'. By this he meant that the high level personnel of different sectors became interchangeable. Representatives of banks sat on the boards of industrial firms, and industrialists sat on the boards of banks. Family and social ties also linked the ruling class together. Smaller capitalists in fact suffered from the rise of monopoly, but Hilferding did not expect them to react against finance capital, because of their dependence on the banks (for loans) and on the monopolies (for orders and supplies). The spread of share ownership was very important in integrating the non-producing classes of landlords, professionals, state employees and rentiers. Rural interests were also incorporated as finance capital penetrated the countryside by setting up plants to process agricultural products and the like. The 'possessing classes' were united politically by the fact that they faced a common enemy, the working class.

The rise of finance capital therefore created a ruling class relatively unified in political affairs under the leadership of the 'magnates of finance capital', corresponding to a relatively unified and hierarchical economic structure (note the similarity to Hobson). This change in the structure of the ruling class naturally involved a change in its relation to the state, a relation which became much more close and direct. Hilferding did not go as far as his successors, who tended to see the state as the more or less direct property of a handful of monopolies, but even so it is possible that he went too far. He was describing tendencies which had not, at that date, fully worked themselves out, and it is doubtful whether the various strata and fractions of the capitalist class and its allies were ever as thoroughly integrated as he suggested.

He also described the growth of new strata of white-collar workers called into existence by the increased size of firms and the consequent mushrooming of administration and paperwork. He foresaw a continuing increase in these groups and fully realized their importance. Although he regarded them as potential allies for the working class, he recognized that they were, at the time, among the most deeply reactionary sections of the population, and that their position would at best be ambivalent. The political position of finance capital was thus very strong.

Hilferding stressed that finance capital needed the power of the state. In the first instance, tariff protection was needed to gain the benefits of monopoly. Given protection, we have seen why finance capital should press for territorial expansion, and thus for a powerful state.

> The demand for an expansionist policy revolutionizes the whole world view of the bourgeoisie, which ceases to be peace-loving and humanitarian. The old free traders believed in free trade not only as the best economic policy but also as the beginning of an era of peace. Finance capital abandoned this belief long ago. It has no faith in the harmony of capitalist interests, and knows well that competition is becoming increasingly a political power struggle. The ideal of peace has lost its lustre, and in place of the idea of humanity there emerges a glorification of the greatness and power of the state. . . . The ideal now is to secure for one's own nation the domination of the world. (FC: 335)

Hilferding did not generally use the word 'imperialism', tending instead to use phrases like 'modern protectionist policy', 'modern colonial policy' and 'the external policy of finance capital'. When he did use it, it was as a generalized descriptive term for militarist and expansionist tendencies in capitalism, so there are phrases like: 'modern protectionist policy, which is inextricably bound up with imperialism', and 'capital can pursue no other policy than that of imperialism' (FC: 365, 366). All these references occur in the last chapter of the book. Imperialism was a word which was around at the time, and Hilferding used it to add punch to his peroration.

The use of words is not of essential importance. What is important is the absence of any clear concept of imperialism, an absence indicated by the variety of phrases Hilferding used to indicate different aspects of the phenomenon. The major elements of the idea were there, but they were never pulled together: the credit for that must go to Bukharin. The reason why Hilferding did not construct a concept of imperialism is fairly clear; his interest was in the internal developments in the major capitalist centres, in the rise of finance capital. That is the title of the book, it is his concept, and nobody can take it away from him.

Pulling together Hilferding's scattered remarks on the phenomena that came to be called 'imperialism', will show immediately how much Bukharin and Lenin took from him. Finance capital has a direct interest in maximizing the extent of the protected national economic territory. In addition there is the search for exclusive fields for capital export. Both point inexorably to a policy of expansion, and thus to conflicts between capitalist powers. Hilferding was rather cautious in discussing the inevitability of conflict. On the one hand, the rise of German finance capital, controlling a relatively narrow territory, and the relative decline of Britain, with a huge empire, in particular, together with other disproportions between economic strength and size of territory, created a set of circumstances which Hilferding summed up: 'This is a situation which is bound to intensify greatly the conflict between Germany and England and their respective satellites, and to lead towards a solution by force' (FC: 331). On the other hand, he argued, the low level of development of finance capital in Britain and France led to the export of capital in the form of loans, often to American and German enterprises, thus creating a 'certain solidarity' of the international interests of capital. He also cited the fear of socialism as a factor deterring capitalist states from going to war. He preferred to remain agnostic as to which of these tendencies would predominate, commenting that it all depended on the circumstances of particular cases, just like the choice for particular firms between entering a cartel or trying to achieve dominance by undercutting its rivals. In the conflict between Kautsky and Lenin over these issues (discussed in the next chapter), Hilferding's position was, as in so many things, somewhere in between. It was, of course, relatively easy for Lenin to announce the inevitability of war when the war had actually broken out.

5.5 SUMMARY

Competition tends to create monopolies, and monopolies can exercise control over the small firms that they deal with. There is therefore a tendency towards the formation of huge blocs of capital organized in a hierarchical way. Financial, industrial, and commercial capital are linked together, as *finance capital*, in these financial groups, which Hilferding saw as dominated by banks. Since monopolies cannot yet control the world market, they need the protection of tariffs, and then seek to extend their protected markets as far as possible, hence the support of finance capital for expansionist policies. By setting out these arguments, Hilferding became the real founder of the classical Marxist theory of imperialism.

6

Bukharin and Lenin

When the First World War broke out, in August 1914, almost all the socialist parties of the Second International abandoned their commitment to internationalism and supported their national governments. The Bolshevik wing of the Russian Social Democratic Party was almost the only organized party which held out against this disintegration. In this desperate situation, exiled and condemned to inactivity, two of the leaders of the Bolsheviks wrote works on imperialism, setting out their analyses of the connections between war and the development of capitalism. These two works, both based on Hilferding's writings, are the foundations of the classical Marxist analysis of imperialism.

Bukharin's *Imperialism and World Economy* (Bukharin 1972a, cited below as *IWE*) was written in 1915, though the manuscript was lost for a time, and it was only published after the success of the Russian revolution. Lenin wrote a laudatory preface to it, which was not rediscovered and published until 1927. In the meantime, Lenin himself had written on the same topic. His *Imperialism, the Highest Stage of Capitalism* (Lenin 1950, cited below as *Imperialism*) was written in early 1916, in other words, shortly after the preface to Bukharin's book, dated December 1915. Lenin's pamphlet had a slightly more successful passage through the hazards of underground activity and was published a few months earlier than Bukharin's. The dating of Lenin's preface, however, establishes as clearly as one can in such circumstances that Bukharin's work came before Lenin's. I shall therefore start with Bukharin, though it should be noted that Bukharin acknowledged a 'debt of deep gratitude' to Lenin, though it is not clear for what; the context suggests that it may simply be for providing the introduction. I make these points not to disparage Lenin but to reclaim for Bukharin the credit that he deserves. Bukharin's subsequent career was erratic, and he ended by being disgraced and executed in the climactic Stalinist purge. (He has now been rehabilitated in the USSR.) This fate must largely account for the subsequent neglect of his work.

Bukharin and Lenin used the term 'imperialism' in rather different ways. Bukharin defined it as a *policy*:

> We speak of imperialism as of a <u>policy of finance capital</u>. However, one may also speak of imperialism as an ideology. In a similar way liberalism is on the one hand a policy of industrial capitalism (free trade, etc.) and on the other it denotes a whole ideology (personal liberty, etc.). (*IWE*: 110n)

However, he insisted that a policy of conquest only counts as imperialism if it is the policy of finance capital, and he also argued that it is inevitably followed by finance capital. Furthermore, looked at on a world scale, what matters is not the fact that any one particular state follows an imperialist policy but the rivalry between them; this comes out clearly in his chapter heading: 'Imperialism as the reproduction of capitalist competition on a larger scale'. His argument moves, therefore, from imperialism as a policy and as an ideology, to imperialism as a characteristic of the world economy at a particular stage of development.

Lenin took this further by treating imperialism as a stage in the development of capitalism. Policies which other writers had called imperialist are part of the characteristics of this stage, but so are other phenomena including the rise of monopoly. All are subsumed under the single heading, imperialism. (For further discussion see Arrighi 1978.) This definition has caused some confusion, since many subsequent Marxists have wanted to talk, more narrowly, of imperialism as the domination of one country over another (yet a third definition), and this has become the most common use of the term. The words we use are, of course, not important in themselves. They only become important when they are a source of confusion. I shall generally use the term 'imperialism' in the sense intended by the writer under discussion at the time.

6.1 BUKHARIN

It is difficult to convey either the quality or the importance of Bukharin's writings on imperialism, since his originality was not essentially in producing new ideas, but in putting existing ideas together to make a coherent and novel whole. Much of his theory was taken from Hilferding; my summary of Hilferding's views in the last chapter concentrates on those elements in his slightly chaotic writing that Bukharin subsequently welded into a coherent picture. The essential difference between them is that where Hilferding saw one process at work, the concentration and centralization of capital, Bukharin saw two: the 'internationalization' and 'nationalization' of capital, the growing interdependence of the world economy, and its division into national blocs. The contradiction between these two opposed tendencies drives the system into war and breakdown. I shall quote extensively from Bukharin, because his theoretical statements are so concise that they frequently defy any shorter summary. The major part of what is, in any case, a short book, is taken up with factual evidence adduced to support each step in his argument.

'Just as every individual enterprise is part of the "national" economy, so every one of these "national economies" is included in the system of world economy' (*IWE*: 17). International trade establishes social relations of production on a world scale. The international division of labour is based on two factors of changing importance: first, on the different natural conditions in different areas of the world and, second, on the different levels of development attained in different areas.

> Important as the natural differences in the conditions of production may be, they recede more and more into the background compared with differences that are the result of the uneven development of productive forces in the various countries. ... The cleavage between 'town and country' as well as the 'development of this cleavage',

formerly confined to one country alone, are now being reproduced on a tremendously enlarged basis. Viewed from this standpoint, entire countries appear today as 'towns', namely, the industrial countries, whereas entire agrarian territories appear to be 'country'. (*IWE*: 20-1; the phrases in quotation marks are from Marx, *Capital* I: 352)

The international division of labour was growing, because of improvements in transport, continued economic development, and unevenness of development, factors that are not accidental and will not go away. The internationalization of economic activity is a fundamental fact.

The international division of labour, the difference in natural and social conditions, are an economic *prius* which cannot be destroyed, even by the World War. This being so, there exist definite value relations, and, as their consequence, conditions for the realisation of a maximum of profit in international transactions. Not economic self-sufficiency, but an intensification of international relations ... such is the road of future evolution. (*IWE*: 148)

A world market for capital develops alongside the markets for goods. Capital export appears in Bukharin's argument as an integral part of the growth of the international division of labour and the internationalization of capital. He did suggest in passing that the movement of capital will be from the more developed to the less developed countries, because there is 'overproduction' of capital in the former and the organic composition of capital is lower in the latter (*IWE*: 45-6). This argument is doubly dubious; the theory of the falling rate of profit is now widely rejected, and its application to inter-country comparisons in a partly integrated world system would need to be worked out properly.

The process of concentration and centralization of capital, the tendency towards monopoly, was also going on, at a tremendous pace. There is no need to go into details: Bukharin followed Hilferding closely in the main lines of his argument. Bukharin took a step beyond Hilferding in asking why the 'organization process' should proceed on a national basis. This question is of great relevance today, when some writers are proclaiming the irrelevance of the nation state in view of the internationalization of capital. Bukharin answered:

> The organisation process ... tends to overstep the 'national' boundaries. But it finds very substantial obstacles on this road. First, it is much easier to overcome competition on a 'national' scale than on a world scale . . .; second, the existing differences of economic structure and consequently of production costs make agreements disadvantageous for the advanced 'national' groups; third, the ties of unity with the state and its boundaries are in themselves an ever growing monopoly which guarantees additional profits. Among the factors of the latter category [is] the tariff policy. (*IWE*: 74)

The role of tariffs in protecting national monopolies has already been discussed (chapter 5). In Bukharin's argument they had a new significance. Instead of being simply reasons for protection, they became reasons both for protection and for the formation of cartels on a national basis. Instead of the link-up between finance capital and the state being a conclusion (as in Hilferding), it becomes a step in the argument.

The essential point is that monopolies, in the first instance, take the form of cartels (agreements to carve up the market). These are rather fragile, because there is a constant temptation for any single firm to break with the cartel and try to increase its share of the market. Cartels can only hold together if their members remain satisfied with the way the market is divided and do not believe that they could improve their profits by breaking with the cartel and trying to win the ensuing competitive struggle. A cartel is particularly liable to break up if the competitive strength of its members is very unequal, so the strongest come to think that they have more to gain by breaking up the cartel than by staying in it, and if the relative strengths of the members change, so that the division of the market agreed at the outset becomes inappropriate. Bukharin argued that both factors operate particularly strongly on an international level, because uneven development is particularly marked between different nations within the world economy.

Since cartelization and the formation of monopolies promised both super-profits and a great competitive advantage in the world market, there was a tremendous incentive for capitalist enterprises to link together on a national basis. Bukharin thus had two processes: the nationalization and the internationalization of capital. 'Together with the internationalisation of economy and the internationalisation of capital there is going on a process of "national" intertwining of capital, a process of "nationalising" capital, fraught with the greatest consequences' (*IWE*: 80). The result is the creation of national blocs of capital set in the context of a world economy:

> various spheres of the concentration and organisation process stimulate each other, creating a very strong tendency towards transforming the entire national economy *into one gigantic combined enterprise under the tutelage of the financial kings and the capitalist state, an enterprise which monopolises the national market.* . . . It follows that world capitalism, the world system of production, assumes in our times the following aspect: a few consolidated, organised economic bodies ('the great civilised powers') on the one hand, and a periphery of underdeveloped countries with a semi-agrarian or agrarian system on the other. (*IWE*: 73-4)

This is a striking description, and one that contains a great deal of truth, but it must still be qualified. Bukharin identified a tendency towards the formation of a single 'gigantic combined enterprise' on a national basis. However, like many Marxists, he often treated a tendency as if it were an established fact and ignored the counter-tendencies. It is not true that competition was, then or later, completely suppressed within national boundaries. I am not concerned here with the remaining fringe of small businesses, though they should not be ignored, but with competition between different big businesses and groups of finance capital. The tendency has been for big corporations to spread out from their national bases and compete all over the world, rather than uniting to face foreign competition. So, for example, one of the major sources of competition in the world motor industry is competition between Ford and General Motors.

Further, Bukharin's treatment of the state was over-simple. He, with many of his contemporaries, seems to have regarded the 'relative autonomy' of the state (a modern phrase) as the product of the division of the capitalist class into distinct fractions and into many competing capitals. With the unification of the capitalist class by finance capital, the separation broke down, and a direct identity between the magnates of capital and the state took its place.

This line of argument has influenced the orthodox communist parties ever since and is still to be found today. It has, however, been widely criticized, first, because the unification of the capitalist class was, as I have pointed out above, never complete; second, because support from the various strata of professionals, state employees, etc., has always been vital, and has generally been mobilized by the incorporation of these groups into political organizations, and finally because of the need to contain and absorb working-class pressure rather than simply repressing it. For all of these reasons, the state has much more autonomy than Bukharin, or the other classical Marxists, admitted.

In a sense Bukharin's vision of the world represents an abolition of the state as a body distinct from 'civil society'. It has often been argued that the state is needed to contain the centrifugal pressures of the anarchy of economic life. In Bukharin's vision, the anarchy of capitalist competition is entirely suppressed at the national level, only to re-emerge in an even more disruptive form at the world level. On a world scale, no state exists to suppress the threats to stability that competitive anarchy generates.

To complete the description of Bukharin's analysis of imperialism, one more point must be made. The tendency towards monopoly, in his framework, does not represent a steady decline in competition. On the contrary, it implies an intensification of competition, as the few remaining firms slug it out for the prize of complete monopoly. Total monopoly, on a world scale, might indeed end competition, but Bukharin did not expect this stage to be reached: capitalism would perish first. The concentration and central-ization of capital therefore does not put an end to competition, but changes its form. Previously competition took place primarily inside national boundaries, and compet-ition in the world market was weak. Now that competition is largely eliminated within each state, it is whole countries that are absorbed by others, instead of small businesses being taken over by large ones. 'Imperialist annexation is only a case of the general capitalist tendency towards centralisation of capital, a case of its centralisation at that maximum scale which corresponds to the competition of state capitalist trusts' (*IWE*: 119-20).

6.2 LENIN

Lenin's pamphlet, *Imperialism, the Highest Stage of Capitalism*, is the most famous Marxist work on imperialism. It was, for me, a surprising discovery that it makes little or no contribution to the development of a theory of imperialism. Its theoretical content is slight and derives from Hilferding, Bukharin and Hobson. This should not, perhaps, be a surprise. The work is a pamphlet (Lenin describes it as such in his preface), a 'popular outline' of the sort that has an honourable and important role in Marxist literature: a factual survey of the current situation together with a summary of the results of theoretical analysis (though not the detailed theoretical argument), designed to provide a basis for political decisions. To argue that the work contains no major theoretical innovations is not, therefore, a criticism of Lenin, but of the orthodox Marxist tradition which turned it into a sacred text. To treat any work as sacred is a thoroughly unscientific attitude; to treat a minor work (with the weaknesses which this one has) as sacred is also a serious lapse of judgement. Since *Imperialism* has been treated as a theoretical work, I shall have to criticise it as such. Lenin's writings on the national question are also relevant, if somewhat lightweight (for example, Lenin 1964: 143-56 and 320-60). Bagchi (1986) argues that they are important, as indeed they are for understanding the development of Lenin's political strategy, but in my view they do not add very much to the theory of imperialism.

Lenin's major purpose in writing *Imperialism* was to counter the propaganda of Kautsky and other 'ex-Marxists' (he included Hilferding in this category) who were, in his view, leading the shattered remnants of the Second International in entirely the wrong direction. From this point of view, the most important sections of the work are those directed against Kautsky's theory of 'ultra-imperialism', and those describing the rise of a 'labour aristocracy', which Lenin saw as the material base for the support Kautsky's revisionism had gained in the major imperialist countries.

Lenin's basic method was to set out a series of trends or tendencies in the development of capitalism in the period in which he was writing, and to document each with factual evidence. One such list reads:

> (1) the concentration of production and capital has developed to such a high stage that it has created monopolies which play a decisive role in economic life; (2) the merging of bank capital with industrial capital, and the creation, on the basis of this 'finance capital' of a financial oligarchy; (3) the export of capital as distinguished from the export of commodities acquires exceptional importance; (4) the formation of international monopolist capitalist combines which share the world among themselves; and (5) the territorial division of the whole world among the biggest capitalist powers is completed. (*Imperialism*: 525)

The problem with this method is that each tendency is described separately, and their interconnections are only examined in passing or in the polemical sections directed against Kautsky. In a theory of imperialism it is precisely the interconnections that are crucial; is it just a matter of chance that these developments occurred at the same time, or are there essential connections that make it inevitable that they should occur together? Lenin did say that the 'briefest possible definition of imperialism' is 'the monopoly stage of capitalism', implying that the rest flows from the growth of monopoly, but he did not specify why.

The first two tendencies in the list, the rise of monopoly and of finance capital, pose few new problems since Lenin followed Hilferding very closely. He quoted a variety of sources to establish that production had become concentrated into fewer and fewer units, as Marx had predicted:

> Marx ... by a theoretical and historical analysis of capitalism proved that free competition gives rise to the concentration of production which, in turn, at a certain stage of development, leads to monopoly. ... For Europe,

the time when the new capitalism definitely supersedes the old can be established with fair precision: it was the beginning of the twentieth century. (*Imperialism*: 448)

He also described the development of monopoly in banking, and the dominance of bank capital over industrial capital. Even more noticeably than Hilferding, he stressed the dominance of the banks, and hence of rentiers, of idle owners of money capital who play no active part in production at all. This foreshadows his discussion of 'parasitism'.

The section on the export of capital raises more problems. Why should the export of capital become especially important at this stage of capitalist development, and what is its significance? Lenin argued:

The possibility of exporting capital is created by the fact that a number of backward countries have already been drawn into world capitalist intercourse; main railways have either been or are being built there, the elementary conditions for industrial development have been created etc. The necessity of exporting capital arises from the fact that in a few countries capitalism has become 'over-ripe' and (owing to the backward stage of agriculture and the impoverished state of the masses) capital cannot find a field for 'profitable' investment. (*Imperialism*: 495)

What are we to make of this? The first half of the quotation gives no difficulty. It is the second half of the quotation, the 'over-ripeness' of capitalism, that is generally quoted and that is very difficult to interpret. Some commentators take it as a reference to the 'law' of the falling rate of profit. This interpretation cannot, however, be accepted, since 'the backward stage of agriculture and the impoverished state of the masses' are not factors that lead to a fall in the rate of profit at all. The backward stage of agriculture should reduce the average organic composition of capital and thus raise the rate of profit (unless, by a strict application of Marx's very dubious theory of absolute rent, we argue that the benefits of a low organic composition of capital are captured by land-owners as rent). Backward agriculture might reduce the rate of profit by raising the value of subsistence goods and thus the value of labour-power, but this should be offset by the 'impoverished state of the masses'.

If the reference to the poverty of the masses and the backwardness of agriculture is to mean anything it must surely represent an under-consumptionist analysis, as must: 'if capitalism could . . . raise the standard of living of the masses . . . there could be no talk of a superabundance of capital. . . . But if capitalism did these things it would not be capitalism' (*Imperialism*: 495). Accumulation is held up by a lack of markets resulting from the low demand for consumer goods, which in turn is a result of the poverty of the masses. This was, of course Hobson's argument, which Lenin seems to have taken over rather uncritically. (He did not take over Hobson's solution, a redistribution of income within capitalism, as the extract cited above shows.) On the other hand, Lenin's major economic work, *The Development of Capitalism in Russia*, was directed specifically against the *Narodnik* argument that capitalism in Russia was doomed to failure because of the lack of a 'home market' resulting from the poverty of the masses. The two works were separated by twenty years, and it is possible that Lenin had changed his mind in the interim, but one would require clearer evidence of a change of mind than these cryptic phrases provide.

There are, of course, other reasons for the export of capital to backward countries beside the 'overripeness' of capitalism, and Lenin mentioned them briefly: 'In these backward countries profits are usually high, for capital is scarce, the price of land is relatively low, wages are low, raw materials are cheap' (*Imperialism*: 496). The strongest motive cited by Lenin was the desire to gain control of sources of raw materials, or at least to prevent others from gaining monopoly control of them. These reasons are perfectly adequate to explain the export of capital, but they do not show that capitalism needs capital export to survive, which might be implied by phrases like 'superabundance' of capital. My conclusion is that Lenin's few remarks about the causes of capital export do not amount to an explanation or to a complete theory and cannot usefully be cited in support of any arguments about the importance of capital export to the more advanced capitalist countries (cf. Michalet 1976).

What of the effects of capital export? In the backward areas the effect was to accelerate development. Here again, Lenin was in the direct line of descent from Marx, and especially from the *Communist Manifesto*. He did not stress the obstacles which this development meets, nor did he stress its one-sided and limited effects, in the way that Hilferding, and more recent writers (for example, Baran) have done.

> The export of capital affects and greatly accelerates the development of capitalism in those countries to which it is exported. While, therefore, the export of capital may tend to a certain extent to arrest development in the capital exporting countries, it can do so only by expanding and deepening the further development of capitalism throughout the world. (*Imperialism*: 498)

The notion that capital export slows development in the capital exporting countries was developed at greater length in the discussion of 'parasitism and decay'. Here Lenin diverged from the Marxist tradition, and recognized the fact by saying that 'the Marxist Hilferding takes a step backwards compared with the non-Marxist Hobson' (*Imperialism*: 536) in not recognizing a 'parasitism, which is characteristic of imperialism'. This is not to say that there is anything inherently un-Marxist in Lenin's argument. Marx argued that a mode of production falls when it becomes a fetter on the forces of production. Lenin, essentially, judged that capitalism, in the imperialist stage, had become such a fetter, a brake on development, at least in the most advanced countries, although, as the quotation above shows, he regarded imperialism as a force for development in the world as a whole. 'On the whole capitalism is growing far more rapidly than ever before; but this growth is not only becoming more and more uneven in general, its unevenness also manifests itself, in particular, in the decay of the countries which are richest in capital' (*Imperialism*: 564).

He followed Hobson rather closely in his account of the effect of capital export on the capital exporting countries:

> Further, imperialism is an immense accumulation of money capital in a few countries. . . . Hence the extraordinary growth of a class, or rather of a social stratum of rentiers, i.e. people who live by clipping coupons, who take no part in any enterprise whatever, whose profession

is idleness. The export of capital, one of the most essential economic bases of imperialism, still more completely isolates the rentiers from production and sets the seal of parasitism on the whole country that lives by exploiting the labour of several overseas countries and colonies. (*Imperialism*: 537)

It is easy to see how capitalists can be called parasitic, but how can one say that a whole country is parasitic? The only circumstances in which it would be reasonable to say this would be where a growing proportion of the workers were drawn into unproductive work, as servants, clerks in the offices of the financiers and so on, and it seems that this is what Lenin had in mind. He quoted Hobson's speculations:

The greater part of Western Europe might then assume the appearance and character already exhibited by tracts of country in the South of England, in the Riviera and in the tourist-ridden or residential parts of Italy and Switzerland, little clusters of wealthy aristocrats drawing dividends and pensions from the Far East, with a somewhat larger group of professional retainers and tradesmen and a large body of personal servants and workers in the transport trades and in the final stage of production of the more perishable goods; all the main arterial industries would have disappeared, the staple foods and manufactures flowing in as tribute from Asia and Africa. (quoted in *Imperialism*: 540-1)

This is, indeed, a possible outcome, but it is not what happened (yet). It is precisely the complaint of the underdeveloped countries today that they have been excluded from 'all the main arterial industries', and it is a major concern of more recent Marxist theorists to explain why the major industries remained centred in the old heartlands of imperialism and took so long to develop in underdeveloped areas. Capital export went, in practice, mainly into the development of raw material production for export from underdeveloped areas to the manufacturing centres of the advanced countries, as predicted by Hilferding and Bukharin. I stress the point for two reasons. First, because it brings out how large is the gap between Lenin and recent Marxist writers, even those who sincerely regard themselves as his disciples, and, second, because a tradition derived from Lenin led Marxists astray for a long time. Since they thought capitalism was in the last throes of decay and dissolution, they were quite unable to explain or to respond to its unexpected capacity not only to survive, but also to advance.

In theoretical terms, the crucial failing in Lenin's pamphlet is its failure adequately to theorise the place of the nation state in the world economy. There are sections headed: 'the division of the world among capitalist combines' and 'the division of the world among the great powers', but no theoretical connection is established between them. This is an extreme example of the methodological weakness of Lenin's pamphlet; he described a number of trends without fully explaining how they are connected.

In discussing the division of the world among capitalist combines, Lenin wrote:

> As the export of capital increased, and as the foreign and colonial connections and 'spheres of influence' of the big monopolist combines expanded in all ways, things 'naturally' gravitated towards an international agreement among these combines, and towards the formation of international cartels. (*Imperialism*: 501)

This was followed by accounts of the various attempts to form such cartels in the electrical industry, the oil industry and so on. The next section went straight on to a mainly descriptive account of the division of the world between the great powers. The central point was that the world had, for practical purposes, been divided already, and that any change had to be by redivision, which would inevitably mean conflict. This was the essential point Lenin wanted to make against Kautsky and it is, in that context, a strong point.

The question that is left open, however, is: who is it that is dividing the world? The implicit answer is: the national groups of finance capital. This invites the further question: why should blocs of finance capital form on a national basis? Perhaps because Bukharin had already dealt with this question, perhaps because it was not relevant to his immediate concerns, Lenin did not try to answer. He took it for granted, with remarks like: 'Monopolist capitalist combines, cartels, syndicates and trusts divide among themselves, first of all, the home market, seize more or less complete possession of the industry of a country' (*Imperialism*: 500). Yes, but why? Why is a 'country' a relevant unit in this context? Lenin gave no answer.

One criticism of the Bukharin-Lenin analysis deserves mention here. It is often argued that their thesis is refuted by the fact that Britain, the country with the largest colonial empire, was relatively late in reaching the stage of monopoly capitalism. This line of criticism is, at least in part, an example of the semantic confusion caused by different uses of the term 'imperialism'. For Lenin, in particular, imperialism did not specifically refer to the possession of colonies. He explicitly recognized that earlier stages of capitalism also involved colonial expansion, but for different reasons and with different results (*Imperialism*: 517). It would, however, be legitimate to criticize Lenin (not Bukharin) for taking England as exemplar of the parasitism and decay characteristic (he says) of imperial centres in the monopoly stage of capitalism. British firms as a group had a monopoly in the colonies, but individual (industrial) firms did not. It is not, in any case, difficult to account for the British empire in the nineteenth century in Marxist terms; Marx's own writings on British rule in India have already been described.

To summarize, Lenin did not provide a full analysis of the key links in his argument. The connections between monopoly, capital export and the division of the world remain obscure. He did, however, write a powerful descriptive account of a world divided between great rival empires. The export of capital led to the internationalization of capitalist production and the extension of capitalist relations of production to the furthest corners of the world, while on the other hand power was concentrated into the hands of great blocs of finance capital and wealth channelled to parasitic rentier classes.

6.3 THE LABOUR ARISTOCRACY

In their writings on imperialism, Lenin and Bukharin were grappling with the most immediate political problems of their time. With the outbreak of the First World War, the majority of workers in the main belligerent countries had supported the war effort of their own states. The working classes of Europe were, at that very moment, killing each other on the battlefields. This horrifying fact ran completely counter to Marx's prediction:

> The working men have no country. ... National differences and antagonisms between peoples are daily more and more vanishing owing to the development of the bourgeoisie, to freedom of commerce, to the world market, to uniformity in the mode of production and in the conditions of life corresponding thereto. (*Manifesto*: 49)

The theory of imperialism explained why there should be antagonism between the ruling classes of different countries, the beneficiaries of the 'state capitalist trusts' or 'monopoly capitalist combines'. It remained to explain how the proletariat could be infected by aggressive nationalism.

Hilferding, writing before the war, saw imperialism as directly opposed to the interests of the working class, even in the dominant countries. He argued that the close links between the state and capital reveal the class character of the state, and lead the proletariat to adopt a stance of opposition to the state and to imperialism.

This over-optimistic estimate could not be sustained when Bukharin and Lenin were writing. They argued that sections of the working class in the dominant countries did benefit from the monopoly position their capitalist masters had in the world market, and that this explains the support that the imperialist powers were able to gain from the working-class movement. They also argued (though not in detail) that this gain only accrued to some workers, and that it was merely a relative gain: workers employed by a monopoly in an advanced country did better than those in a weaker position, but all would do better in a socialist society. The main argument that Lenin, in particular, relied on, however, was that imperialism made war inevitable, and that the horrors of war totally wiped out any gains the workers might get from monopolistic privilege. I shall discuss this argument in the next section.

Bukharin set the context like this:

The first period of the war has brought about, not a crisis of capitalism ... but a collapse of the 'Socialist' International. This phenomenon, which many have attempted to explain by proceeding solely from the analysis of the internal relations in every country, cannot be more or less satisfactorily explained from this angle. For the collapse of the proletarian movement is a result of the unequal situation of the 'state capitalist trusts' within the boundaries of world economy. (*IWE*: 161)

His argument was fairly straightforward. There is always a tendency in capitalist economies for workers to identify with their employers, on the basis that: 'the better the business of our shop, the better for me'. The evolution of trades union struggle has largely wiped out this attachment to a particular enterprise or industry and replaced it with an awareness of the need to unite against the capitalist employers. At the same time, however, the formation of 'state capitalist trusts' has created a basis for solidarity between classes on the national level, the 'so called working class protectionism with its policy of safeguarding "national industry", "national labour", etc.' (*IWE*: 162-3). The competitive struggle has been transformed into a struggle in the world market between state monopoly trusts. The stronger trusts gain monopoly profit. They also gain extra profit by exploiting native labour in the colonies. These extra profits are the basis for the payment of increased wages. The workers in the dominant countries therefore gain from the success of 'their' states in the competitive struggle.

Lenin's arguments follow the same lines, but are rather broader and less specific (on Lenin's version, see Szymanski 1981, ch. 14). He was more insistent that it is only a section of the workers who gain, and he also emphasized the possession of colonies more strongly, quoting Engels, who had discussed the reactionary political stance of the English working class as early as 1858. The significance of this, though Lenin did not bring it out, is that Engels (and Lenin) described the emergence of a 'labour aristocracy' *before* the rise of monopoly (in the sense of control of a market by a single enterprise or organized group of enterprises). This seems inconsistent with Lenin's own comment 'the economic possibility of such bribery, whatever its form may be, requires high monopolist profits' (*Imperialism*: 540).

Let us first consider the case of an enterprise which gains high profits because of its monopoly control of markets. It is clearly possible for such a firm to pay higher wages to its workers than it could without a protected monopoly position. There is, however, nothing in its monopoly position that compels it to pay higher wages. If workers are effectively organized in trades unions, they can try to insist on higher wages, and the sheltered economic position of the employers may reduce their resistance to this pressure. Alternatively, a firm may decide to pay higher wages in order to forestall trades unionism, or to gain the loyalty of its workers. The gains are very likely, in this case, to go to a privileged minority, if the management chooses to 'divide and rule'. Workers' gains may be in terms of better working conditions, shorter hours or better conditions of work, rather than in higher wages. Against this must be set the possibility, emphasized by Hilferding, that a larger firm with greater financial resources may be in a stronger position to resist wage claims and to suppress trades unions, especially if it can call on state support in these conflicts. The stronger economic position of large monopoly firms may thus lead to better or worse conditions for workers, depending on the precise balance of forces. Lenin, in particular, seems to suggest a conscious policy of the ruling class in his repeated use of the word 'bribe' to describe the gains of the workers.

There is a difficulty. All the classical Marxists tended to overstate the extent to which monopoly had triumphed. In fact, it was still the exception, rather than the rule, for a single firm or organized cartel to have complete control over the market for a product, even within the protected boundaries of a single advanced country, and in the world market as a whole, price competition was very far from being suppressed. This difficulty is compounded by Lenin's insistence on tracing the history of the 'labour aristocracy' back to nineteenth-century England, when there certainly were many competing firms.

We must, therefore, look at the case where a particular country has a monopoly position in the production of some commodity, either in the world market or in colonial markets, but where there are many small firms competing with each other within the country concerned. The main point is that no single firm can afford to concede higher wages unless its competitors do the same. The fact that the firms in the industry have a monopoly as a group makes little difference when there is competition within the group. The only way workers can gain is by a general wage increase across the whole industry, and this can only be achieved by some force that operates at that level. A general shortage of labour in the industry is one such factor (which might be the product of its success in gaining control of markets), a strong trades union organization is another, and the intervention of the state is a third. Marx discussed the latter possibility in relation not to wage increases, but to statutory limitations on hours of work. Emmanuel's theory of 'unequal exchange' follows the same lines, with trades union action as the driving force (see chapter 9). Very much the same considerations apply where the industry has a technical lead over its overseas competitors, and thus an advantage in productivity. This was probably the main factor in the dominant position of British capitalism in the nineteenth century.

Lenin also hinted (the text is not very clear) that profits from investment abroad provide a further basis for the bribing of the working class. This is much more dubious. In general the firms that receive profits from abroad will not be the ones that employ the workers to be bribed in the home country. The profits from British investment abroad went mainly to individual rentiers, and it is hard to see any plausible mechanism by which the money was transferred to the 'labour aristocracy'. Rentiers, it is true, often employed servants, but these were generally among the lowest paid sections of the working class. Butlers and housemaids do not make a very plausible basis for revisionist politics.

It is true that there are many interconnections that I have not discussed, which provide some basis for working-class support for imperialism. Protected markets, for example, may improve security of employment. Workers producing luxury goods have, at least, a short-run interest in the prosperity of buyers of such goods, and so on. These sorts of connections provide a basis for talking of 'national prosperity' and of a 'national interest', in the way that Bukharin did, but to deal with them adequately would require a detailed analysis which neither Bukharin nor Lenin provided.

Both Bukharin and Lenin correctly identified skilled workers as the better-off stratum of the working class, and therefore tended to identify them as the beneficiaries of imperialism. In fact, differentials between skilled and unskilled workers were of great antiquity, and it is not clear that skilled workers, as a group, did particularly well out of imperialism. To analyse the point further would require an analysis of the world division of labour. One could argue that the work done by unskilled workers is more easily transferred to establishments in colonies where cheap labour can be employed, and that skilled workers are more protected from this kind of competition.

It should also be pointed out that capital export works counter to the workers' interests, at least in the longer run, by creating jobs abroad at the expense of jobs at home, although it may, in the short run, encourage the production of capital goods for export and thus keep up employment in the industries concerned.

To sum up, Bukharin and Lenin observed that the living standards of some workers in some advanced countries had risen significantly, and that they no longer had 'nothing to lose but their chains'. At the same time, the countries where this was happening were also those which were coming out on top in the struggle for world dominance. Our authors deserve great credit for recognizing that a 'national interest' does exist, at least to a certain degree, and that sectional and nationalistic sentiments among the working class have a real material basis. There can be no doubt that stratification of the working class is a very important issue, but subsequent writers have not generally sought to explain it in terms of colonial profits or in terms of monopoly in world markets.

6.4 ULTRA-IMPERIALISM

In the years before the First World War, the centre of gravity of the socialist movement and of theoretical Marxism was in the German Social Democratic Party. The dominant figure, both in theoretical debates and in practical politics, was Karl Kautsky. A tradition of Marxist thought grew up around Kautsky, which was, in its time, the established Marxist orthodoxy (though it is difficult to remember this today, when, with the benefit of hindsight, we tend to focus on Lenin and the Bolsheviks). At the time, the various Russian groups seemed relatively insignificant.

The leaders of the German Social Democrats had a long tradition of support for free trade, which they associated with low prices and, in particular, low food prices. When Hilferding built his analysis of the rise of monopoly around the role of tariffs, and the connection between protection and monopoly, he was working firmly in this tradition, but when he argued that the rise of finance capital had unified the capitalist class and that finance capital had definitely seized control of the state, he broke sharply from the orthodox approach, which was still rooted in the idea that state policies were the outcome of a clash of interests representing different fractions of capital. Kautsky and his school thought of imperialist policies as expressing the interests of finance capital and of certain monopoly groups, but held that some sections of industrial capital still retained an interest in peace and free trade. The social democrats hoped that by throwing the weight of the working class into the scales against imperialism and militarism, the balance could be tipped in favour of peace.

Immediately before the First World War, Kautsky came up with a further reason for optimism about the prospects for peace, in the theory of *ultra-imperialism*, that is, the idea that the major powers would agree to exploit the world jointly, rather than fighting over the division of the world. A similar line of argument had been advanced earlier by Hobson (as Lenin pointed out), using the term 'inter-imperialism'. The importance of this argument in the theoretical framework of the social-democratic centre was that inter-imperialist cooperation would draw its support from those sections of the ruling class who would otherwise have an interest in supporting imperialist policies, and would thus strengthen the political forces working for peace and weaken those prepared to risk war. This idea helped to lull the working-class movement into a false sense of security on the eve of the First World War, and thus contributed to the debacle of the Second International on the outbreak of war.

When the war broke out, Kautsky transferred his hopes for peace to the post-war period. In a key article, published soon after the start of the war, he wrote:

What Marx said of capitalism can also be applied to imperialism: monopoly creates competition and competition monopoly. The frantic competition of giant firms, giant banks and multi-millionaires obliged the great financial groups ... to think up the notion of the cartel. In the same way the result of the World War between the great imperialist powers may be a federation of the strongest, who renounce their arms race. ... Hence from the purely economic standpoint it is not impossible that capitalism may still live through another phase, the translation of cartelisation into foreign policy: a phase of ultraimperialism, which of course we must struggle against as energetically as we do against imperialism, but whose perils lie in another direction, not in that of the arms race and the threat to world peace. (Kautsky 1970: 46)

Kautsky argued that this policy of 'peaceful' joint exploitation of the world by the united finance capital of the great powers would be forced on them by the threat they faced from the oppressed colonial peoples and from their own proletariat. It is clear, incidentally, that in describing ultra-imperialism as 'peaceful', Kautsky did not mean that exploited peoples or the proletariat at the centre would be treated with kid gloves. He simply meant that the ruling classes of the major capitalist powers would not go to war with each other.

The way this theory was posed, and the way it was attacked by the left, reveal a great deal about the concepts of imperialism shared by both sides in the debate. Kautsky argued that the stress might shift from conflict between imperialist powers to maintenance of a world system of exploitation. It is surely the latter, the world-wide suppression of colonial peoples by the metropolitan bourgeoisie, which is generally understood by the term 'imperialism' today, but Kautsky was careful to distinguish it from imperialism as the term was then understood, and to give it a different name. The very suggestion that such a shift was possible aroused vehement hostility from the left. For both sides, inter-imperialist rivalry leading to war was the very essence of imperialism. As I suggested at the beginning of this chapter, the concept of imperialism has shifted its meaning between then and now.

There are three different issues that arise in considering the theory of ultra-imperialism. First, does it make sense on a purely theoretical level as a possible tendency in capitalist development? Second, if so, was this tendency in fact dominant at the time of the First World War, or, alternatively, was it reasonable to expect it to become dominant within a fairly short time? Third, does this theory have anything to offer in understanding the world today? There is no space here to deal fully with the second of these questions, since detailed historical and empirical material would be required. Those who criticized Kautsky at the time could, of course, only consider the first two of these questions.

The central reason for left-wing opposition to the theory of ultra-imperialism is obvious. Lenin and his allies thought that a socialist revolution was on the cards for the near future, and they wanted to argue that war and misery were the only alternative to revolution. In the context of the First World War, idle dreams of the possibility of lasting peace after the war were a diversion from the real issues. Both Bukharin and, especially, Lenin wrote about imperialism primarily to challenge Kautsky's view, and to repair the damage done to the international socialist movement by the capitulation of the parties of the Second International at the outbreak of the war. As far as they were concerned, the intimate connection between capitalist development, imperialism, and war was the central theoretical basis of their stand against abandoning the struggle for socialism for the duration. No compromise on this issue was possible.

Lenin vehemently rejected any idea of ultra-imperialism: 'development is proceeding towards monopolies, hence towards a single world monopoly [is] as completely meaningless as is the statement that "development is proceeding" towards the manufacture of foodstuffs in laboratories' (*Imperialism*: 530). Bukharin was more moderate: in the abstract a world trust is thinkable, but in reality it cannot come about. He advanced two reasons for this. First, any agreement between 'state capitalist trusts' must be disrupted by uneven development. The strong will not in any case accept agreements since they will hope to gain more without. Second, if the proletariat became strong enough to prevent aggressive policies, as Kautsky hoped they might, they would be strong enough to establish socialism. Hilferding, who wrote before Kautsky's theory of ultra-imperialism was devised, put the same argument, but did not come to any conclusion as to whether force or peaceful division of the market would prevail, though he thought that agreements were only likely to be temporary.

The first of Bukharin's arguments rests on the assumption that national blocs of capital, each exploiting exclusive possession of a national economic territory, must remain the basic units between which any ultra-imperialist peace would be made. However, in addition to the reasons Bukharin put forward for the formation of nationally based 'state capitalist trusts', there is a counter-tendency, also arising from factors included in his analysis. For Bukharin, as for Hilferding, an important motive for capital export is the desire to penetrate the protected markets of other nation states from within. Over a long period of time, this can lead to interpenetration of national capitals, with the same group of firms operating within each national economic territory. In this case, a struggle to enlarge one nation's territory at the expense of others becomes economically pointless. To give an example, there would be no point in Ford or General Motors seeking to extend their markets by sponsoring US annexation of parts of the EEC, when they are securely established in the European industry already. In the same way, tariff barriers between different markets become a hindrance rather than a benefit once multinational firms are well established.

As for the second argument, that if the working class is strong enough to compel the adoption of peaceful policies it will also be strong enough to overthrow capitalism, this seems an extremely schematic argument which does not do adequate justice to the complexity of political developments. All of our authors anticipated socialist revolutions in the advanced countries within a fairly short period of time. We have, in fact, seen the emergence of a socialist bloc, and of Third World liberation movements which pose a massive threat to world capitalism, forcing the major capitalist states onto the defensive, together with a political absorption of the working class into a reshaped political system. It is clear that the orthodox objections to the theory of ultra-imperialism no longer have the same force.

I am not arguing that Kautsky's theory is correct as applied to our own times, only that the arguments that Lenin and

Bukharin put against him are not decisive on a purely theoretical level. The First and Second World Wars provide strong evidence that rivalry leading towards war was indeed the dominant tendency at that time, but here, as elsewhere, they allowed themselves to be drawn by the pressures of debate into overstating their case.

6.5 THE COMMUNIST INTERNATIONAL

After the Bolshevik revolution and the establishment of the Soviet Union, Lenin, Bukharin, and other communist leaders were faced with a new situation. Among many other issues, they had to take a view on communist strategy in under-developed areas, and on the relations between the USSR and colonial areas. Little of theoretical substance emerged (there was too much else to do, to spend much time on theory), but the positions taken by Lenin and, after his death, by the newly formed Communist International, had a lasting effect on Marxist thinking. During the 1920s, the Communist International discussed communist attitudes to anti-colonial movements: almost the first serious Marxist discussion of the issue. Lenin argued that communists should form a temporary alliance with bourgeois democratic movements, while remaining independent, and he also flirted with the idea that it was possible for backward areas to move to communism without passing through a capitalist stage. By 1928 (after Lenin's death), the International reversed the traditional Marxist position, arguing that capital export and imperialism hindered development in colonial territories rather than accelerating it (see Szymanski 1981: 44-51; Warren 1980: 84-109).

Warren (1980) made this period the linchpin of his account of the development of theories of imperialism. There was undoubtedly a break between Marx's assessment of colonial expansion as broadly progressive, if brutal, and the wholly negative judgement on imperialism of most Marxist writers after the Second World War. Warren blamed Lenin for this shift in opinion, arguing that although Lenin paid lip service to the classical view (which Warren supported; see chapter 11), the tone of his condemnation of imperialism as 'parasitic' told a different story. As far as *Imperialism* is concerned, I disagree. It is true that some dependency theorists (see chapter 8) have claimed Lenin for their view, but this is because they have been determined to do so, not because they found much in the text to encourage them. The extracts cited in section 6.2 above, in which Lenin argued that capital export expands and deepens the further development of capitalism throughout the world, make the point. Bukharin and Hilferding came closer to the dependency theorists than Lenin did.

Warren was on firmer ground in claiming that Lenin's political strategy in the 1920s, and the shift of opinion recorded in the resolutions of the Communist International, marked a fundamental change of direction. It is important to recognize that support for national independence in colonies does not in any way conflict with the classical Marxist position. It is clear from Marx's writings that he saw the construction of a modern independent state as impossible until development had progressed to a certain stage, and both inevitable and desirable thereafter. However, once Marxists were committed to national liberation movements, it was fatally easy to slide into blaming foreigners for economic backwardness. The 1928 resolution of the Communist International was an early example of this, but it was not backed by any serious economic analysis.

6.6 SUMMARY

Bukharin combined the analysis of the internationalization of capitalist relations of production (Marx, Luxemburg) with Hilferding's analysis of the formation of blocs of finance capital, to show why these blocs formed on a national basis. The competitive struggle continued in the era of finance capital, but it took the form of military and political rivalry between 'state capitalist trusts'. Lenin's *Imperialism* followed the same lines on a lower level of abstraction, providing a forceful descriptive account of imperialism. Both argued that capital export accelerated development in underdeveloped areas (though Bukharin was more cautious in his predictions), both discussed how workers in imperialist centres gain some (limited) advantages from the success of 'their' nations, thus explaining the material basis of working-class nationalism, and both thought that inter-imperialist rivalry made inter-imperialist war inevitable.

7

Baran

From theories of imperialism developed between 1900 and
1920, I turn to theories put forward after the Second World
War, since the period between the wars produced no notable
innovations in the Marxist theory of imperialism. The success
of the Russian revolution and the defeat of revolution in
western Europe widened the rift between social democrats,
and communists, institutionalized with the formation of the
Third International, the 'Comintern', and of separate communist parties in the various countries of Europe. The rise of
Stalin in Russia was followed by the imposition of a grey
orthodoxy in matters of theory, not only in Russia but in all of
the communist parties. The victory of fascism in much of
continental Europe further disrupted any serious development of Marxist theory. I will not discuss the textbooks of
Marxism produced in the Soviet Union; they reproduced
Lenin rather mechanically and tended, as far as imperialism
is concerned, to draw on the weaker aspects of Lenin's
writing, stressing the 'overripeness' of capitalism and
interpreting it in an under-consumptionist sense (see Kemp
1967, ch. 7 on some of these works). In the early 1920s, before
Stalin had consolidated his power, there were notable debates
on economics in Russia, but they were, naturally, directed
mainly to problems of post-revolutionary economic policy.

Marxist economics, understood as the study of capitalist
(not socialist) economies, was kept alive through this period
by a handful of writers working in isolation in the West.
Maurice Dobb wrote a number of valuable works, but had
little new to say about imperialism (Dobb 1940, ch. 7; Dobb
1963: 311 ff.). Paul Sweezy's textbook, *The Theory of Capitalist*

Development (Sweezy 1942), is an important bridge between classical Marxist writings and more recent work.

Paul Baran's *Political Economy of Growth* (Baran 1973, cited below as *PEG*), published in 1957, marked an important shift in Marxist theory, both in the problems to which it was addressed and in its theoretical content. Rivalry and war had receded into the background in the new circumstances of American dominance. Baran stigmatized monopoly capital as a cause of stagnation, in both advanced and underdeveloped countries. At the same time, he was the first major Marxist theorist to treat underdeveloped countries as worthy of study in their own right. Lenin, it is true, had written about the *Development of Capitalism in Russia* (1974), but Russia was semi-developed rather than underdeveloped. Baran differed from his predecessors in treating the development of capitalism in underdeveloped countries as a different process from that which the advanced countries had gone through earlier. This approach dominated Marxist thinking about underdevelopment until at least the 1970s.

Baran worked closely with Sweezy over a long period, a collaboration which culminated in their joint work, *Monopoly Capital* (1968). It is rather unprofitable to try to determine which was the original author of the general line of thought that they represent. There is a consistent line of development from *The Theory of Capitalist Development*, through the *Political Economy of Growth* to *Monopoly Capital*, starting fairly close to classical Marxism, and evolving into something distinctively different. As Marxist economics revived in the 1960s, Baran and Sweezy provided an important starting point, especially in America, North and South; *Monthly Review* (edited by Sweezy and others), nurtured a whole school of writers.

7.1 MONOPOLY AND STAGNATION

Baran and Sweezy were, as remarked above, 'underconsumptionists', who thought that capitalist economies suffer from a chronic lack of demand because of the restricted purchasing power of the workers. Their whole argument is remarkably close to Hobson's, though they seem to have been rather unwilling to acknowledge the fact. I have already discussed Hobson's version (chapter 4), so I will be brief. In

The Theory of Capitalist Development, Sweezy argued that continuous expansion in a capitalist system is logically impossible, if one takes account of various tendencies described by Marx. This argument applies at all stages of capitalist development. He also argued that it was unlikely that monopoly enterprises would carry out enough investment to sustain demand. The second argument is the one developed by Baran. They are combined, in a rather different form, in *Monopoly Capital*.

Sweezy's first argument runs as follows: as capitalism develops, the share of wages and hence of wage earners' consumption in total output falls, while the concentration of capital into fewer hands means that a falling share of profit is consumed. Consumption therefore absorbs a falling share of total output (this prefigures the 'law of rising surplus' in *Monopoly Capital*), and the falling share of consumption must be matched by a rising share of investment. Consumption and investment both increase over time, but if demand is to expand in line with output, investment must rise faster than consumption. Sweezy argued that new investment is only required to expand the capacity to produce consumer goods (this point is implicit, not explicit), and that there is a technically fixed ratio between new investment and the additional output of consumer goods produced, so the two can only expand in step. There is then a contradiction between the requirements that investment should increase faster than consumption, to maintain demand, and the technical requirement that they increase at the same rate. He concluded that demand will fail to match output, unless some way is found of absorbing output in unproductive uses (military spending, etc.) or through capital export.

The flaw in the argument (which is exactly the same as Hobson's) is obvious; Sweezy assumed that means of production are only used to produce consumer goods, but investment also goes into the industries that produce means of production. A lower share of consumption could be balanced by faster growth, with more investment going into industries that produce investment goods. There is no assurance that this will happen, of course, but if enough profitable investment opportunities exist then the opportunity to accelerate accumulation will be taken. The prospect of profit drives capitalism, not the expansion of consumption.

Rejecting Sweezy's under-consumption analysis, leaves the rate of investment, itself determined by investment opportunities, to determine whether the gap between output and consumption will be filled.

Sweezy had a further argument, distinct from the under-consumption argument, which predominates in Baran's *Political Economy of Growth*, and in their joint work, *Monopoly Capital*. I shall concentrate on Baran's formulation, since it seems more complete than those in the other works cited. He argued that there are two motives for investment: to introduce new techniques of production and to expand output. A monopoly will hold back on the introduction of new techniques, because they threaten to make its existing equipment obsolete, while it will not expand output because it would have to cut prices to sell more, reducing its profits. He contrasted competitive capitalism with a capitalism dominated by monopolies. In competitive capitalism, any firm which holds back on cost-reducing innovations will be driven out of the market by the low prices of its competitors. Competitive firms invest to expand output because they are each trying to expand their share of the market, heedless of the effect on the total output and price. A firm which held back on expansion would fall behind its competitors, would end up with higher costs, and would lack resources to introduce new methods of production.

There is a noticeable shift here from the classical Marxist position. The classical Marxists regarded the tendency towards monopoly as a factor intensifying competition, not suppressing it, although it is true that they were not wholly consistent in this. Baran and Sweezy, by contrast, argued that the competitive struggle virtually vanishes when there are only a few large firms operating in each market, since they will generally adopt a 'live and let live' policy towards each other. Hilferding had discussed this possibility in a rather open-minded fashion, but Lenin and Bukharin had rejected it as part of their rejection of 'ultra-imperialism'. There is something of a paradox here. While the classical Marxists, especially Bukharin, tended to talk as if each national economy was dominated by a single 'state capitalist trust', their thoughts were influenced by the fact that concentration had not gone that far in reality. The main form of monopoly was the relatively fragile cartel agreement between rather a large number of firms, liable to break down into furious competition. Baran and Sweezy, writing later, stressed that there were typically several firms, not just one, in each market, but that they were few enough and established enough to maintain a stable 'balance of power'.

It is necessary, however, to evaluate the theoretical argument. Will monopolies in general invest less than competitive firms would do? I do not believe that Baran and Sweezy established this central point. Consider technical innovation first. There has been a massive debate on the effect of market structure on technical advance, and no clear empirical evidence has emerged of the superiority of competitive markets. Any greater incentive that small firms may feel to innovate is offset by their reduced capacity to do so. (See, for example, Hay and Morris 1979, ch. 13 and references cited there.) On the level of theory, the case is not clear cut anyway. Both a monopoly and a competitive firm have an incentive to minimize their costs: there is, therefore, an incentive to adopt any innovation that reduces costs. In both cases it pays to introduce new equipment and throw away the old only if the total cost of production with the new equipment is lower than the direct cost of production on the old (since the capital cost with the old equipment is already sunk: the alternatives are to throw it away, or go on using it as long as it gives any return at all towards the capital costs). Baran was aware of this (*PEG*: 198-9) but introduced other arguments resting on the risk of committing capital and the limited supply of capital to the firm. He argued that these will lead monopolies to hold back where competitive firms are forced to go ahead. One can argue, on the other hand, that large firms devote much resources to the deliberate search for new methods of production and new products, and thus have more opportunities to innovate, even if they are slower in taking up some of them. What Baran's argument comes down to is not that monopolies slow down technical change in the long run, but that they will introduce new techniques less wastefully and thus with less investment. Whether this helps or hinders capitalist development depends on whether, in the long run, capitalist expansion is more often slowed by lack of demand or by lack of resources to exploit the technological opportunities open to it. In other words, the way monopolies respond to technical change only leads to a shortfall of demand in a framework in which a shortfall of demand is a problem anyway.

The main weight of the argument thus falls on the claim that monopolies restrict the expansion of output to protect monopoly profits. This is a static argument applied to an essentially dynamic problem. For a given level of costs and of demand, there is a particular price and output which give the maximum profit. A monopoly will continue to produce this output, and will not invest for expansion, as long as the given conditions remain the same. To analyse investment we must look at changes in costs and demand. The static model cannot help. A similar static model of a competitive industry can be constructed. Again, with given costs and demand, there is a determinate equilibrium output. Any expansion of the industry would depress profits and induce an outflow of capital. In this case too, the rate of investment is governed by changes in costs and demand (see Matthews 1959: 33 ff.).

The determinants of changes in demand must be sought in the economy as a whole. Expansion in one industry creates demand for investment goods, and also creates jobs, expanding demand for consumer goods. The expansion in demand, if not offset by contraction elsewhere, has a cumulative effect. Other industries step up investment, and this generates further expansion. This cumulative process will work through whether the economy is competitive or monopolistic, though not necessarily in exactly the same way. The same process works in reverse when demand contracts. As a result, a capitalist economy moves through a sequence of booms and slumps. The major factors determining the overall rate of investment over a long period of time must therefore either be forces that manifest themselves slowly but steadily through boom and slump, or forces that actually work through the mechanism of the cycle, through the relative strength of boom and slump and through the limiting factors that halt a boom or a depression. The desire of monopolies to avoid spoiling a given, static, market by overexpansion does not fit the bill at all.

It has to be admitted that nobody has a really satisfactory theory of the determinants of investment, or their relation to the predominance of monopoly or competition in the economy. In default of any theory, we must turn to the evidence. Baran, writing in the 1950s, looked for evidence mainly to the period before the Second World War. The depression of the 1930s, the deepest and most prolonged in history, made it easy for him to find examples of the failure of monopoly capitalism. The 'long boom' of the 1950s and 1960s suggests strongly that monopoly capitalism is not incompatible with growth. The 'long boom' was a period of rapid growth in the world capitalist economy which far outstrips any such episode in the epoch of competitive capitalism. Baran and Sweezy should have realized this when they wrote *Monopoly Capital* in the 1960s, but they seem to have been misled by an excessive concentration on the American economy. It was, of course, Japan and Europe that were the main centres of growth.

7.2 GROWTH AND SURPLUS

The idea of an economic surplus goes back to the classical economists and the 'physiocrats', who thought in terms of a physical surplus, available to society or to the state, over and above the part of output needed to maintain the population and the capital stock intact. This surplus or 'net product' could be used for accumulation, for military purposes, or for the development of culture (see, for example, Ricardo's *Principles*, 1951, ch. 26). Marx transformed the idea into an expression of class relations; *surplus labour* is the labour that an exploited class has to do to produce goods for its exploiters. In a capitalist society, this takes the form of *surplus value*, corresponding to a *surplus product*, goods appropriated by capitalists for their own consumption, for investment, or for unproductive workers and hangers-on.

Baran reverted, essentially, to the classical, pre-Marxist, definition, for very much the same reasons as the classical economists: to discuss the 'nature and causes of the wealth of nations'. He defined economic growth as 'increase over time in per capita output of material goods' (*PEG*: 128). To measure growth, we must have some way of aggregating the output of material goods; Baran discussed the issue, but decided to assume that 'increases of aggregate output can somehow be measured' (*PEG*: 129). The point is not the technical problems of measurement, but the fact that Baran conceptualized growth in quantitative terms, unlike earlier

Marxist writers whose focus was on qualitative change in the social relations of production. In some ways this represents a step forward, since ideas like the 'development of the forces of production' and 'increases in the productivity of labour', which are central to a Marxist analysis of capitalism, are essentially quantitative. There is, however, a danger that qualitative changes will be overlooked and that socialism may be seen solely as a means to more rapid growth.

Baran had a very simple theory of the determinants of economic growth. He listed a number of factors generating growth (*PEG*: 129-31), but emerged with new net investment in means of production as the dominant factor. Since net investment is part of the economic surplus, he concluded that the size and use of the surplus is the key factor in economic growth. He defined net investment as the net addition to the stock of means of production, the definition used by mainstream economics. Marx, on the other hand, defined capital by reference to a specific social relation, so capital accumulation, for Marx, includes wages advanced to new workers, but excludes additions to means of production used in non-capitalist sectors of the economy. Marx included, under the heading of 'primitive accumulation', the transformation of means of production (and consumption goods) into capital by transfer from a non-capitalist to a capitalist sector. In Baran's framework, its only significance lies in the changes in the use of the surplus that follow from it.

Baran's purpose was to argue that capitalism was, at one stage, a (moderately) efficient engine of growth, but that socialism would now do the job better, so he needed to conceptualize growth independent of social relations, in order to be able to compare growth in socialist and capitalist systems. This is, in a way, fully consistent with the perspective of classical Marxism: he was arguing that capitalism has become a fetter on the development of the forces of production and has thus come to the end of its historically allotted span.

He defined the *actual surplus* as the difference between current net output and current consumption. Since virtually all uses of output other than investment in new means of production are to be counted as consumption, the actual surplus is equal to net investment plus any outflow (or minus any inflow) of funds across the boundaries of the country concerned. This does not mean that surplus necessarily determines investment; if investment is insufficient to absorb the (potential) surplus, either output falls or surplus must be diverted to current consumption. In a capitalist system goods will not be produced if there is no demand for them. For the world as a whole, the actual surplus must equal net investment (plus additions to stocks of gold, which can be ignored), so any discrepancy for one country must constitute a transfer of surplus for investment in another country. In a capitalist world, this transfer can come about by exports of capital (which remain the property of capitalists from the capital exporting country) or by flows of profits, dividends and interest as a result of previous acts of investment. It can also take the form of flows of 'tribute' directly extracted from colonies by a dominant power.

The *potential surplus* is the amount that a totally growth-orientated society could devote to investment without reducing current consumption below some minimum necessary level. It is thus 'the difference between the output that could be produced in a given natural and technical environment with the help of employable productive resources, and what might be regarded as essential consumption' (*PEG*: 133). There are considerable conceptual and practical difficulties of measurement here (Taylor 1979: 79), but Baran did not use the concept in a quantitative way, being content to indicate that a large gap exists between the potential surplus and the actual level of investment.

Baran spent some time discussing which kinds of labour are productive and which are unproductive. From the point of view of the definitions, it is more relevant to think of the way in which different products are to be treated, since the definitions of surplus are cast in terms of the output and use of products. Put simply, any outputs that Baran disapproves of ('that would be absent in a rationally ordered society') are to count as part of actual consumption, but not of necessary consumption. They thus account for part of the gap between the potential and actual surplus. (I cannot resist the thought that the working class might, in a 'rationally ordered society', allot themselves a chromium-plated Cadillac each, if only to annoy puritanical intellectuals like Baran. Who, after all, is to decide what is rational?)

The third concept of surplus is the *planned surplus*, a concept relevant only to a socialist society, which plays little part in the further development of Baran's arguments. It is the difference between an 'optimal' level of output (perhaps less than the maximum possible output because of shorter working hours, etc.) and an 'optimal' level of consumption. It thus represents the outcome of a deliberate and conscious collective choice between consumption and investment.

Baran's procedure is now fairly obvious: the planned surplus represents the use that a rational society would make of its potential surplus. In a capitalist society, the actual surplus falls short of the potential surplus, and it is the size and use of the surplus, the relation between actual and potential surplus, that is the focus of investigation.

7.3 THE DEVELOPED COUNTRIES

Baran's discussion of the advanced capitalist countries was really a discussion of the USA, though he did not say so. Virtually all of the examples and evidence that he gives are American, and the whole story makes much more sense in that context than it would applied to, say, Japan or West Germany. It is worth noting that the concept of a 'nation state' or a 'national economy' is taken for granted as the unit of analysis, with no serious discussion. It becomes clear, from the discussion of concepts like surplus, investment and so on, that they are aggregates at a national level.

For the advanced capitalist countries, the argument turns on a contrast between competitive and monopoly capitalism, though it is presented, rather confusingly, in terms of a contrast between the idealized model of competition held by the classical economists and the reality (as Baran saw it) of monopoly capital; the idealized model 'indicates, at least approximately, the essential principles of the mechanism that has actually provided for . . . an unprecedented development of productive forces' (*PEG*: 165). In this account, competitive capitalism maximizes the surplus by depressing workers' consumption to a minimum, encouraging capitalists to save, and eliminating unproductive spending. The surplus is directed mainly into investment because of competitive pressures to innovate and to expand. Competitive capitalism is thus a powerful agent of growth.

The evolution of the surplus under monopoly capitalism proves rather difficult to pin down:

> The economic surplus generated under monopolistic capitalism is, however, as large as is possible in the only relevant sense of the notion, that is, taking into account the prevailing level of output, the market mechanism responsible for the distribution of income under capitalism as well as the more or less steady rise of conventional standards of subsistence. (*PEG*: 177)

In other words, it is what it is. It is, however, large and rising. Baran seems here (it isn't very clear) to have used a concept of surplus as total profit plus other property income. He returned, in other words, to Marx's concept, though in terms of prices, not values.

He concentrated on the use of the surplus, arguing that monopolies will tend to invest less than they might, so there is a chronic lack of demand unless other stimulating factors take over. I have already described (and rejected) this picture of monopoly as a cause of stagnation, which is the heart of Baran's case against monopoly capitalism. If surplus is not used, however, it will not be realized in money terms at all. Goods that cannot be sold will not be produced. The resulting unemployment will reduce consumption, cutting total sales and output still further. The central problem for monopoly capitalism, therefore, is to avoid a slump of the dimensions of the 1930s or worse. This is achieved, in Baran's account, by the absorption of surplus in various forms of waste, some a response to the lack of demand, some a fortuitous result of other developments in capitalism. Because of the chronic lack of demand, sales effort is stepped up and part of the potential surplus is diverted into advertizing, wasteful product differentiation and so on. (This argument is more fully developed in *Monopoly Capital* than in *The Political Economy of Growth*.) Another part of the surplus is devoted to a proliferation of unproductive activities within the giant firm, for reasons not directly connected with the lack of demand, but tending, all the same, to relieve it.

146

State spending absorbs large chunks of the potential surplus in various wasteful ways, notably through military spending. Baran discussed the possibility of useful state spending, but judged it unlikely on political grounds. The ruling class is, first, ambivalent about state spending; it wants demand to be maintained, which requires that the surplus be used, but at the same time wants to retain ownership of the surplus and resents parting with it in taxes. Second, there is fierce opposition to any collective provision that competes with private provision. The state will, in any case, not aim at genuinely full employment, since a certain amount of unemployment is necessary to maintain labour discipline and keep wages down. These arguments allowed Baran to accept the substance of a Keynesian analysis of unemployment while rejecting the Keynesian argument that state intervention can produce a stable and conflict-free capitalism. In the same way, Baran rejected the argument that an increase in wages or in transfers to the poor could relieve the problem by raising consumption. This was Hobson's prescription, but Baran joined Lenin in arguing that it was not a possible way out in a capitalist framework.

Military spending, with related forms of expenditure, such as spying, military aid to allies, and so on, emerges as one of the few forms of state spending which can absorb the surplus without harming the interests of any powerful fraction of the ruling class. Military spending is, in Baran's analysis, intimately tied up with imperialism.

Baran did not give a definition of imperialism, nor is it clear from his use of the word exactly what he meant by it. He used the word broadly to indicate a policy and an ideology of expansionism (like Bukharin) rather than a stage of development (Lenin). It does not necessarily imply a policy of formal territorial expansion, but includes more general policies designed to forward the interests of the country's citizens and, specifically, its giant corporations, all over the world. It does not necessarily imply rivalry between imperialist powers (though Baran did mention rivalry in a rather muted form; PEG: 242-3). To put it very briefly, Baran's account of the origins of imperialism follows broadly classical Marxist lines, but he argued that its effects in the advanced countries were mainly felt through the military and other spending involved; in effect, imperialism ends up virtually as

an excuse for state spending. This rather surprising conclusion needs further examination.

The export of goods does not help to absorb surplus, since
it must be balanced by a corresponding import of goods or
export of capital, or the balance of payments is disturbed and
will force a readjustment (by revaluation of the currency or
by other means). This does not prevent individual enterprises
from trying to alleviate their own problems of deficient
demand by seeking export markets.

The export of capital, on the other hand, leads to a
balancing export of goods (to keep the balance of payments
in line), and thus does help to absorb surplus. At the same
time individual monopolistic enterprises, unwilling to
expand at home for fear of spoiling the market, are anxious to
expand abroad. The world market is not as thoroughly
carved up as national markets are (*PEG*: 240), though the
same desire to avoid competition that holds them back at
home is at work here too (*PEG*: 239). Baran was very
ambivalent. On the one hand he needed capital export as an
important link in his argument, but on the other hand he
wanted to retain his picture of monopoly as a force holding
back investment on a world as well as a national level. For
reasons which will be examined later, he maintained that
underdeveloped countries only offer very limited scope for
profitable investment. In any case, as his critics have pointed
out, the export of capital only helps to absorb surplus in a
very temporary way, since he argued that the return flows of
profits and dividends, which augment the surplus, soon
outweigh the outflow of capital. This does not really damage
his argument, since it is individual corporations that decide
to invest abroad, and they are trying to maximize their
profits.

Baran argued that corporations call for, and get,
government support for their activities abroad, in the form of
military, economic and diplomatic pressure on the government of the host country, leading to massive spending on the
maintenance of a military establishment, on foreign aid,
technical assistance and so on. This is the real significance of
imperialism:

> What matters here is not whatever increases in income
> and employment an imperialist country may derive from

foreign trade and investment. These need not be very large, even if of vast importance to the individual corporations involved and the groups associated with them. . . . The issue appears in an altogether different perspective when not merely the direct advantages of imperialist policies to the society of an advanced capitalist country are taken into account but when their effect is visualised in its entirety. The loans and grants to so-called friendly governments, the outlays on the military establishment . . . all assume prodigious magnitudes. . . . Thus the impact of this form of utilisation of the economic surplus on the level of income and employment in an advanced capitalist country transcends by far the income- and employment-generating effect of foreign economic activities themselves. The latter assume actually only incidental significance compared with the former – an errant stone setting in motion a mighty rock. (*PEG*: 245-6)

At first sight it is difficult to accept this argument. It is surely irrational to incur all the real risks (of war, for example) involved in an imperialist policy purely to gain the benefits of state spending which could be gained anyway by redirecting state spending to more useful ends. This is precisely Baran's point; it is irrational but (he claimed) it happens, because capitalist politics is not rational, and because certain powerful interests gain from this policy while others would be threatened by any alternative. The argument is in fact a neat inversion of an old radical critique of colonialism. It has often been argued that the possession of colonies gives advantages to a favoured few, but that on balance the costs to the 'nation' exceed the benefits. Radicals have therefore argued that the people as a whole should oppose imperialist policies. Given his under-consumptionist stance, Baran can argue that the 'costs' of imperialism are, in fact, benefits, since they help to maintain demand and employment by absorbing the surplus. There is thus a coincidence of interests between the direct beneficiaries of imperialism and the mass of the people (as long as the only alternative to monopoly capitalism with imperialist policies is monopoly capitalism without these policies). Hobson, of course, considered exactly the same argument, but claimed that income redistribution could remove the need for an imperialist policy within a capitalist framework.

Baran mentioned Lenin's idea of a 'labour aristocracy' in this context, but it is clear that his ideas were not the same. All he took from Lenin was the possibility that 'the policy of imperialism may actually be of benefit to the ordinary man in an imperialist country' (*PEG*: 245). Lenin, however, saw the benefits as a sharing of monopoly profits in the form of higher wages for a minority of the working class while Baran saw them primarily in terms of better employment prospects for the working class in general.

Baran's case depends, first, on the general presumption that monopoly capital has difficulty in absorbing the surplus and that waste is therefore, paradoxically, good for monopoly capital and for the population as a whole (so long as the basic framework remains unchanged), and, second, on the existence of a particular political constellation that permits some forms of state spending while barring others. Both of these presumptions looked more plausible in the USA in the 1950s and 1960s than they would in other places and at other times. A final comment: Baran's argument, as presented in this section, was virtually a carbon copy of Hobson's. Regrettably, Baran did not give Hobson his due credit.

7.4 THE ORIGINS OF UNDERDEVELOPMENT

Baran divided the world economy into two parts: advanced capitalist countries and underdeveloped countries. Socialist countries were only discussed as models for others to follow; as long as they engage only in planned and balanced trade with the rest of the world, they have little direct economic effect on the capitalist world. Countries in an intermediate stage of development are also largely ignored.

The interactions between advanced and underdeveloped countries can be gathered under three headings: flows of trade, flows of surplus, and political–military influence. Trade flows serve to provide cheap sources of primary products to the advanced countries, while the development of industry in underdeveloped areas is discouraged by the competition of manufactured products imported from the advanced countries. Surplus flows, in the form of profits and dividends, deprive the underdeveloped countries of much-needed resources for investment (though they might not be used even if they were available), while adding to the problems caused by an excessive surplus in the heartlands of monopoly capital. The political influence of the advanced countries helps to maintain governments in underdeveloped areas which are well disposed to foreign investors and which hold back indigenous development. All these forces, as they affect the underdeveloped areas, will be discussed in more detail in subsequent sections.

To set up this bipolar model of the world system, Baran had to explain the origins of the massive discrepancy in accumulated capital, wealth, and power between advanced and underdeveloped areas. The high level of development in the heartlands of capitalism was no problem; according to Baran, competitive capitalism was a force for rapid development, and the advanced capitalist economies had been dominated by competitive capitalism during a long period. The problem is to explain why the same process did not occur elsewhere.

Baran argued that before the period of European colonialism, there was 'everywhere a mode of production and a social and political order that are conveniently summarised under the name of feudalism' (PEG: 268). Despite differences between areas, this order 'had entered at a certain stage of its development a process of dissolution and decay', which created the possibility of capitalist development. Marx, by contrast, thought that there were major differences between the mode of production in Europe (feudalism) and that in Asia ('Asiatic').

Baran identified three pre-conditions for capitalism: an increase in agricultural output accompanied by the displacement of peasants from the land, a growth of commodity production and of the division of labour, and the accumulation of capital by merchants and rich peasants. Of these, he assigned strategic significance to the third, the accumulation of capital in the form of merchant capital, on the grounds that the other two were proceeding at a roughly even pace everywhere. The development of merchant capital in Europe was the basis of European expansion, and of a process in which European capital siphoned off surplus from the rest of the world. The world economy, starting from a state of near parity between its different parts, was divided into rich and poor areas by a redivision of surplus. This explanation is set out mainly in terms of a comparison of India, massively looted and exploited by its British conquerors, with Japan, which remained independent and became a major capitalist power. In addition, Baran stressed state support for capitalist development. Independent states took measures to protect new industries from competition, to provide infrastructure, and so on, while the colonial administrations of subject territories systematically discriminated against local producers who might compete with the ruling country.

Baran's work represents a move towards seeing capitalist development as the development of one area at the expense of others. Ultimately this can lead to a view of history as a zero sum game, a struggle for the division of a fixed world income. It would be unfair to accuse Baran of this, given his stress on the progressive character of competitive capitalism and its creation of 'an unprecedented development of productive forces, . . . a gigantic advance in technology, and . . . a momentous increase in output and consumption' (*PEG*: 165). His successors, notably Frank, moved further away from the classical Marxist analysis.

7.5 THE PERSISTENCE OF UNDERDEVELOPMENT

Whatever the origins of underdevelopment, Baran argued that a fairly uniform and characteristic social and economic structure had come into existence in the underdeveloped countries, where it blocks further development. The main elements of this structure are: a large and very backward agricultural sector with small-scale peasant production and a parasitic landlord class; a small but relatively advanced industrial sector, partly foreign owned, producing for the restricted local market; a number of enterprises producing for export, typically foreign owned and producing primary products; and finally a large sector of traders, including large-scale merchants who control foreign trade and have close links with foreign capital, as well as petty traders who penetrate into the remoter rural areas.

Baran described this a 'capitalist order' (*PEG*: 300), but the agricultural sector seems to be characterized by pre-capitalist relations of production. Baran did not in fact differentiate at all clearly between capitalist and pre-capitalist modes of production in his discussion; the correct way to draw this distinction has since become a matter of fierce debate. Read in terms of an 'articulation of modes of production', Baran's description would amount to identifying a capitalist urban industry and export sector and a predominantly pre-capitalist rural sector, with merchant capital forming the principal link between the two. This is, I think, how Amin interprets it. On the other hand, we could regard these as being different levels in a 'chain of metropolis-satellite relations' in which towns are satellites of the imperialist countries, and the villages are satellites of the towns, as Frank did (cf. Barone 1985, ch. 4). Baran made the internal structure of under-developed countries into a central issue in Marxist theory, but his rather descriptive and practical approach leaves the way open for a number of different interpretations.

The starting point of the analysis was, naturally, the economic surplus in underdeveloped countries. He argued that the surplus, while small in absolute terms because of the low level of output, is large in relative terms because mass consumption is depressed to the lowest possible level. The economic surplus is therefore large enough to permit a fairly rapid rate of growth, although from a low starting point. The explanation for lack of growth in underdeveloped countries must lie in the use of the surplus, not in its size.

He put forward a double explanation for the lack of productive investment in underdeveloped countries. The surplus is not available for investment because it is either drained away to the advanced countries or absorbed in unproductive uses, but even if it were not diverted it would not be used for investment, because the incentive to invest is too low. Baran did not separate these two arguments, and so did not explain why he put both forward. Presumably, if the surplus were available for investment but was not invested, this would show up in a chronic lack of demand, falling prices, and an outflow of capital, while if the investment opportunities were there without the available surplus, there would be a permanent boom and a capital inflow. With both a low available surplus for investment and a low incentive to invest, there is a sort of low-growth equilibrium. The two arguments are, in any case, not wholly separable since the low incentive to invest is, in some instances, the cause of the diversion of surplus into other uses. Savings and investment decisions are not entirely separated. I shall follow Baran by going through the different sectors in turn, looking at the generation and use of surplus.

The largest sector in most underdeveloped countries is agriculture. Baran described two ways in which agricultural production may be organized: small-scale peasant production or a system of large estates. These may be combined in different proportions in different areas. Where subsistence peasant farming predominates, productivity is very low because of the small scale of production and the archaic methods used. Despite this, a large fraction of total output is taken by landlords, demonstrating the existence of a substantial surplus. Peasants do not invest in improved methods of production, because they cannot afford to (the surplus is being drained away from them), and because there are, in any case, few opportunities for mechanization as long as the land is subdivided into very small holdings.

Landlords do not invest in improvements because they cannot be sure of getting a return in the form of higher rent, because the smallness of holdings makes many forms of investment impossible, and because the surplus that they control is largely absorbed by 'the necessity of maintaining the style of life appropriate to their status in society' (*PEG*: 304). What savings they do carry out are diverted into money lending or into the acquisition of additional land, and thus, presumably, into consumption by impoverished peasants who are driven to borrow or to sell off their land. Here it is clear that it is the social relations of production that are the obstacle to development, and that these are essentially pre-capitalist relations. This point has been argued more explicitly and forcefully by subsequent writers.

Where there are large estates worked by hired labour, where, in other words, agriculture is capitalist (Baran did not say this), investment is deterred because labour is cheap and machinery relatively expensive, while the returns on investment are typically uncertain and slow to materialize. Here we see a different argument; capitalism in underdeveloped areas suffers from difficulties which hamper its full development.

This line too has been followed by a number of writers; on the effect of low wages, see chapter 9.

Baran was not enthusiastic about agrarian reform as an answer, if all it does is to relieve the burden of rent and subdivide the larger estates. Since they are so poor, peasants spend any increased income on consumption, while the barriers to progress caused by subdivision of the land are intensified. In the (now) advanced capitalist countries, the development of capitalist agriculture centralized agricultural production, and expelled peasants from the land, raising productivity and providing simultaneously an industrial proletariat, a market for industrial products and a supply of agricultural products to feed the industrial workers. (See Marx's account of primitive accumulation.) Baran argued that agrarian reforms can only succeed in the context of industrial development, and of state policies to encourage the expansion of capitalist industry. They are not, by themselves, any answer and may make matters worse. The exact reasons why the capitalist road in agriculture can only be followed if there is simultaneous industrial development are not clear. It is true that labourers expelled from the land by capitalist agriculture will only find jobs in industry if there is industry to employ them, but need that be any concern of the capitalist farmer? Capitalist agriculture has in fact developed fairly rapidly in many underdeveloped areas, with a corresponding growth of urban unemployment. Baran's hostility to small-scale farming may have stemmed from a preference for collectivization in agriculture; if so, few will now agree.

An important part of the surplus accrues to 'merchants, money lenders and intermediaries of all kinds', who can be described collectively as merchant capital (Baran avoided this convenient term). Merchant capital can exploit the many opportunities for monopoly profit in the 'disorganized and isolated' markets of underdeveloped countries but, at the same time, monopoly profits attract new recruits to this stratum from declassed landlords, rich peasants and so on. Intensified competition leads not to an erosion of monopoly profit but to the creation of ever-smaller and more local monopolies. The result is a large, and parasitic stratum of traders, absorbing large parts of the surplus despite the relative poverty of many of its members. The subdivision of merchant capital, like the subdivision of land, is a barrier to progress. Baran recognized that large-scale merchants exist too (just as large plantations do in agriculture); they are deterred from investing their profits productively by the relatively low returns on productive investment and the attraction of alternative uses of funds. Baran's description of the parasitic hold of merchant capital is convincing (*PEG*: 308-13), but his explanation of this stage of affairs is sketchy. In the advanced countries too there was a stage in which merchant capital dominated, but it was thrust aside by industrial capital. The persistent hold of merchant capital in rural areas of the underdeveloped world must be explained by the restricted development of both agriculture and industry, especially, in Baran's account, the latter.

Baran's explanation for the lack of industrial development is the crux of his explanation of underdevelopment, and has several interconnected elements. Competition from abroad stifles infant industries, narrow markets discourage development, and what industrial development there is rapidly takes a monopolistic form and becomes a barrier to further progress. These handicaps applied, to a degree, to present advanced countries in the initial stages of their growth, but were overcome with resolute state support; the lack of equivalent support from the state is a further factor in holding back similar development today.

Competition from abroad is a factor many Marxists (and others) have emphasized in explaining lack of industrial development. Amin developed this argument in more detail, so I will postpone discussion to the next chapter. Competition from abroad can, in any case, be prevented by protection. State support is therefore the critical factor. The narrow home market is a result of the generally low level of output and income. Baran did not put forward an under-consumptionist argument here; it is the low general level of development that is to blame. His argument is slightly odd though. 'Under such circumstances there could be no spreading of small industrial shops that marked elsewhere the transition from the merchant phase of capitalism to its industrial phase' (*PEG*: 314). A narrow market can hardly prevent the spread of *small-scale* production. The real importance of narrow markets, to Baran, was that larger-scale production leads to an early development of monopoly, the real villain of the piece throughout.

Completing swiftly the entire journey from a progressive to a regressive role in the economic system, they [industrial firms] became at an early stage barriers to economic development rather similar in their effect to the semi-feudal landownership prevailing in underdeveloped countries. . . . Monopolistic industry on the one hand extends the merchant phase of capitalism by obstructing the transition of capital and men from the sphere of circulation to the sphere of industrial production. On the other hand, providing neither a market for agricultural produce nor outlets for agricultural surplus labour and not supplying agriculture with cheap manufactured consumer goods and implements, it forces agriculture back towards self sufficiency, perpetuates the idleness of the structurally unemployed and fosters further mushrooming of petty traders, cottage industries and the like. (*PEG*: 315-16)

I have already described Baran's argument that monopoly deters investment, and its weaknesses. The case he puts forward may be stronger in an underdeveloped country where a large part of total demand derives from a rather static and inflexible agricultural sector, since, as I have argued above, it is the expansion of the market that must be the main stimulus to development in a monopolistic system.

Foreign firms catering for the domestic market are even more likely to operate on a large scale and to have a monopoly position. The fact of foreign ownership makes no difference to the stifling effect of monopoly on investment. They are additionally charged with sending surplus abroad and with importing many of the things they buy. Neither charge is very convincing (Szymanski calculated that there has been a net flow of wealth from the advanced to the underdeveloped countries; 1981, ch. 9). Foreign firms would presumably re-invest profits locally if it were profitable to do so, and would buy goods locally if they were cheaper or better. More important is the political backing they can get from their home countries, and the fact that by displacing local firms they retard the growth of a national bourgeoisie.

There are also firms producing for export, mainly producing primary commodities and mainly foreign-owned. Baran claimed that they typically pay out only a small part of their revenue in wages, that the surplus is correspondingly high and is predominantly taken out of the country. There is thus little stimulus to consumer demand (which might stimulate investment) nor is there a large contribution to the local investible surplus. I will reserve the main discussion of these questions for later chapters; again Baran is the source of ideas that have been developed further. Since Baran's time, manufactured exports from newly industrializing countries have boomed, a development he did not foresee.

The political structure of underdeveloped countries is shaped, first, by the enormous weight of foreign capital, because of its economic and political power within the country and its ability to call on the support of its home country. Foreign capital is opposed to economic development, Baran claimed, because it would threaten cheap supplies of labour, and because it would involve higher taxes and a diversion of state support to the promotion of internal development to the detriment of the 'needs' of the export sector for specialized infrastructure. Second, there is a powerful bloc of mercantile interests attached to foreign capital: enterprises acting as suppliers, agents, and sub-contractors, as well as those who handle import and export business. These Baran calls the *'comprador'* bourgeoisie. In representing their own interests, they represent, to a large extent, the interests of foreign capital as well. Third, there are feudal or semi-feudal landed interests, who have their own reasons for opposing any disturbance in the status quo, and for lining up with foreign capital. Finally, industrial capital, although it has a relatively small weight in the economy, is concentrated into a few powerful monopolies which oppose any developments which threaten their position. These are not the only class forces: workers, peasants and intellectuals have their own interests, opposed to those of the ruling oligarchy, and must be represented or somehow bought off (or both), while a progressive industrial bourgeoisie, though weak, may exist.

It is clear that there are many possible alignments that could arise from this complex web of classes and class fractions, and Baran's importance in the development of the political analysis of underdeveloped countries, as in other aspects of his writing, is largely in the possible lines of analysis suggested by his work. His own stress was mainly on the role of foreign capital, and the imperialist states that lie behind it, in stifling development. This makes sense, since if we take away the element of foreign dominance we are left with very much the same classes and fractions as were contending for power in the advanced countries at an early stage in their development. We may doubt Baran's presumption that mercantile and feudal classes must be uniformly hostile to development; they were not always so in the countries where capitalism first emerged.

Baran discussed three different kinds of government in underdeveloped countries, which he called colonial administrations, *comprador* regimes and 'New Deal' governments. This division looks less relevant now that decolonization has almost eliminated formal colonial rule. Colonial territories are, of course, directly dominated by foreign capital, interested in natural resources, cheap labour, and cheap government. *Comprador* governments were described by Baran as little different from colonial regimes. The job of government is farmed out to local interests that can be relied on to support their paymasters (or be thrown out if they give trouble), so privileged sections of the local population get hold of substantial chunks of surplus which they squander ostentatiously. He cited oil sheikhs as examples (this was before OPEC, of course).

'New Deal' governments are more interesting. Baran described, without very deep analysis, the formation of a popular coalition to demand independence. At the time he was writing, only a few colonial territories had achieved formal independence, and they were at an early stage in their development. He did not wholly rule out the possibility that some of these countries might achieve genuinely independent economic development on the lines of Japan, but he foresaw enormous difficulties. The central point is that it is not only foreign capital which is threatened by economic development. There are powerful interests within the country which also have much to fear. Once independence is attained, the nationalist movement splits into a right and a left wing, and the outcome depends on the precise balance of forces. If popular pressures for reform are strong, Baran argues, there is likely to be to a rapid reconciliation between reactionary local interests and foreign capital; independence will become a sham and the pretence of democracy will be abandoned. It is not difficult to think of examples. The prospects for capitalist development are better where the working class is weak and the industrial bourgeoisie relatively strong.

Although capitalist development was not impossible, Baran thought it unlikely, and expected it at best to be slower than the potential surplus makes technically possible. The only sure road to development is by the adoption of socialist planning. He advocated a Soviet model of development with the surplus in agriculture used to develop heavy industry first and consumer goods industries afterwards.

Since Baran made a clear prediction that monopoly capitalism will lead to slow growth in both advanced and underdeveloped areas, one might try to test this prediction against the facts. It does not fare well. In almost every country in the world, total output has grown more rapidly since the Second World War than in any previous epoch. Industry has grown more rapidly in underdeveloped than in developed countries (Warren 1973, 1980). Per capita output in underdeveloped countries, especially in the agricultural sector, has, it is true, grown more slowly than might have been hoped, but even here it is doubtful whether any previous period has a better record. It might be argued that Baran was comparing monopoly capitalism with socialism, which would have done even better, but this is not my reading of him. In any case, socialist countries do not have an impressive record. The prospects for capitalist development will be discussed further in chapter 11.

7.6 SUMMARY

Baran argued that monopoly leads to a diversion of the surplus of output over necessary consumption away from productive investment towards wasteful uses. It is thus a cause of stagnation in both advanced and underdeveloped countries (an argument that is theoretically weak and conflicts with the facts). Underdeveloped countries are dominated by foreign capital with its local hangers-on, and by mercantile and landlord interests. All are hostile to development. He directed Marxists' attention to the analysis of underdeveloped countries, and provided many of the ideas built on by subsequent writers.

8

Dependency Theories

Andre Gunder Frank's most influential book, *Capitalism and Underdevelopment in Latin America* (Frank 1979a, cited below as *CULA*), starts with a sentence which sums up his position admirably:

> I believe, with Paul Baran, that it is capitalism, both world and national, which produced underdevelopment in the past and which still generates underdevelopment in the present. (*CULA*: xi)

It is essential to realize how drastic a break with the classical Marxists this is. Compare it with Marx:

> National differences and antagonisms between peoples are daily more and more vanishing, owing to the development of the bourgeoisie, to freedom of commerce, to the world market, to uniformity in the mode of production and in the conditions of life corresponding thereto. (Marx, *Manifesto*: 49)

Frank's claim that capitalism causes underdevelopment is characteristic of the *dependency theories* which dominated Marxist (and radical non-Marxist) thinking on the world economy from the late 1960s to the late 1970s. These theories see the world capitalist system as divided into a *centre* and a *periphery* (terminology varies; metropolis and satellite, or core and periphery, are alternatives). The normal processes of the system cause the gap between centre and periphery to widen, as the centre develops at the expense of the periphery, while the periphery is reduced to a state of *dependence*. Imperialism, in the usual sense of political and military dominance, plays a secondary role in dependency theories, which were intended to explain what was seen as a continued failure of development in the Third World, in the era of decolonization. In so far as dependency theorists discussed the history of underdevelopment, one can distinguish a strong form of the theory (Europe found countries that were developed for the time, and made tham underdeveloped), and a less common weak form (Europe prevented underdeveloped countries from developing) (Griffin and Gurley 1985). During the 1970s, dependency theory came under increasing fire, and by the 1980s those writers still working in the dependency framework were visibly on the defensive.

I shall concentrate on a few of the most influential writers in the dependency tradition, primarily Andre Gunder Frank, Immanuel Wallerstein, and Samir Amin, with the emphasis on the works which were most discussed and emulated. By contrast with the earlier periods surveyed in this book, a great variety of work in the dependency framework exists, so the discussion has to be selective. This book is about Marxist theories of imperialism, not about modern theories of economic development, and topics for discussion have been selected accordingly. Dependency theory emerged from debates on development economics, and by no means all of its adherents claimed to be Marxists; were I writing the history of dependency theory in its own right, I would have more to say about writers like Cardoso and Dos Santos.

Frank is sometimes treated as the inventor of dependency theory (Simon and Ruccio 1986), though others could dispute the honour with him. His work has typically taken the form of essays, subsequently collected and published in book form. The most important collections are *Capitalism and Underdevelopment in Latin America* (*CULA*, 1969a, first published in 1967) and *Latin America: Underdevelopment or Revolution* (*LAUR*, 1969b). *Lumpenbourgeoisie: Lumpendevelopment* (*LL*, 1972) was a reply to his critics, and represents a minor modification and restatement of his position. *Dependent Accumulation and Underdevelopment* (*DAU*, 1978) represents a further shift on some issues, and was influenced by other writers, notably Amin. *DAU* contains a historical account of the world economy interspersed with more theoretical essays. Of Frank's many subsequent publications, three (1981,

1983, 1984) deserve mention. I shall concentrate on the earlier works, since they have become part of the intellectual history of the period, even where Frank has subsequently changed his views. Frank was criticized by Laclau (1971), among others.

Wallerstein's *The Modern World System* (*MWS*, 1974a) is the first instalment of a promised four-volume analytical history of the capitalist world economy, continued in *The Modern World System II* (1980); between them they cover the period from 1450 to 1750. A more accessible introduction to his views is to be found in *Historical Capitalism* (1983), and in an article (1974b) which is included, with others, in a useful collection, *The Capitalist World Economy* (*CWE*, 1979; see also 1984). Wallerstein's views (and those of Frank) have been critically analysed by Brenner (1977).

Amin's major works are *Accumulation on a World Scale* (1974, cited below as *AWS*), *Unequal Development* (1976, cited as *UD*), and *Class and Nation: Historically and in the Present Crisis* (1980), which all cover very similar ground. *Imperialism and Unequal Development* (1977, cited as *IUD*) is a collection of essays, one of which, 'The End of a Debate', sets out Amin's main ideas very clearly. He has also written a considerable amount about particular areas, notably North Africa (1966) and West Africa (1971). Addo (1984) contains useful essays by Frank and Wallerstein as well as Amin. Amin has been criticized for eclecticism (Barone 1982; cf. Griffin and Gurley 1985), though it is not clear why that should be a vice.

8.1 FRANK

Frank identified capitalism with a system of (world-wide) exchange, characterized by monopoly and by exploitation. He also (implicitly) argued that any part of the world which is affected in any fundamental way by 'capitalism' (exchange) is 'capitalist'. He had little difficulty in showing that the effects of the capitalist world economy have penetrated so deep into Latin America that no part of the continent has been unaffected. Even areas substantially devoted to self-sufficient, subsistence farming (such as north-east Brazil – see *CULA*: 153-4) are the products of the decay of earlier export industries, while *latifundias* (large estates worked by peasant

163

cultivators) originated as a response to commercial opportunities even where they have subsequently declined into almost self-sufficient isolation.

Incorporation into the world capitalist system leads to development, in some areas, and to the *development of underdevelopment* elsewhere. Underdevelopment, as Frank uses the word, is not an original state; he coined the name *undevelopment* for the state of affairs before capitalist penetration (though neither he nor his followers have used it much, on the grounds that all vestiges of older forms have long since been reconstructed by capitalism). The 'development of underdevelopment' occurs because the world capitalist system is characterized by a *metropolis–satellite* structure. The metropolis exploits the satellite, surplus is concentrated in the metropolis, and the satellite is cut off from potential investment funds, so its growth is slowed down. More important, the satellite is reduced to a state of *dependence* which creates a local ruling class with an interest in perpetuating underdevelopment, a 'lumpenbourgeoisie' which follows a 'policy of underdevelopment' (*LL*, passim). I shall first discuss Frank's conception of the structure of the world capitalist system, the 'chain of metropolis–satellite relations', then the transfer of surplus from satellite to metropolis and its consequences, and finally the economic and political structures that result.

Consider first the idea of a chain of metropolis–satellite relations.

> The monopoly capitalist structure and the surplus expropriation/appropriation contradiction run through the entire Chilean economy, past and present. Indeed, it is this exploitative relation which in chain-like fashion extends the capitalist link between the capitalist world and national metropolises to the regional centers (part of whose surplus they appropriate) and from these to local centers and so on to large landholders or merchants who expropriate surplus from small peasants or tenants, and sometimes even from these latter to landless laborers exploited by them in turn. At each step along the way the relatively few capitalists above exercise monopoly power over the many below, expropriating some or all of their economic surplus, and to the extent that they are not

expropriated in turn by the still fewer above, appropriating it for their own use. Thus at each point, the international, national and local capitalist system generates economic development for the few and underdevelopment for the many. (*CULA*: 7-8. Similar statements may be found throughout Frank's work, e.g. *CULA*: 146-8, about Brazil)

This 'chain' of metropolis–satellite relations has existed, according to Frank, since the sixteenth century; changes since then represent only changes in the forms of dominance and exploitation of the satellite, not changes of substance. This is the principle of 'continuity in change' (cf. Addo 1986).

As a description, Frank's 'chain of metropolis–satellite relations' is plausible. Relations of dominance and surplus extraction exist not only between the direct producers and their immediate exploiters, but at all levels in the world system. The idea is essential to Frank, since the 'chain' serves both to channel surplus to the metropolis and to create the class interests that sustain underdevelopment. As an analysis, however, it raises more questions than it answers. I shall criticize Frank primarily for conflating very different kinds of relations on the basis of purely superficial similarities. In particular, I shall argue that merchant capital and modern monopoly capital are quite different.

The basic idea is of an exchange relationship in which the metropolis has a monopolistic position because each metropolis has several satellites, while each satellite confronts only one metropolis. The concept of monopoly used here is familiar from economics textbooks: a single seller facing a multitude of small buyers or, conversely, a single buyer facing many sellers. The monopolist can set the terms of exchange, and capture any surplus controlled by the other party. Frank, however, generalized the idea to cover any exploitative or unequal relationship: 'the source or form of this monopoly varies from one case to another' (*CULA*: 147). One can say, for example, that landlords monopolize access to the land, capitalists monopolize the means of production, and so on. But if one does not distinguish between different forms of monopoly, and in particular between class monopolies and individual monopolies, between monopoly control of the means of production and monopoly in exchange, then the assertion that exploitation is the result of monopoly becomes an empty tautology.

At the international and inter-regional levels of Frank's hierarchy, there are two distinct kinds of monopoly involved. The first, and the one that fits Frank's account best, is the monopolistic system of merchant capital, established in Latin America following the Spanish and Portuguese conquests and dominant into the twentieth century. Merchants collect products for export and for inter-regional trade, and distribute foreign and urban products. They are usually not involved directly in production; where they are, their activities in organizing production are secondary. Mercantile monopoly may be associated with either pre-capitalist or (small-scale) capitalist relations of production. The second kind of monopoly, which Frank does not distinguish clearly, is modern monopoly capital, characterized by large-scale capitalist production. In underdeveloped countries, it typically appears in the form of multinational companies, though national monopolies also exist. In contrast to merchant capital, modern monopoly capital exercises direct control over production and normally introduces fully capitalist production relations and the most modern technology. To confuse the two is a major mistake. It is true that some cases are hard to categorize, for example where multinational firms are engaged in buying agricultural products from small-scale producers, or where they organize production on a relatively primitive technical basis (e.g. plantation agriculture), but the existence of borderline cases does not invalidate the classification.

At the local levels of the hierarchy, closer to the direct producers, Frank mentions merchants, landlords and (occasionally) capitalists. These must be clearly distinguished from each other. Frank argues that it is often difficult to disentangle these relationships in practice, but this surely makes it even more essential to be clear in analysis. I am not arguing that these different exploitative relations exist independently of each other. In each different historical period they have interacted and reinforced each other – this is what gives Frank's account its descriptive verisimilitude.

The next major point to note is that Frank identifies an economic hierarchy of individuals or classes (the 'relatively few capitalists above' exploiting 'the many below') with a

spatial or geographic hierarchy (world and national met-
ropolises, regional centres, local centres). This coincidence of
economic and spatial relations is characteristic of some, but
not all, systems of exploitation. Merchant capital, for example, sometimes creates a geographical hierarchy, when the
output of scattered production units is gathered in regional
centres for export in bulk, or for shipment to urban markets.
This is the case that fits Frank's picture best: the economic
and geographical hierarchies coincide.

Modern monopoly capital is often administered through a
superficially similar geographical hierarchy. The head office
is in a major world centre, regional offices or local
subsidiaries are established in large cities, while productive
activities are located wherever manpower, markets and raw
materials supplies dictate (see Hymer 1972; Chandler and
Redlich 1961). This hierarchy of administration is not in any
real sense a 'chain of metropolis–satellite relations'. The
intermediate levels of management are no more than agents
of the corporation, with no independent economic base.
There is a direct wage relation between the workers and the
corporation as a unit of capital. Another kind of hierarchy is
created by the existence of subcontractors and the like,
subordinate to the large corporations. This was discussed by
Hilferding and is still important (Friedman 1977). As with
merchant capital, it involves exchange relations, but the units
involved are producing units, and are often located within a
single urban area. All of these hierarchical structures differ
from competitive capitalism, which is characterized by a
'chain' with only one link: the relation between workers and
capitalists.

There are superficial similarities between Frank's 'chain'
(and also Wallerstein's core–periphery relation) and the
classical Marxist theories of imperialism. Lenin said that
finance capital 'spreads its net' over the world, and Bukharin
wrote of a 'few consolidated, organised economic bodies'
confronting an agrarian periphery. However, for Bukharin
and Lenin, this was part of a process of internationalization
that was transforming the world system by concentrating
power and wealth at the centre, but simultaneously developing production and creating a true proletariat in the
periphery. Where Frank and Wallerstein saw an essentially
static system of redistribution persisting for centuries, the

167

classical Marxists saw a process of development that was transforming the world. The essential difference between these views is to be found in the classical Marxist emphasis on the relations of production. Frank is only able to argue that the 'chain' has remained essentially unchanged by ignoring the real changes in the relations of production which followed the displacement of merchant capital by modern monopoly capital.

The 'chain of metropolis–satellite relations' is, according to Frank, the cause of the 'development of underdevelopment'. This latter phrase is not very clearly defined, but part of its meaning seems to be a quantitative retardation in the growth of output, employment and productivity. (The other aspect of its meaning is a qualitative deformation of the system.) I now turn to the argument (used, in rather different forms, by Baran, Frank, Wallerstein and others) that the transfer of surplus from the satellite to the metropolis leads to a retardation of development in the satellite.

First, consider the concept of surplus. Frank referred to Baran's definitions (chapter 7 above), but there are additional difficulties in using this definition in Frank's framework. Baran defined surplus as the difference between output (actual or potential) and consumption (actual or necessary). For a self-sufficient producing unit, the surplus is simply the physical excess of what is produced over what is consumed.

Frank, however, was explicitly concerned with production units that are not self-sufficient, but are involved in a network of exchange relations. In this case, the goods that are consumed are not produced within the unit concerned, so production and consumption must be valued in comparable units before the difference between them can be calculated. The problem of valuation was a major preoccupation of the English classical economists; Marx tackled it by using labour values. Neither Frank nor Baran suggested any solution. It is not a mere technicality; to argue that there is exploitation in exchange, it is necessary to compare the prices that are actually paid with some reference set of 'correct' prices. At the prices actually paid, obviously, producers get the 'value' of what they sell. I know of no simple or universal solution to this problem, which greatly reduces the usefulness of the concept of surplus. Labour values make sense only in a relatively homogeneous system, in which competition leads to a certain uniformity in levels of technique by eliminating inefficient producers. This is the context implied by Marx in his discussion of value. As Frank himself insisted, the world economy is not now, and has never been, homogeneous in this sort of way, so the concept of surplus can only be used in a rather loose and qualitative fashion.

If we accept a concept of surplus, we must still ask: what are the effects of a transfer of surplus from satellite to metropolis? Here Frank's conflation of the economic and geographical dimensions of exploitation adds powerfully to the confusion. To say that one region extracts surplus from another suggests strongly that some physical goods are being seized from one place and shifted to another. Within a system of exchange, however, what is happening is that an exchange of goods of unequal value (in some sense) is taking place, and that control over the use of certain sums of value is being transferred from individuals (or groups) who live in one place to individuals (or groups, or corporate bodies) who live (or have their head offices) in another. Without analysis of the use of the surplus, this tells us nothing about the geographical location of new investment. The whole point of Baran's concept of surplus is that surplus represents potential investment and hence economic growth.

As a starting point, consider what determines the geographical pattern of investment in a fully developed (ideal) capitalist system. Here, investment will be directed into the activities that yield the highest profits (this is what leads to the formation of a general rate of profit, see Marx, *Capital*, III, ch. 10). In geographical terms, investment will be located where costs are lowest (allowing for transport costs), and thus, other things being equal, investment will go to low wage areas, i.e. underdeveloped areas. I do not argue that these ideal conditions have ever existed, nor that an allocation of investment according to profitability would be desirable. The real point is that the geographical pattern of investment need not correspond at all to the geographical location of the owners of the surplus. If anything, the super-exploitation of underdeveloped countries should mean more rapid development, as the classical Marxists expected. A large part of Frank's argument is therefore misdirected; the transfer of surplus from satellite to metropolis cannot in itself explain the lack of development in the satellite. The pattern of development depends on the factors that govern the *use* of the surplus.

Part of Frank's answer to this criticism would no doubt be to refer to his discussion of the distortion of the satellite's economy as a result of economic dependence, to be discussed below. He could also argue that the structure of the chain of metropolis–satellite relations impedes the return flow of investment from metropolis to satellite. Here, the distinctions between merchant capital and modern monopoly capital are relevant.

In the case of a mercantile hierarchy, there are very real barriers to the productive use of the surplus in the satellite. The production units are separate from the capitalist enterprises that exploit them. If mercantile profit is ploughed back into the expansion of the mercantile enterprise itself, this does nothing to expand actual production. Where production is in the hands of pre-capitalist producers, there may be no way in which investment funds could be channelled into production, at least without transforming the social relations of production, a task which merchant capital may have neither the means nor the desire to undertake. Where production is organized in small capitalist firms or in pre-capitalist units which can absorb money capital productively (for example, slave plantations), the problem is that investment funds will not be forthcoming unless production is profitable, and production is not profitable if the potential profits are being creamed off by mercantile middlemen.

In the case of modern monopoly capital, especially in the form of multinational companies, the case is different. It has been argued by many commentators (e.g. Hymer 1972; Adam 1975) that multinational companies look over the whole world to select sites for investment, potentially profitable markets, and so on. They have no special reason to concentrate investment in their home countries, indeed they are multinational precisely because they have not done so in the past. The investment decisions of multinational companies should approximate more closely to the 'pure' capitalist pattern than those of any preceding form of capital.

Frank cited evidence showing that the outflow of profit from Latin America to the USA in various forms greatly exceeds the return flow of investment funds from the USA. This is not really surprising, since it is generally true that only

170

a small part of profit is reinvested, whether the profits are
generated in advanced or underdeveloped countries, by local
or foreign capitalists. In all these cases, a large fraction of
profit is consumed. This may be an indictment of capitalism,
but not particularly of foreign capital. Baran argued that
monopoly capital is particularly prone to waste the surplus. I
have criticized this view, and in any case it is a charge
directed against monopoly capital in general, not foreign or
multinational corporations as such. The relevant question is
whether multinational companies reinvest less than locally
owned capitalist enterprises. In Frank's treatment of foreign
firms, nationalist rhetoric often supplants sober analysis.

My conclusion, then, is that the transfer of (control over)
surplus to the metropolis is not, in itself, an explanation for
lack of development in the satellite, which must be explained
by looking at the uses of surplus. Of course, the fact that
surplus is in different hands may be relevant to determining
its use, but it is not the only factor. In particular, the relations
of production and of exchange are crucial factors. Where
production is in the hands of multinational corporations, the
scope for productive use of surplus is far greater than it is
where production is pre-capitalist and surplus is captured by
merchant capital. In all cases, however, the incentives and
opportunities provided by the economic environment are
critically important.

The transfer of surplus is not the only cause of the
'development of underdevelopment'; Frank also claimed that
participation as a satellite in the capitalist world system leads
to a distorted and dependent economic structure. This idea
was developed independently by a number of writers, and
led to them becoming known as the *dependency school*. The
point is that even a nationalist government cannot succeed in
promoting capitalist development because of the constraints
imposed by the international environment.

Dos Santos (1970) defined dependence as follows:

> By dependence we mean a situation in which the
> economy of certain countries is conditioned by the dev-
> elopment and expansion of another economy to which the
> former is subjected. The relation of interdependence ...
> assumes the form of dependence when some countries
> (the dominant ones) can expand and be self sustaining,

171

while other countries (the dependent ones) can do this only as a reflection of that expansion.

The story runs as follows: underdeveloped countries produce a narrow range of staple raw materials for export (this is the result of earlier stages of development). Incomes are very unequal and much of the surplus flows out of the country, so the mass market for consumer goods is limited. 'Import substituting' industrialization involves capital-intensive techniques, so employment is low, as are wages, leaving a large part of the population 'marginalized', either unemployed or in low productivity traditional activities. (The concept of 'marginalization' has much in common with dualistic theories, except that here it is the lack of dynamism of the modern sector that excludes people, forcing them back into low productivity activities, where theories of dualism originally saw the modern sector as held back by the traditional sector.) The market remains narrow, further constricting development. Furtado (1973) suggested a further factor: consumption patterns among the elite are copied from those of more advanced countries, and the result is to bias demand towards imports or towards goods produced by capital-intensive methods, reinforcing the problem. Modern production methods require imported capital goods, imported components and materials, while multinational companies remit profits abroad (openly or by devious means). The balance of payments is therefore a constant problem, halting growth, and compelling the retention of traditional export industries as foreign exchange earners.

Consider, first, the problem of narrow markets. There are two issues: the absolute size of the market and its rate of growth. A small market limits the opportunities for use of modern large-scale techniques; there is no doubt that small underdeveloped countries are at a disadvantage here, though larger underdeveloped countries (Brazil, India, etc.) are not. Production for the (potentially almost unlimited) export market can overcome both this problem and the problem of a slowly growing market. Relatively slow growth in the market for consumer goods is the result not of a high rate of exploitation, but of a rising rate of exploitation. Correspondingly, the market for means of production could expand relatively rapidly. This is the standard argument against under-consumptionism, an argument Frank accepted (*DAU*, chapter 5). It is argued, however, that means of production are predominantly imported, so the growth of local industry is limited by the slow growth of the market for consumer goods. The case thus hinges on assumptions about the pattern of international specialization. Exports (which generate income, and hence demand) are assumed to be confined to traditional exports. Production for the local market is assumed to be limited to consumer goods. An explanation of the pattern of specialization is needed to give these arguments a solid foundation.

What of the balance of payments? Suppose a country exports a limited range of traditional staples, and cannot easily expand its exports. Growth in export earnings is limited, so import growth must be limited too (since imports must, in the end, be paid for by exports). If imports, say of capital equipment or materials, are essential for growth, the growth of the whole economy can be limited by the balance of payments constraint. The argument is familiar to development economists (it is a form of 'structuralism'; see Little 1982), and is perfectly coherent. The problem is that it, like the 'narrow markets' argument, rests on the assumption that nothing can be done about the pattern of specialization; indeed, it is just a variant of the 'narrow markets' argument, for the special case in which export markets are narrow.

What is needed to add some substance to these arguments is some explanation of *why* a country should be so limited in the range of goods it can produce and export. All the evidence is that many Third World countries have, in fact, widened the range of goods they produce, either to replace imports of manufactures (this is called 'import substituting industrialization' in the jargon) or by exporting manufactures themselves ('export-oriented industrialization'). Some countries which shifted to exporting manufactures became net importers of primary products themselves, creating markets for exporters of primary products. The benefits have not been evenly spread, of course, but what is needed is an explanation of why some countries have succeded while others, as yet, have not. To deny the possibility of something which is visibly happening is not very helpful.

Finally, Frank stressed the political consequences of dependency. The ruling classes in underdeveloped countries owe their position to their place in a 'chain' that runs from the countryside to the imperialist metropolis, and thus have an interest in maintaining it.

> This colonial and class structure establishes very well defined class interests for the dominant sector of the bourgeoisie. Using government cabinets and other instruments of the state, the bourgeoisie produces a policy of underdevelopment in the economic, social and political life of the 'nation' and the people of Latin America. (*LL*: 13)

This part of Frank's argument is at its best in his historical analysis of a crucial turning point in Latin American history, the period after independence in the nineteenth century. At this time there was a bitter conflict between the 'Europeans', the advocates of free trade, and the 'Americans', the advocates of protection for domestic industries. The 'Europeans' were led by merchants who handled the export and import trades and by agricultural export interests, and they were the stronger party precisely because the preceding centuries of dependence had created an economy dominated by the groups that stood to gain from continuation of the system. Free trade made imported manufactured goods available cheaply to the export agriculturalists, and the weakness of the local currency increased the value of exported products in terms of the depreciated currency, transferring income to those who sold goods for export. Local manufacturing industry was unable to compete with imports without protection, so perpetuating the imbalance (*LL*: 61). State policy was geared to the needs of the export sector in other ways as well: taxes, distribution of land, immigration policy, ports, railways, and so on. Frank summarizes: 'the "European" lumpenbourgeoisie built "national" lumpenstates which never achieved real independence but were, and are, simply effective instruments of the lumpenbourgeoisie's policy of lumpendevelopment' (*LL*: 58).

By contrast, the United States did not offer suitable conditions for export agriculture except in the south.

> Consequently, the class structure which developed there, based at the start on small farmers, did not present any

obstacle to a development policy which permitted the Northern bourgeoisie to become strong enough to use independence to promote integrated development, to defeat the planter/exporters of the South in the Civil War, to impose a policy of industrialisation and arrive at their own industrial 'take-off' point. (*LL*: 58-9)

Frank was surely right to argue that state policy is a critical element in economic development, that state policy is the outcome of conflict between classes and fractions of classes with conflicting interests, and that classes and fractions which benefit from an existing economic structure have an interest in perpetuating it and are in a strong position to succeed. However, his political analysis was radically impoverished by the presumption that international trade is bad for development, and self-sufficiency good, so classes and fractions were classified by whether they were for or against trade. The issues in development policy are far too complex to be captured by this simple opposition. In any case, the idea that state policy since the Second World War has been hostile to industrial development is simply ridiculous. In the majority of Third World countries, levels of industrial protection have been very high (absurdly high in some cases), and state investment has been poured into infrastructure and 'heavy' industries. It can be argued that some countries, at least, have lost out by neglecting agriculture and primary production, not the reverse. The interesting question is: how did industrial capital succeed in enlisting such wholehearted state support, when it was, to begin with, so weak? This, and related issues, will be taken up in chapters 10 and 11.

A final comment: Frank's arguments were presented in a distinctive way, which seems to me to be an important source of weakness. His normal procedure was to make brief, sloganistic assertions, and then to justify and expand on them by giving a series of historical examples, frequently quoting at length from other writers or from original sources. The problem with this style of argument is that it leaves no room for systematic theoretical exposition; one is left repeatedly saying: yes, it happened like that in those cases, but why, and must it be the same everywhere? In addition, crucial terms (development, underdevelopment, metropolis, satellite, capitalism, and so on) are never explicitly defined. The reader is

175

left to infer their meaning from the essentially descriptive uses they are put to. They often have a spectrum of meanings rather than a single precisely defined sense, blurring the logic of some of his most important assertions.

8.2 WALLERSTEIN

I shall summarize Wallerstein's arguments briefly, since they have a great deal in common with those of Frank. He insisted that any social system must be seen as a totality. Nation states, in the modern world, are not closed systems and cannot be treated as if they were.

> We take the defining characteristic of a social system to be the existence within it of a division of labour, such that the various sectors or areas within are dependent upon economic exchange with others for the smooth and continuous provisioning of the needs of the area. (*CWE*: 5)

The only kinds of social system that have existed are 'mini-systems' (closed local economies), 'world empires' (defined by the extraction of tribute by a central authority) and 'world economies' (formed by a market exchange). A 'world' system does not necessarily have to cover the whole globe; it is a 'unit with a single division of labour and multiple cultural systems'. A world economy, then, is a world system without a single central authority. The modern world system is capitalist, since it is a world economy (as defined).

> Capitalism and a world economy (that is, a single division of labour but multiple polities) are obverse sides of the same coin. One does not cause the other. We are merely defining the same indivisible phenomenon by different characteristics. (*CWE*: 6)

The capitalist world system is divided into three tiers of states, those of the core, the semi-periphery and the periphery. The essential difference between them is in the strength of the state machine in different areas, leading to transfers of surplus from the periphery to the core, which further strengthen the state machines in the core. State power is the central mechanism since 'actors in the market' attempt to 'avoid the normal operation of the market whenever it does not maximise their profit' by using the state to alter the terms of trade. The link with imperialism in the traditional sense, the dominance of one state over others, is obvious.

At least in origin, the core–periphery division is explained through a sort of technological determinism. Western Europe specialized in manufacture and animal raising, activities which require relatively high skills, and are better carried out by relatively well-paid free wage labour. The resulting social structure is the foundation of relatively strong 'core' states, able to manipulate markets to their advantage. Hispanic America (mining) and Baltic east Europe (grain) specialized in activities requiring relatively little skill, hence capitalists chose (through state intervention) forms of coerced labour, and a difference of interests emerged between manufacturing and primary product export interests. Local states were weak, and readily subjugated by the core, so these areas became 'peripheral'.

Once in existence, the core–periphery division is maintained by the ability of the core states to manipulate the workings of the system as a whole to suit their needs. They deliberately weaken peripheral states or eliminate them altogether by conquest, and also alter the workings of markets by imposing monopolistic restrictions, protecting their own industries, forbidding corresponding protection in the periphery, and so on.

The 'semi-periphery' is a sort of labour aristocracy of states or geographical areas. Without it, a world system becomes polarized and liable to revolt, while an intermediate tier diffuses antagonisms. This argument is hard to accept as an explanation of the existence of a semi-periphery. Was the creation of a semi-periphery deliberate? The particular cases Wallerstein cites (Italy in the sixteenth century, Russia later, including the USSR) do not seem to have been deliberately created by the core states. In any case, if the core is divided into distinct national states (by definition), who is there to oversee the interests of the system as a whole? The notion of a semi-periphery is rather convenient for the theory because it provides, so to speak, a site for change. New core states can emerge from the semi-periphery, and declining core states can sink into it. On the other hand, the notion of a semi-periphery can easily become an excuse for *ad hoc* explanations; core states are expected to succeed, so any core state that does badly can be redescribed as semi-peripheral, and so on. There is a risk of leaving the theory with no substance at all.

Critique

At this stage, one might well ask what has happened to relations of production and to classes in the ordinary Marxist sense. Wallerstein seems to count anybody who produces for profit in the market as a capitalist. Labour-power is indeed a commodity but 'wage labor is only one of the modes in which labor is recruited and compensated in the labour market. Slavery, coerced cash-crop production, sharecropping and tenancy are all alternative modes' (*CWE*: 17). Marx's concept of capitalism in terms of a relation between free labour and capital is ruthlessly ditched. 'Class analysis' amounts, in Wallerstein's view, to the analysis of the interests of 'syndical groups' within particular states, and is legitimate provided we look at the 'structural position and interests in the world economy' of these groups. At the same time, classes have no permanent reality and are no more fundamental than 'ethno-nations'. That, at least, is my interpretation of some more than usually opaque passages in Wallerstein's writings. (See *CWE*: 24, 224-6.) The central point, which has been the subject of much debate, is that 'modes of labour control' (wage labour, slavery, etc.) are secondary results of the functioning of a world system defined by the existence of market links. The situation in the core is such that free wage labour tends to be chosen (by the ruling class, with state support) while in the periphery more coercive systems are used.

Social classes

modes of labour control

Overall, Wallerstein's primary assertion is that a world system must be analysed as a whole. Few are likely to disagree. Beyond this, I find little more than a series of definitions and phrases, with a mass of detailed historical material that often seems to have little connection with his overall generalizations. What is lacking is a level of theory that would connect the two, by specifying exactly how, and under what conditions, the structure produces the results he claimed for it.

8.3 LACLAU'S CRITIQUE

Both Frank and Wallerstein defined capitalism as a system of exchange relations. They did so, quite deliberately, to include relations of exploitation such as those between landlords and peasants, which do not involve wage labour in the strict sense. This approach has been criticized by a number of Marxist writers. Laclau, in an article which has been the starting point for much debate (1971, reprinted in Laclau 1977), stated his essential point as follows:

Of course, Frank is at liberty to abstract a mass of historical features and build a model on this basis. He can even, if he wishes, give the resulting entity the name of capitalism. . . . But what is wholly unacceptable is the fact that Frank claims that his conception is the Marxist concept of capitalism. *Because for Marx – as is obvious to anyone who has even a superficial acquaintance with his works – capitalism was a mode of production.* The fundamental economic relationship of capitalism is constituted by the free laborer's sale of his labour-power, whose necessary precondition is the loss by the direct producer of ownership of the means of production. (Laclau 1977: 23)

Marx regarded exchange, and the development of merchant capital, as perfectly consistent with the persistence of pre-capitalist modes of production. I have already described this aspect of Marx's analysis.

Laclau distinguished between 'modes of production' and 'economic systems'. A mode of production is 'an integrated complex of social productive forces and relations linked to a determinate type of ownership of the means of production' (1977: 34). The feudal and capitalist modes are the only two that are relevant:

The feudal mode of production is one in which the productive process operates according to the following pattern: 1. the economic surplus is produced by a labour force subject to extra-economic compulsion; 2. the economic surplus is privately appropriated by someone other than the direct producers; 3. property in the means of production remains in the hands of the direct producer.

> In the capitalist mode of production, the economic surplus is also subject to private appropriation, but as distinct from feudalism, ownership of the means of production is severed from ownership of labour power. (Laclau 1977: 35)

An 'economic system' consists of 'the mutual relations between the different sectors of the economy, or between different production units, whether on a regional, national or world scale' (1977: 35), so 'an economic system can include, as constitutive elements, different modes of production.' (Similar ideas were developed by a number of writers in the 1970s, and will be discussed further in chapter 10; Laclau's version is discussed here, because it was presented as a critique of Frank and Wallerstein.) According to Laclau, Feudal production for exchange is not ruled out, so Frank's evidence that supposedly feudal areas of Latin America have been deeply influenced by exchange becomes irrelevant, and *'to affirm the feudal character of the relations of production in the agrarian sector does not necessarily involve maintaining a dualist thesis'* (1977: 32).

Wallerstein responded: 'The substantive issue, in my view, concerns the appropriate unit of analysis for the purpose of comparison. . . . Sweezy and Frank better follow the spirit of Marx if not his letter' (*CWE*: 9). The essence of his reply is that the system must be viewed as a totality, and that the only totality that actually exists is the world economy. This brings out the key point very well. Both Frank and Wallerstein were looking for descriptive generalizations, based directly on the observed facts. Marx, by contrast, insisted on the necessity of abstraction. The capitalist mode of production was not, for Marx, a directly observable empirical thing (like the capitalist world economy); it was instead a conceptual object, the product of thought. The aim is to pick out key relationships and examine them in isolation before elaborating the analysis to deal with the complexities of the real world. Wallerstein's reply, therefore, misses its target, since Marx was not looking for a totality that really exists.

However, an appeal to the authority of Marx only settles the issue for dogmatists (cf. Foster-Carter 1979). Marx did indeed define a mode of production in terms of relations of production, but it remains to be shown that this approach gives better results in explaining reality than any other. I have argued that major weaknesses in Frank's analysis follow directly from his neglect of relations of production. If this is accepted, then it strengthens Laclau's case. On the other hand, Laclau's own explanation of underdevelopment and of the persistence of pre-capitalist modes is most unconvincing.

Laclau wrote '[Frank] shows us how the advanced countries have exploited the peripheral countries; what he at no time explains is why certain nations needed the under-development of other nations for their own process of development' (Laclau 1977: 35-6). And again: 'if we want to show that ... development generates underdevelopment, what we have to prove is that the maintenance of pre-capitalist relations of production in the peripheral areas is an inherent condition of the process of accumulation in the central countries' (Laclau 1977: 37).

There is a clear logical fallacy here. Laclau claims that if development requires underdevelopment, then underdevelopment will happen, but not otherwise. This is the crudest kind of functionalism; whatever is necessary for capitalism will happen. It cannot be sustained. If underdevelopment were necessary for development, it might still fail to happen, either because owners of metropolitan capital, not having understood Marx, fail to realize the necessity, or because they lack the means to enforce their wishes. On the other hand, underdevelopment might not be necessary, but could happen all the same, just as an innocent bystander might be killed in a shoot-out without his death being necessary to anybody. Then again, underdevelopment might contribute to develop-ment without being necessary to it, it could be the jam on the bread. I stress this point, perhaps too heavily, because this logical fallacy is all too common in Marxist writings. Laclau tried to show the necessity of underdevelopment to develop-ment through the theory of the falling rate of profit, which I have already criticized (chapter 2). The organic composition of capital, he claimed, rises in the advanced countries, bringing down the rate of profit, which must be offset by expansion into areas where the organic composition is low. Even if true, however, this would not explain the persistence of pre-capitalist modes; rather, one would expect investment in underdeveloped areas to lead to the replacement of pre-capitalist modes by capitalism (as Lenin, for example, expected).

Brenner (1977) developed Laclau's critical points and added a very thorough critique of Wallerstein, while advancing quite different positive arguments. His central point is that capitalism is unique, above all, for the way in which it promotes technological development, increased productivity and hence increased profits (through relative surplus value). This tendency to develop the forces of production is one of Marx's main conclusions. Brenner showed that other modes of production ('modes of labour control' in Wallerstein's terms) do not have the same dynamic. Equally, 'modes of labour control' are not freely chosen by ruling classes. They are the result of class struggle.

Different parts of the world economy, therefore, have their own tendencies that derive from the modes of production installed there. This does not mean that they evolve independently of each other, but that analysis should start from the workings of distinct modes of production, and then go on to analyse how they interact with each other. This line of argument will be developed further in chapter 10. Note, incidentally, that if increasing productivity is the essence of capitalist development, the prosperity of the 'core', or the 'metropolis', does not have to be at the expense of anybody else; development is not necessarily the 'other side of the coin' of underdevelopment (which is not to deny that international flows of surplus can and do take place). This is not a new idea; it is a reassertion of the classical Marxist perspective.

8.4 AMIN

Amin's guiding vision is summed up by the titles of his two main works: *Accumulation on a World Scale* and *Unequal Development*. The process of accumulation, of development, must be analysed as a single process on a world scale, but it takes place in a world divided into many distinct national social formations, containing different modes of production. Accumulation does not tend to create uniformity between these social formations, but divides them into two categories: those of the *centre* and those of the *periphery*. Accumulation at the centre is *autocentric* (self-centred); it is governed by its own internal dynamic, as analysed by Marx. In the periphery, by contrast, accumulation is dependent or *extraverted*, constrained by the centre–periphery relation.

At the heart of Amin's analysis, as I read it, is an explanation of unequal specialization, to be discussed in detail below. Put very simply, he argues that the pattern of international specialization is determined by absolute cost levels (not by comparative advantage, as Ricardo thought), and that cost levels depend on productivity and on wages. The countries of the centre developed capitalism earlier, or under especially favourable conditions, and got a huge lead in productivity during a period in which wages were held down to something close to physical subsistence levels in both centre and periphery. This established a pattern of unequal specialization. Later, wages started to rise at the centre, but the centre's lead in productivity remained enough to ensure lower costs at least in most sectors of industry. Unequal specialization is thus both cause and consequence of unequal development; both are anchored in the conditions of production and reflected in exchange relations.

Given this pattern of unequal specialization and development, capitalism at the centre evolved as the classical Marxists predicted, driving out pre-capitalist modes of production, while capitalist development in the periphery was blocked, since the periphery could compete only in resource-based activities (minerals, tropical agriculture), and there could only be limited development oriented to the narrow domestic market. The larger part of the population was excluded from the capitalist sector, so pre-capitalist modes of production were not eliminated. This provides an explanation for the typical structure of underdeveloped countries, 'peripheral capitalism'.

After a certain stage of development, wages started to rise at the centre, while massive unemployment and the persistence of pre-capitalist modes of production held wages down in the periphery. Amin's explanations of increased wages at the centre are both obscure and inconsistent; I shall not go into detail here; see Brewer (1980a; 1980b: 250-6). High wages at the centre and low wages in the periphery lead to unequal exchange, as analysed by Emmanuel (discussed in chapter 9 below). Very briefly, Emmanuel argued that low wages in the periphery mean low prices for its products, while the products of the high wage centre sell at high prices. Some care is needed here; according to Amin, the centre has advantages in productivity that more than outweigh its higher wages, so one might expect its prices to be low. However, he argued that although the centre has relatively high productivity in most lines of (industrial) production (thus maintaining unequal specialization despite the wage gap), the periphery has relatively high productivity in the few lines of production in which it specializes. In its export industries, therefore, the periphery combines high productivity with low wages, the recipe, given international equalization of profits, for unequal exchange.

Amin criticized Emmanuel for treating wages as an 'independent variable', without adequately explaining them. In Amin's words: 'Which is cause and which effect: the international prices, or the inequality in wage levels? The question is pointless. Inequality in wages, due to historical reasons (the difference between social formations) constitutes the basis of a specialisation and a system of international prices that perpetuate this inequality' (UD: 151). There are thus no independent variables, only a self-perpetuating process (see also Amin 1977: 185).

The social formations of the periphery are characterized by disarticulation between sectors, since most of the industries producing means of production are absent. The links between industries producing means of production and consumer goods, analysed by Marx in his schemes of reproduction, exist at the world level but are incomplete within the national economy. The periphery is also characterized by unevenness of productivity; export sectors operated by foreign capital on the most modern lines coexist with primitive pre-capitalist sectors. The capitalist mode of production is dominant but does not tend to become exclusive, and the tertiary sector becomes overexpanded as a result of the pattern of demand and the lack of opportunities for investment in industry. These features of peripheral capitalism are not at all characteristic of 'traditional' pre-capitalist societies, they are the product of the 'development of underdevelopment'.

How does Amin's account of the world system fit in with those of other writers? He took the analysis of international prices from Emmanuel, adding his own account of unequal specialization to complement it. Together these theories amount to the first serious analysis of international trade in the Marxist tradition. Other writers have, of course, described the destruction of industries in the periphery by foreign competition (Marx on the destruction of Indian handloom weaving, etc.), but Amin developed the idea and made it the centre of his analysis. Unequal specialization provides a foundation for an analysis of peripheral capitalism that has much in common with Baran and with dependency theories. On the other hand, Amin analysed social formations in terms of the interaction of different modes of production, like a number of writers discussed in chapter 10. Monopoly, as such, plays very little part in his analysis, but the mobility of capital is of central importance.

Amin argued that economic laws of the sort elaborated by Marx in *Capital* only apply to a pure capitalist system, while capitalism, in fact, coexists in the world system with other modes of production. An 'economistic' analysis which deals only with quantitative relations between narrowly economic variables can only be a subordinate part of the story. Real history can only be understood by the analysis of concrete social formations and cannot be reduced to a preordinated succession of modes of production. A major part of his work is therefore devoted to historical analysis (*UD*, chapters 1, 5). I cannot hope to give an adequate account of this aspect of Amin's writing here, and I will not try to do so; I will only pick out some points of theoretical interest and try to indicate the main outlines. Amin's discussions of the Arab world and of Africa are especially notable for their combination of wide-ranging knowledge and analytical insight.

He defined five modes of production, of which four are familiar: the primitive-communal, slave owning, simple petty-commodity and capitalist modes. The one that stands out as unusual is:

> the 'tribute-paying' mode, which adds to a still existing village community a social and political apparatus for the exploitation of this community through the exaction of tribute; this tribute-paying mode of production is the most widespread form of precapitalist classes, and I distinguish between (a) its early and (b) its developed forms such as the 'feudal' mode of production, in which the village

community loses its *dominium eminens* over the soil to the feudal lords. (*UD*: 13)

The 'tribute-paying' mode is clearly an old friend, the Asiatic mode, under another name. It covers a spectrum of social structures, from African societies little removed from the primitive-communal mode, though the great Asiatic cultures, to feudal Europe. The all-inclusive nature of this concept rather reduces its usefulness, though it has to be said that this is an area in which it is hard to make any very firm distinctions.

Pre-capitalist societies can incorporate several modes of production and, as a result, a very complex class structure. A formation dominated by the tribute-paying mode may contain commodity production and exchange, though the pure form of the tribute-paying mode does not. Different social formations interact, for example by trade, which can form the basis for societies living on a surplus produced elsewhere. The key to the analysis of any social formation is the production and circulation of surplus, defined, much as in Baran, as 'an excess of production over the consumption needed in order to ensure the reconstitution of the labour force' (*UD*: 18). This amounts to a rich and flexible framework for historical analysis.

Amin described a pre-capitalist world made up of three 'central' tribute-paying formations (China, Egypt, India), with a 'periphery' around them which was much less stable and was influenced more by the centre than *vice versa*. The Mediterranean periphery produced a society dominated by the slave-owning mode, and dependent on its own periphery (Europe) for supplies of slaves. The collapse of this society faced with barbarian invaders produced European feudalism and, finally, capitalism. On the far eastern periphery of China, Japan evolved a feudal society and thus an indigenous capitalism. All this bears a suspicious resemblance to Marx's (now usually derided) judgement that Asiatic societies have no real history, but with the reversal that these Asiatic societies are now called 'central'. One point is that progress took place on the periphery; Amin argued that today the transition to socialism must start from the periphery. It is an interesting thought, though the feudalism–capitalism transition is so different from the transition to socialism that the analogy cannot really be regarded as a proof of anything.

Amin's treatment of feudalism is somewhat inconsistent. It is the most developed form of the tribute-paying mode: 'when well developed [the tribute-paying mode] nearly always tends to become feudal (this happened in China, India and Egypt)' (*AWS*: 140), so that the 'central' tribute-paying formations are described as moving towards feudalism. On the other hand, feudalism is peripheral because it is a borderline case analytically (*IUD*: 16) and because it develops on the borders (geographically) in areas where natural conditions were less favourable and centralizing tendencies weaker (*UD*: 55-6). This may represent a shift in position between the two works cited, but I suspect that it is a reflection of the unsatisfactory state of the definitions. The point, of course, is that capitalism emerges from 'peripheral' feudalism, so the erstwhile periphery becomes central.

The emergence of capitalism from its feudal origins is a familiar story, explained both by the formation of a landless proletariat and by mercantile accumulations of loot; which is the determining factor is not clear. It is clear, however, that capitalism emerged where it did because it was preceded by feudalism. The 'new' capitalist centres of the USA, Canada, and the like, were by-products of proletarianization at the centre, which led to emigration and to the formation in areas of settlement of societies which had an unusually large element of petty-commodity production, and thus an unusually favourable context for capitalist development.

Amin divided the development of the capitalist world economy into three (familiar) stages. The first, mercantilist stage, is marked by the emergence of capitalism in its homelands and by the establishment of a net of exchange relations connecting capitalist with pre-capitalist formations. The next stage is that of developed pre-monopoly capitalism ('competitive capitalism' for short, though relations with the periphery were often monopolistic), lasting from about 1800 to about 1900. This stage, according to Amin, was characterized by approximately equal exchange between centre and periphery (since wages were still low at the centre). Productivity increases were passed on as price reductions under competitive conditions. It was a 'pause' of a century while 'Europe and the United States withdrew into themselves'

(*UD*: 187). Again, there are inconsistencies in Amin's phraseology, if not in his story, in that his 'pause' was also a period in which 'external extension of the capitalist market was . . . of prime importance as a means for realising surplus value' (p.188, i.e. the following page). During this period, in any case, the foundations of a new pattern of international specialization were laid, and the dividing line between centre and periphery was established.

Amin was, of course, mainly interested in the imperialist stage (from 1900). Wages started to rise (with productivity) at the centre, capital became fairly mobile, and world markets became closely integrated, creating the conditions under which unequal exchange takes place. In the emerging periphery, capitalist development was blocked by the competitive strength of the centre, and pre-capitalist modes of production survived. Peripheral social formations developed in a variety of ways, according to the pre-existing social structure, the date of capitalist penetration, the opportunities offered by natural conditions and so on. It is in the analysis of these different paths to peripheral capitalism that Amin's skills as a writer of analytical history are most evident, and I will not try to summarize.

All of these varied peripheral formations, however, move towards a common pattern of peripheral capitalism. There is some ambivalence in Amin's account; on the one hand peripheral capitalism is defined by the persistence of pre-capitalist modes of production while, at the same time, pre-capitalist modes have become a mere 'shell, whose content has become the sale of labour power' (*IUD*: 191).

> We too often confine ourselves to looking for the capitalist relation at the 'microeconomic' level, that of the firm. . . . In peripheral capitalism . . . the petty commodity production mode may appear to be integrated within the capitalist market, but in reality capital dominates the direct producer. The latter is not a petty commodity producer. . . . In fact he is very like the cottage industry proletarian as he formerly existed in Europe; that is exploited by capital to which, in fact, he sold his labour power rather than his product. Here the failure to see that it is the sale of labour power which gears the system is a

failure to understand the unity of the world system. (*IUD*: 90-1; see also *UD*: 361)

The absorption of pre-capitalist modes by capitalism (as opposed to an articulation between distinct modes) has developed very rapidly recently. Amin also conceded that the rise of multinational companies could change matters drastically, as they shift their activities to sources of low-cost labour. Taken together these hints could be the basis for a prediction that 'peripheral capitalism' is in the process of changing very fundamentally and rather rapidly.

At the heart of Amin's argument is an economic process: the development of capitalism in the periphery is blocked by the superior competitive strength of the industries of the centre, manifested in an ability to undercut the industries of the periphery or to establish a price level which prevents new industries emerging at all. This mechanism works, according to Amin, at all stages of development, both of the centre and of the various social formations of the periphery, at least from the industrial revolution onwards.

> The distortion towards export activities (extraversion), which is the decisive one, does not result from 'inadequacy of the home market', but from the superior productivity of the centre in all fields, which compels the periphery to confine itself to the role of complementary supplier of products for the production of which it possesses a natural advantage: exotic agricultural produce and minerals. When, as a result of this distortion, the level of wages in the periphery has become lower, for the same productivity, than at the centre, a limited development of industries focussed on the home market of the periphery will have become possible, while at the same time exchange will have become unequal. The subsequent pattern of industrialisation though import-substitution, together with the (as yet embryonic) effects of the new international division of labour inside the transnational firm, do not alter the essential conditions of extraversion, even if they alter the forms that it takes. (*UD*: 200)

The destruction of craft production and the blockage of capitalist industrialization forced the population into pre-capitalist agriculture, in the first instance, and later into an overexpanded tertiary (service) sector, forcing down wages and reinforcing the hold of landlords and other pre-capitalist exploiting classes. Both low wages and the persistence of pre-capitalist modes follow from the absence of a fully fledged industrial sector. There are other mechanisms at work as well. Capital never scorns extra-economic coercion when it is the most cost-effective means to maximize profits, and co-ercion is absolutely necessary to break into societies where commodity production is not well established. State power, and the economic power of monopoly, also play a role at all stages of development. However, Amin stressed the conver-gence of the formations of the periphery towards a common path, despite their very different histories; the economic mechanism summarized above is his general explanation of the persistence of underdevelopment.

Amin's line of argument can be related to the theory of 'comparative advantage' or 'comparative costs'. There are two elements to it. First, for simple geographical reasons, the peripheral formations have a comparative advantage in the production of 'exotic agricultural produce' and (certain) minerals. This is not difficult to accept. Second, the employment created is not sufficient to absorb the whole labour force. Historical experience suggests that this may be true, but the exact mechanisms involved are not clear from Amin's account, and need further examination. A prelim-inary point must be dealt with at the start. In mainstream economics, the productivity of labour in different branches of production in different countries is taken as given. Amin, rightly, criticized this. The periphery is not ordained by nature to be a supplier of raw materials; the productivity of labour in different activities is the result of a historical process of development. What a theory of specialization can do is to show how unequal development manifests itself in trade relations. These relations, in turn, modify the subsequent pattern of development.

Standard post-Ricardian theories of international special-ization are based on an assumption of full employment. This is not so obvious in the usual Ricardian example with only two goods, since if one country specializes in one, the other country must specialize in the other. In practice, of course, there are a multiplicity of commodities. Suppose there are two countries, A and B. If one, say A, has twice the labour force of the other, then it must specialize in the production of commodities that absorb two thirds of the total labour of the two-country system. If we think of a spectrum of commodities, arranged in order, with those in which A has the greatest comparative advantage at one end, a dividing line must be established between A's exports and its imports, at a point that allows full employment in both countries. How could this happen? If there is unemployment of resources in A, then factor rewards (wages, profits, etc.) must fall there, until A is able to undercut B in some additional branches of production. The dividing line is moved along the spectrum of activities until full employment (or at least equal unemployment) is established everywhere.

In Amin's account, by contrast, the industries assigned (by the 'invisible hand') to the periphery are not enough to absorb the productive resources available there, so there is massive unemployment and, at the same time, money capital is diverted away from productive uses. It seems that his argument is incomplete; falling wages (and other factor rewards) should restore the periphery's capacity to compete in enough areas to offset the fall in demand.

In fact, his analysis is in an even worse position. He claimed that trade with a more advanced economy will create unemployment. Ricardo's classic analysis (1951, chapter 7) is intended to show that trade will raise incomes in the less advanced as well as the more advanced economy, so there is no need to force down wages in order to restore full employment. The point of the Ricardian argument is simple: exchange of commodities can only transmit a structure of relative prices. If one country can produce every commodity with, say, a hundred times lower real costs than the other country this makes no difference at all provided that relative costs are the same. I will examine the analysis, to begin with, for the case where both countries are wholly capitalist; the basic point applies to any commodity-producing system.

There are two distinct cases in which Amin's account can be rescued. First, there is the case in which the comparative advantages are such that the less developed area is excluded from activities which are relatively labour-intensive given the techniques used in that area. This is exactly Amin's case; the periphery was excluded from 'industrial' activities, which were carried out by labour-intensive (craft) methods, and forced to specialize in agriculture (land-intensive). The result is increased pressure on the land, raising rents and either forcing down wages or creating unemployment. (This is an application, in different circumstances, of the Stolper–Samuelson (1941) argument.) Here, it is the pattern of comparative costs that matters.

The second case is quite different. The Ricardian argument assumes that only commodities are mobile between different countries, so only (relative) commodity prices are equalized. Suppose, instead, that capital is mobile as well. Capitalists set up production wherever costs are lowest. Costs depend largely on unit labour costs, and hence on wages relative to productivity. This is still not enough to ensure that there will be de-industrialization and unemployment in the periphery. If the wage differential matches the (assumed) productivity differential, there is no reason for the periphery to be uncompetitive. Amin considered this possibility (new 'light' industries are established in the periphery once wages in the centre have risen far enough), but it plays only a subsidiary part in his argument. We therefore have to assume that wages are, at least to some extent, fixed in real terms; for example, in the nineteenth century wages were close to subsistence in both centre and periphery, so wages could not be cut in the periphery. (On the theoretical argument underlying this paragraph, see Brewer 1985.)

It follows, then, that trade can cause unemployment, as Amin claimed it did, when capital is mobile and productivity differences outweigh differences in wages. The more advanced country has the higher rate of profit (lower costs), so capital flows out of the less developed country, leaving unemployment. Specialization is determined by absolute and not comparative costs. Ricardo commented on this possibility in a passage cited by Amin (Ricardo 1951: 136). Amin referred to the outflow of capital from the periphery to the centre, which fits in with this analysis, though he also argued that profits are higher in the periphery than in the centre as a result of super-exploitation, which is not consistent with the analysis presented here.

The level of productivity in different activities, and its evolution, are clearly crucial to the argument as I have presented it. Amin discussed the pattern of relative advantages under the guise of a discussion of 'sectoral unevenness of productivity' (in the periphery):

> It is not, of course, possible to compare productivities in the strict sense of the word except between two enterprises that produce the same product. ... Between one branch and another one can speak only of different *profitabilities*, as Emmanuel has reminded us. All the same, if, with a given price structure, conditions are such that labour, or capital, or both, cannot be rewarded in one branch at the same rate as in another, I say that productivity is lower in that branch. In the capitalist mode of production ... the effective tendency is for labour and capital to be rewarded in all branches at the same rates. If, however, this price structure [of the centre] . . . is transmitted to the periphery, the result will be that factors cannot be rewarded at the same rate in the different branches if the technical conditions (and so the productivity) are distributed otherwise than at the centre. (*UD*: 215-16)

Note the assumption here that the price structure of the centre determines world prices. This rules out unequal exchange in Emmanuel's sense, since the point of unequal exchange is precisely that low wages in the periphery are incorporated in low prices for the periphery's products (see chapter 9 below). Amin could, perhaps, argue that prices are intermediate between those corresponding to the costs of the centre and of the periphery, giving both unevenness of productivity (as defined) and unequal exchange.

In *IUD*, Amin went much further in rejecting Emmanuel's analysis, asserting that the same products are produced at the centre and in the periphery and even denying that 'the productions exchanged on the world market are specific, that they have irreducible use values' (*IUD*: 209). The point seems to be that it doesn't matter what is produced, since a demand can be created for anything, say for plastic flowers. However, even if the goods produced are constantly changing they must still be distinct from each other, or there is no basis for exchange or for a social division of labour. In particular, if use values are not 'specific', there is no room for unequal specialization, and Amin's analysis evaporates, along with the theory of unequal exchange. If the periphery produces the same range of goods as the centre, they must sell at the same prices, and super-exploitation must appear as super-profits for firms producing in the periphery, rather than through unequal exchange. Super-profits and unequal exchange could coexist if capital were only partly mobile. Amin did not specify the assumptions involved clearly.

Levels of productivity, and their evolution, remain to be explained. Amin largely took them for granted. At an early stage in the evolution of the world economy, when commodity exchange was the only integrating factor, productivities in different areas would differ according to the level of development reached. Specialization would depend on comparative (not absolute) costs. Given a pattern of costs such that the periphery was excluded from the main lines of industry, the pattern would tend to persist, or to be reinforced, since there would be no opportunity to gain experience in industry.

Once capital becomes mobile, it is difficult to see why technology, and hence productivity levels, are not transferred, along with capital. They clearly have been in some cases, as Amin knew (*IUD*: 212). A major part of the answer must surely lie in external economies: conditions of production that an individual enterprise either cannot provide for itself or need not provide where the industry is already well established. Examples are a skilled labour force, a network of suppliers, suitable transport services, and so on. These are, of course, all reasons why it is difficult (i.e. in a capitalist context, costly and hence unprofitable) to establish production in a new location. In the earlier parts of the imperialist stage, say around 1900, when wages in the centre were still fairly low and technology was still largely in the hands of skilled workers rather than being systematized and brought fully under the control of capital (cf. Braverman 1974), it is easy to see that there was little incentive for established capitalist firms in the centre to shift production to the periphery.

In the present stage, however, wage differentials are large, and multinational firms have great experience of transferring technology, so it is much harder to see why a productivity gap should persist. Without it, Amin's main arguments would collapse. He admitted that transfer of industries from the centre to the periphery is indeed the tendency, but gave a number of reasons why this tendency does not dominate. First, it takes time, and is only beginning. This is true, but why should it take much more than, say, the turnover time of capital equipment? Second, capitalism needs the high wages of the centre to provide a market (*IUD*: 213). Even if this were true (it is yet another version of under-consumption, which I have already criticized at length), it would still not explain why individual companies should continue to produce where wages are high. Third, he referred to the need for balance of payments equilibrium (*IUD*: 213). This is no argument: large-scale capital outflows from the centre would not disturb its balance of payments, if accompanied by exports of capital goods. Once industries have been transferred, the centre's capacity to pay for imports would be reduced, but so would the general level of activity and hence the demand for them. Amin was willing to accept this argument for the periphery; why not for the centre in its turn? Fourth, development in the periphery must be blocked and distorted in order 'to re-produce its own conditions of existence' (*IUD*: 218). This simply restates the problem. Why and how does it reproduce itself? He finally, rather desperately, asserted that if, say, Mexico were to become a fully developed province of the USA, 'the contradiction would shift from the economic to the cultural and political domains' (*UD*: 381).

To sum up, Amin provided a plausible account of the evolution of a periphery which is integrated, by stages, into a world market, while retaining a distinct wage level, a distinct social structure (persistence of pre-capitalist modes) and a lagging productivity level, at least in some sectors. He did not, however, have an adequate explanation of the evolution of productivity, especially in the era of multinational companies. De Janvry (1981: 9) treated Amin as part of the revival of classical Marxist ideas ('to some extent'); his overall framework, however, was recognizably in the dependency tradition, even if his use of the concept of a mode of production was more sophisticated than most.

8.5 DEPENDENCY THEORY: THE BALANCE SHEET

The essential elements of the dependency approach seem to be: (1) the (capitalist) world system is divided into a centre and a periphery (or equivalent terms); (2) the societies of the periphery are 'dependent', while those of the centre are not; (3) dependency restricts or distorts development in the periphery in some harmful way. I will consider these three elements in turn.

Dependency theory divides the world system into centre and periphery. Frank, it is true, allowed for a chain of satellites, satellites of satellites, and so on, while Wallerstein introduced a 'semi-periphery', but the terminology clearly shows the underlying bipolar model. If such a classification is to be useful, there must be important features shared by all peripheral economies which differentiate them from all the centre economies. It is very hard to see what they are. Consider, for example, Korea, Ethiopia, India, Singapore, and Argentina. All would, I think, be counted as peripheral by most dependency writers, but what is gained by lumping them together? The only way to justify classifying them all as 'peripheral', is to claim that all are 'dependent'.

It is surprisingly hard to discover what 'dependence' means. The root meaning seems to be that the countries of the centre are in some sense masters of their own fate, while the dependent countries of the periphery are not. In any simple sense, this is clearly ridiculous; in the modern world, no country is unaffected by external events. Size matters, of course; the USA clearly relies less on external markets (for example) than Singapore does, but equally, Belgium is more 'dependent' (in that sense) than India. Something more must be meant. One possible meaning is that the countries of the centre gain from their involvement in the world system, while the countries of the periphery do not. I postpone discussion of this possibility for a moment. Another element in the idea of dependence, I suspect, is the notion that the world system is somehow shaped by the centre countries to suit their own purposes. This might reasonably be said of the political role of the major countries; imperialism in the traditional sense was exactly the reshaping of the world to suit the dominant imperial powers, and it is entirely possible to claim that imperialist powers continue to exert political dominance after formal independence, or over countries that have never been formally subjugated. The point of dependency theory, however, seems to be that the impersonal mechanisms of the market maintain the dependence of some countries on others, without the need to use state power overtly (Wallerstein is an exception to this rule). If this is what is meant, it betrays a failure to understand how capitalism works. There is no central planning agency in a market system, no overall purpose. Huge numbers of individual businesses and households, in many different countries, make their separate plans, which interact through the market. In the absense of state intervention, countries are not relevant units, at this level of analysis.

The crucial element in dependency theory, then, has to be the claim that development in 'dependent' countries is restricted or distorted in some way, while development in the centre countries is not. This is not an easy claim to assess, since it presupposes some standard rate and pattern of development which the dependent countries are unable to attain. Early writers in the dependency tradition were fairly clear about what they meant; the periphery would lag even further behind the centre, would be unable to develop a significant industrial sector, and would continue to depend on primary product exports to pay for their imports of manufactures. This is not what has happened. I postpone fuller discussion to chapter 11, merely noting here what any standard statistical source will show; output has grown more rapidly in less developed countries than in more developed countries. Population has also grown faster, but even so per capita output has at least kept pace. Industrial output and exports have grown even more rapidly; a widespread process of (capitalist) industrialization is underway. The point is not that capitalism is doing a good job, in some abstract or ideal sense; there is poverty, working conditions are often very bad, and so on. The point is that dependency theory gives no useful guidance to the analysis of these problems. There were some attempts to define a concept of 'dependent industrialization', but this impressed few apart from those with an intellectual investment in dependency theory to protect.

An even more telling indictment of dependency theory is the gross unevenness of capitalist development in the Third World. A few countries have experienced extremely high rates of growth, and will clearly join the centre countries soon. The most widely discussed examples are in east Asia, though there are examples in southern Europe and elsewhere. By contrast, other parts of the Third World have grown very slowly, and in some cases per capita incomes have actually fallen substantially over decades. Growth of manufactured exports has been even more heavily concentrated into a few exceptionally successful places. To force these very different cases into the single category of 'dependence' is simply not helpful.

It is slightly difficult to understand how dependency theory came to dominate radical thought in the way it did, given its visible weaknesses, and even harder to explain why Marxists accepted a framework of analysis so alien to the mainstream of Marxist thought. It can be argued (Harris 1986, ch. 7) that dependency theory, and related ideas, served the interests of the emerging middle classes of the Third World. Certainly, a system of thought which blamed all ills on foreigners, and legitimized state intervention to support domestic industry, was very convenient both for the personnel of the state apparatuses and for emerging industrial capital. Dependency theory emerged at a time when classical Marxism was very weak, and had its roots in development economics, from which it inherited the concepts of national interests and national development. It has come to look like a blind alley, and attention has switched to examination of the differences in the internal structures of different 'peripheral' countries.

8.6 SUMMARY

Both Frank and Wallerstein identified capitalism with a network of exchange relations, on a world scale, that channel surplus from satellite (periphery) to metropolis (core). Both insisted that the internal structure and development of different parts of the world economy is primarily determined by their place in the whole, and that the organization of production at a lower level (enterprise, sector, nation state) is secondary. Both asserted that development and underdevelopment are opposite sides of the coin, that one is the result of the other. My main criticism of both writers is that there is little connection between their grandiose general statements and their (sometimes illuminating) discussion of particular historical cases. What is lacking is real theory. Frank and Wallerstein did, however, make an important contribution by insisting on the importance of underdevelopment and the necessity of analysing it in terms of the development of a world system.

Amin argued that the capitalist world economy is divided into two distinct types of social formation, those of the centre and those of the periphery. In the centre, the capitalist mode of production eliminates other modes, and generates a process of development of the sort analysed by the classical Marxists. In the periphery, capitalist development is 'blocked' by the competition of the more advanced industries of the centre, so pre-capitalist modes persist for a long time, and an economic and social structure quite distinct from that of the centre arises. Amin's explanation of unequal specialization hinges on relative levels of productivity in the centre and the periphery, which he did not explain fully. His is the most sophisticated version of dependency theory, and contains many valuable insights.

On a more general level, dependency theory fails, because it cannot explain the burst of industrialization in the so-called periphery in the decades since the Second World War, nor can it help to account for the extreme unevenness of capitalist development in the Third World.

9

Emmanuel

Arghiri Emmanuel's theory of unequal exchange is in complete contrast to the main traditions of Marxist thought on imperialism and the world economy, and is equally distant from conventional non-Marxist theories. It is a genuinely original contribution. Marxists have generally identified the mainspring of imperialism either with the development of monopoly (in exchange or in production) or with the expansion of capitalism at the expense of pre-capitalist modes of production. Emmanuel's break with these traditions is indicated by the subtitle of his book: 'a study of the imperialism of trade'. He claimed that free trade between two wholly capitalist countries can still be 'unequal', and that this unequal exchange is the foundation of the massive inequalities that exist in the world economy. His explanation does not rest on any monopoly by capitalist firms, nor does it involve any exercise of state power in international relations. Note that 'imperialism', in this context, refers to exploitation and inequality, but not (as it usually does) to military or political domination of some countries by others.

Emmanuel extended Marx's theory of 'prices of production' to the determination of international prices, making the key assumption that goods and capital are internationally mobile, while labour is not, so prices and profit rates are equalized internationally by competition, but wages are not. This seems at least a reasonable starting point. I shall argue that Emmanuel's theory provides a potentially useful component of a theory of the world economy, but cannot be regarded as complete in itself or as a complete account of the way the world system works.

The term 'unequal exchange' is not new, and has often been used by other writers, usually very loosely. Unequal exchange, so called, may be ascribed to monopoly pricing, to 'transfer prices' used to evade tax, and so on. Alternatively, it may be argued, following Marx, that high productivity labour in an advanced country produces more 'value' (in the terms of the labour theory of value) than lower productivity labour in more backward areas. The product of an hour's labour in an advanced country will then exchange for the product of a great deal more labour in an underdeveloped country. In this case 'unequal exchange' is merely a reflection of divergences in productivity that have other causes. Mandel (1975, ch. 11) seems to combine all of these arguments at once in an account which is both eclectic and lacking in rigour. Roemer (1982: 55-60) presented a model in which returns to capital are equalized, even without capital mobility, so countries with more capital have higher average incomes. Lewis (1969) is more interesting, and will be discussed briefly at the end of this chapter.

Emmanuel's theory is set out in his book *Unequal Exchange* (1972, cited below as *UE*), which also contains, in the edition cited, a debate between Emmanuel and Bettelheim. See also Amin (1977, part IV) and Gibson (1980) for discussion of Emmanuel's theory. An article by Emmanuel (1974), which is really a contribution to a different debate, elaborates some of his views, especially on demand and capitalist development. His more recent work has taken a rather different direction (e.g. Emmanuel 1982); I shall concentrate on *Unequal Exchange* because of the influence it has had.

9.1 UNEQUAL EXCHANGE

The statement of the theory in the body of Emmanuel's book was modelled on Marx's solution to the transformation problem, so international exchange was presented first in terms of labour values, which were then 'transformed' into prices of production. Following Bettelheim's criticisms of some of his statements (from a more orthodox Marxist standpoint), Emmanuel counter-attacked by elaborating a consistent treatment of prices of production rather than retreating under fire. I will, therefore, present the theory in its more developed form (as set out in Appendix V to the English edition) without using labour values at all. In this section the presentation will be informal; for a more formal statement, see the appendix to this chapter.

Emmanuel defined a factor of production as 'an established claim to a primary share in society's economic product'. Criticized by Bettelheim for looking at production only in terms of monetary magnitudes and not at the material basis of these magnitudes, he replied that the social relations of production are precisely relations of property ownership, of appropriation, and hence of claims to a share of the product. In a capitalist economy, there are two factors (two classes). Mobility of labour tends to equalize wages between industries, while competition between capitals (mobility of capital) tends to equalize profit rates. Prices of production (equilibrium prices) are thus made up of money costs (wage costs, materials, depreciation of fixed capital) plus a profit margin sufficient to give the general rate of profit on the capital invested. Prices and the rate of profit can only be determined simultaneously, since the prices of materials and capital goods enter as costs, while profit must be calculated on the capital required, which depends on the price of capital goods. This is a standard problem in Marxist economics, and the algebra is now well understood (see *UE*, Appendix V or any modern text on Marxist economics, e.g. Howard and King 1985). The first complete solution was by Bortkiewitz: Emmanuel's solution is modelled on Sraffa (1960). The formal statement is in the appendix to this chapter.

In Emmanuel's story, as in Marx's, the real wage is assumed to be fixed. I will discuss the determinants of wages later, in section 9.2. In simple terms we can think of the profit rate as determined by the gap between what is produced and the fixed wage level, together with the methods of production used and hence the capital intensity of production, and we can think of prices as determined by costs (of which wages are a major component) plus profits (determined in the way just described).

Turning to the world economy, Emmanuel made the key assumption that capital is mobile internationally, so a single rate of profit is formed at the world level, while labour is not mobile between countries, so workers in different countries are not (directly) in competition with each other, and different national levels of wages may be formed. Products are assumed, at this stage in the argument, to be freely traded (transport costs are ignored) so a single set of prices of production exists for the whole world.

If two countries (or groups of countries) have different wage levels there are two ways in which the profit rate can be the same in both, without any product having two different prices (free trade and competition rule out multiple prices for the same good). First, if they produce the same products, profits can only be equalized if the high-wage country has higher productivity, so costs are the same (or, more strictly, so labour and other costs plus the general profit rate add up to the same price of production). In this case, differences in wages correspond to, and are explained by, productivity differences. Although Emmanuel accepted that this explanation applies to some goods, he did not treat it as the normal case, on the grounds that there is an international division of labour in which countries (or groups of countries, advanced and underdeveloped) specialize in different goods.

The second possibility is the one in which 'unequal exchange' can occur. The two countries may produce wholly different commodities, so they are not in direct competition with each other. If one good is produced only in the high-wage country and the other only in the low-wage country, the price of each must incorporate wage costs, so their prices reflect the differences in wages. To put it simply, the products of the high-wage country are dearer and the products of the low-wage country cheaper than they would have been if wages were the same in the two countries; this is what Emmanuel calls unequal exchange. Two points should be noted here for later discussion. First, it is assumed that wages are given independently of prices: 'wages are the independent variable', so wage differences are the cause of unequal exchange. Second, there must be some barrier that prevents all production moving to the low-wage country and enjoying lower costs of production. The theory thus assumes a predetermined pattern of international specialization.

Exchange is 'unequal' because the low-wage country has to pay more for its imports than it would if wages were the same in both countries, without getting higher prices for its own exports. It thus has to export more to get a given amount of imports. Correspondingly, the high-wage country gets more imports in return for a given amount of exports. Whether the actual amounts traded would stay the same at different prices is another matter; the argument is concerned only with the terms of trade.

To see how the theory works, I will take a very simple and unrealistic numerical example, to illustrate the principles involved. I have deliberately set it up so that the two countries are as alike as possible. Suppose there are two countries (A and B) and two goods (1 and 2). Country A produces only good 1, while country B produces only good 2. I will compare two cases: with wages the same in the two countries, and with wages higher in A. I assume that the production of five units of good 1 (in country A) requires one unit of labour, together with inputs of one unit of good 1 itself and one unit of good 2, as means of production, at the beginning of the period. For good 2 (in country B) conditions of production are exactly the same; five units are produced by one unit of labour and one of each commodity. Wages are assumed to be fixed in real terms. In the first case, with wages the same in A and B, each worker must be paid enough, at the beginning of the year, to buy one unit of good 1 and one unit of good 2. For each worker employed, a capitalist must lay out, at the beginning of the year, enough money to buy one unit of each good to use as means of production, plus a wage enough to buy one unit of each good.

To calculate profits, we must know the money costs and money receipts. We cannot, in general, calculate costs without knowing the prices of the goods, and we cannot calculate the price without knowing the costs and profit. What we must do is to find both simultaneously. (In this case we can get to the rate of profit directly since it is obvious that the two goods must sell for the same price; this is not so in general.) In this particular case, all costs are in the form of capital outlays at the beginning of the year, so annual costs are the same as capital employed. We can write:

$$\text{selling price} = \text{cost} + \text{profit},$$

but

$$\text{rate of profit} = \text{profit}/\text{capital} = \text{profit}/\text{costs};$$

so, writing r for the rate of profit:

$$\text{selling price} = (1+r)\ \text{costs}.$$

The price equations follow directly, given that the rate of profit must be the same in both countries:

$$5p_1 = (1 + r) (2p_1 + 2p_2)$$
$$5p_2 = (1 + r) (2p_1 + 2p_2)$$

where p_1 is the price of good 1, and p_2 the price of good 2. From these equations, it follows immediately that $p_1 = p_2$ and $r = 0.25$ or 25 per cent. The actual levels of p_1 and p_2 cannot be determined, but this does not matter; it is only the terms of exchange that count, together with the real purchasing power of the wage, already fixed by assumption.

Now suppose that the wage rate in country A goes up, so it will now buy one and a half units of each commodity, while the wage in B is enough to buy one unit of each, as before. Following exactly the same procedure, the price equations can be set out again:

$$5p_1 = (1 + r) (2.5p_1 + 2.5p_2)$$
$$5p_2 = (1 + r) (2p_1 + 2p_2)$$

The rate of profit, r, falls to $1/9$ or 11.1 per cent (add the equations and $(p_1 + p_2)$ cancels out), and relative prices follow; $p_1 = 1.25p_2$. The low-wage country, B, now has to export 1.25 units of its export, good 2, in order to buy one unit of its import, good 1. Its 'terms of trade' (export price divided by import price) have worsened by 20 per cent. Since real wages have gone up, if only in one country, and productivity is still the same, the profit rate is reduced.

Nothing has been said about the amounts produced and traded; to say anything about this would require additional assumptions. The theory of unequal exchange is, in the first instance, a theory of prices, of the terms of exchange, which depend on costs per unit of each product and on the wage rate for a unit of labour-power. As an illustration, I will set out a possible outcome, in terms of production, consumption, and trade, of the example of pricing given above. Suppose that goods 1 and 2 are always used in fixed proportions, one unit of good 1 to one of good 2, both as means of production, and when they are bought as consumer goods by workers or by capitalists, regardless of their relative price, and that all wages and profits are spent on consumer goods with no net investment. Both assumptions are very restrictive; more realistic cases will be discussed later. Suppose that 100 workers are employed in each country. With wages equal, as in the first set of price equations, we get the pattern of production and consumption set out in table 9.1. In constructing the table, I have assumed that profits are consumed in the country in which they originate. With free mobility of capital this need not be so, since profits in one country may accrue to capitalists elsewhere, but this is a rather different matter from unequal exchange, and will be discussed later.

Table 9.1 Sources and uses of goods; equal wages

		Output	Used as input	Used by workers	Used by capitalists	Net imports
Country A	Good 1	500	−100	−100	−50	−250
	Good 2	0	−100	−100	−50	+250
Country B	Good 1	0	−100	−100	−50	+250
	Good 2	500	−100	−100	−50	−250

Notes: (1) Sources of goods (production, imports) shown as +, uses as −
(2) Assumptions given in text

Table 9.2 Sources and uses of goods; wages increased in A

		Output	Used as input	Used by workers	Used by capitalists	Net imports
Country A	Good 1	500	−100	−150	−27.78	−222.22
	Good 2	0	−100	−150	−27.78	+277.78
Country B	Good 1	0	−100	−100	−22.22	+222.22
	Good 2	500	−100	−100	−22.22	−277.78

Notes as for table 9.1

Now compare table 9.1 with the situation where wages are higher in country A, as in the second set of price equations above. The results are given in table 9.2. Since country A's product now exchanges at a higher price, consumption in country A can be higher without any increase in production and productivity. Instead of importing 250 units of good 2 in exchange for 250 units of good 1, they import 277.78 units and only export 222.22. Although wages have gone up in A and not B, the total profit in country A now exceeds that in B, where they were previously equal, because the rate of profit is equalized, and the capital advanced is increased in A by the wage increase (remember that wages are paid in advance, so the capitalist expects profits on the advance of wages).

Before leaving the example, consider how the cases shown in the tables would be recorded in conventional national income measurements. These figures are normally shown in money terms, so let the price of good 2 be fixed at $1. In the first case each country would have a gross product of $500, and a net product (output – replacement) of $300 ($500 – $200). In the second case, country A's gross product is valued at $625 (500 units at $1.25) and its net product (net national income) at $400 ($624 – $225), while country B's gross product is still $500 and net product $275. Just looking at national income figures, therefore, gives the impression that the high wages in country A are justified by a higher level of productivity, but this higher 'productivity' is an illusion produced by the prices at which the output is valued and is a result, not a cause, of the higher wages. Physical productivity is, of course, the same before and after the wage increase.

The 'prices of production' calculated in the example are equilibrium prices, determined by the equilibrium condition that the profit rate should be equalized. Actual prices fluctuate around these levels, but always tend back towards them because whenever the price of (say) good 1 is above the equilibrium level, profits will be higher in country A than country B, and capital will flow into A, expanding supply and pushing the price down.

An objection to the theory that will occur to many economists is that a wage increase will lead to a balance of payments deficit, and hence to a devaluation of the currency of the country concerned. However, exchange rate changes make no difference, because of the key assumption that wages are fixed in real terms, as a given quantity of commodities. A devaluation can only affect equilibrium prices if wages are fixed in money terms, and can be reduced in real terms by reducing the value of the currency. As for the balance of payments, a deficit on the current account can only arise if domestic investment is greater than domestic saving but, with freely mobile capital, any excess of investment over saving is financed by an inflow of capital, and any current account deficit is matched by a capital account surplus.

To give some impression of what this theory might mean in reality, consider an example given by Emmanuel (*UE*: 338,

367-8; I have made some of the calculations more explicit). His critics had pointed out that imports into the advanced countries from the Third World amounted to $25 billion (in 1965), which was only 2.5 per cent of the advanced countries' national income of about $1,000 billion. In reply he argued that if wages account for 50 per cent of the cost of these imports, and if wages in the Third World would have to increase by twenty times to bring them to the level of those in advanced countries, then the price of Third World exports would have to rise roughly tenfold (there would be repercussions on profits to take into account), to $250 billion, 25 per cent of the advanced countries' national income, a very considerable amount. One can, of course, doubt whether anything like the same volume of trade would take place at these prices; Emmanuel's argument is concerned only with prices, and not with the amount traded.

Note that it does not matter what kind of goods are produced in the high-wage countries, so long as they do not face competition from low-wage producers. There is no presumption that high wage, high price goods are high technology products, or anything of the sort, though they might be. Emmanuel's example is the price of timber: since wages in Sweden, Canada, and other softwood exporting countries have been high and rising, softwoods have sold at high and rising prices, while African hardwoods have not.

9.2 WAGES

The key factor in Emmanuel's theory of international prices is the difference in wages between advanced and underdeveloped countries, so an account of wage determination is needed. It is essential for wages to be independent of market forces, over the time span required to establish equilibrium prices, since wage costs could not underpin an equilibrium set of prices if they were themselves liable to fluctuate. This rules out any market theory of wages. The classical wage theory (Ricardo, Malthus), in which wages are determined by physical subsistence needs, would not help either, since there is no reason for these needs to differ markedly between countries.

Instead, Emmanuel's starting point was Marx's famous, if rather cryptic, statement that the 'quantity of commodities necessary for the worker' contains an 'historical and moral element' (which may therefore differ between countries and over time), but 'nevertheless, in a given country, at a given period ... is also given' (*Capital* I: 171). This can be interpreted as meaning that the real wage is very resistant to downward pressure in the short run, even over decades, since workers have adopted a certain pattern of life and entered into commitments which cannot easily be changed (the historical element). So, for example, the layout of cities may compel certain spending on transport, the physical character of the stock of housing may be such that it requires certain spending on maintenance, heating, and so on, if workers are to be able to function at all. The moral element can be read as a claim that once a certain standard of life has become the norm, there will be great resistance to changing it. The wage may fluctuate around this given standard of living according to market influences, but any fluctuations are too short-lived to be incorporated into it (hence wages are the independent variable). According to Emmanuel, 'historical and moral' factors operate relatively uniformly within each country, but not between different countries, so unequal exchange operates between countries. On a purely analytical level, his pricing model could just as well describe relations between high and low-wage industries in a single country.

He still had to explain how the 'historical and moral' element changes over time and why it differs between countries. He argued that trades union pressure and political action can change the equilibrium wage by sustained action over a long period of time. Economic development does tend to raise wages, but not directly. Rather, economic development, by centralizing workers, creating needs for higher levels of skills and so on, makes conditions more favourable for trades union and political action to raise wages. Emmanuel also claimed that high wages are good for development, for reasons to be considered later, so a circle is set up in which relatively high wages lead (over a long period) to higher wages still, and so on.

Emmanuel's model thus divides economic forces into three groups which act over different time scales. In the short run, prices and wages fluctuate around their equilibrium levels. In the longer run, equilibrium prices are determined in the way that has been described, while equilibrium wages are relatively fixed and act as the 'independent variable'. Given an even longer time scale there is no equilibrium state, since the process is cumulative.

Is this account of wage determination acceptable? The difficulty in forming a judgement is that although Emmanuel's arguments are plausible enough, there are other theories that are equally plausible. The factors involved are so ill defined that it is difficult to settle the issue by using historical or empirical evidence; indeed, it is not clear that the theory has any real content at all, beyond acting as an excuse for treating wages as given.

Suppose prices in international trade are systematically biased in favour of the high-wage countries and against the low-wage countries: why does it matter? In Emmanuel's basic model, with products and capital freely mobile between countries, it is not clear that it matters at all. There are three classes: the working class in each country and a single capitalist class. It is clear that no distinct national capitalist classes with distinct interests can exist when capital is freely mobile between countries and a single profit rate is formed. If workers in one country succeed in raising their (equilibrium) wage, they do so at the expense of profits; this clearly follows from the idea (on which Emmanuel insists) that wages are the independent variable, so a wage increase in one country cannot reduce the (given) wage in the other. All that happens is that a wage increase anywhere harms capital on the world scale, and a wage reduction anywhere benefits capital. If capital were not freely mobile the effect would fall on the national capitalist class alone. Can we say that the high-wage country benefits as a country? Clearly not, since there is no national interest, but two diametrically opposed class interests. High wages benefit the workers, of course, but no one ever supposed otherwise. They are not gaining from unequal exchange but from high wages.

9.3 DEMAND AND DEVELOPMENT

Emmanuel claimed that unequal exchange acts as the basis for a process of unequal development, on two different counts. First, capital is attracted to demand, so the high incomes generated by unequal exchange attract further investment, and start a cumulative process of development. Second, high wages lead to the use of capital-intensive methods of production, which raise productivity and promote development.

The argument that demand attracts capital investment is clearly out of place in the models discussed so far, which assume free movement of goods and a predetermined pattern of specialization between countries. High incomes in a country as a result of high wages and unequal exchange may mean more demand, but this demand is just as likely to be demand for the products of the low-wage countries as for home-produced goods and, correspondingly, the low-wage country's low level of demand will also be divided between both countries' products.

There is, in fact, one good reason to expect the opposite, that high wages and prices will repel capital. If the products of the high-wage country sell at high prices, as the theory requires, then this will generally mean that less will be sold, and, correspondingly, income and employment in the high-wage country will be reduced. The critical factor is the 'elasticity of demand' for the country's products: the percentage fall in the quantity demanded when price increases by one per cent. If this is greater than one, then the fall in the quantity sold will outweigh the increase in prices, and total sales revenue will be lower. If it is less than one, then a price increase will lead to increased receipts and an increase in national income. In the numerical example of section 9.1, I assumed that demand was independent of price (elasticity of demand, zero) to get the result that a higher wage level corresponds to a higher level of national income and expenditure. There are complications (a change in output will also affect spending on imported means of production and, in addition, income changes will affect the composition of demand: increased demand for particular products from countries with increased income may not exactly offset reduced demand where income has decreased), but the basic principle should be clear. Price increases have a double effect: they increase income for each unit, but they reduce the number of units sold. The overall effect may go either way.

Is anything then left of Emmanuel's argument that high wages and prices generate increased demand which attracts capital? If we accept his (implicit) assumption that high wage and price levels mean increased incomes, then his argument can be rescued by a simple change in the assumptions, a change implicit in his arguments. Suppose some goods are traded internationally but others are not. Non-traded goods include perishable and bulky goods, construction, and many services. Protective tariffs can also artificially prevent certain goods being traded which otherwise would be. In this case, high incomes in a country will mean high levels of demand for non-traded as well as traded goods. Since non-traded goods can only be produced locally, capital will flow into a high-wage country to meet this demand, generating more employment in these industries, more incomes and hence more demand. If, for example, half of income is spent on non-traded goods then each dollar of income from the production of traded goods will generate another dollar of income for producers of non-traded goods, taking the repercussions into account. This model, which Emmanuel did not make explicit, is reminiscent of a Keynesian foreign trade multiplier, or of the theory, in urban economics, of a city's 'economic base' of 'exports'.

It is essential to the argument that each country should produce both traded and non-traded goods. Traded goods are necessary for unequal exchange to have something to bite on; you must trade to benefit from favourable terms of trade. Non-traded goods are essential to convert high incomes into an attraction to capital from outside. High prices reduce employment in the export industries by reducing the quantity sold, but the increased demand for non-traded goods may offset this. If, on the other hand, the fall in sales as a result of increased prices outweighs the increased income per unit, the mechanism works the other way round and multiplies the reduction in income and employment through a reduction in demand for non-traded goods.

Non-traded goods must, of course, be produced by local labour. Their prices are determined in the same way as those of traded goods, so identical non-traded goods will have higher prices in high-wage than in low-wage countries, since their prices incorporate higher wage costs. This introduces a complication, as Emmanuel realized. If real wages in one country are to be, say, twice those in another, then money wages (translated at current exchange rates) will have to diverge much more, perhaps by four or even ten times, since high wages and a high cost of living (high price of non-traded goods) go together. To put it another way, if productivity in non-traded goods is the same everywhere, and so is the rate of profit, then higher standards of living in one country compared with another can only come from a high purchasing power in terms of traded goods (whose prices are the same everywhere), so if the fraction of traded goods in workers' consumption is rather low, it will require a large difference in money wages to generate a moderate difference in living standards. The divergence in money wages determines international prices, since capitalists' production decisions are governed by money costs and not by what money wages will buy. Relatively moderate divergences in real wages may thus be the foundation for extreme inequality in exchange.

In discussing the role of unequal exchange in creating local demand and attracting capital imports, I have assumed that demand depends on the total incomes generated locally. It is not clear that this is correct, since with international mobility of capital we cannot specify in advance where capital has come from, nor can we predict where profit incomes will be spent. Profits accruing to British capitalists from production in Africa may well be spent in the Bahamas. Workers, on the other hand, must clearly spend the main part of their wages in the locality where they are employed. Emmanuel, rightly, stressed the importance of wage incomes as generating a local demand which attracts capital. If the stress is laid on workers' demand for consumer goods, however, the role of unequal exchange is altered. It is high wages, rather than unequal exchange as such, which create an enlarged market. The role of unequal exchange is to permit the equalization of profits between countries, so that the effect of high wages falls on profits everywhere, not just in the high-wage country. Without this equalization of profits, high-wage countries would be low-profit countries and could not attract capital.

I should stress that the model built up in this section is mine rather than Emmanuel's, though I think it embodies the essential points of Emmanuel's arguments. I have tried to indicate the points taken directly from Emmanuel by linking his name clearly with them.

It is worth pausing to take a general look at the picture of the world economy built up in this section. It might appear to be an under-consumptionist model, in that development is made to depend on demand, and specifically on workers' consumption demand, but it is not. There is no assumption that demand is lacking on a world scale. The question under discussion is: where does growth take place? With free mobility of capital between countries, the critical factor is the division of new investment between different locations. With a predetermined pattern of specialization between countries in the production of traded goods (which is essential to the theory, as presented so far) the scope for expansion is determined outside any given country, on the world scale. What the pricing mechanism of unequal exchange does, is to determine the terms on which a country participates in this world division of labour, and that, in turn, governs the scope for expansion in the non-traded goods sector.

In this model, then, unequal exchange does not generate a cumulative growth of inequality between countries unless there is a cumulative growth in wage differentials. Emmanuel did indeed predict a cumulative enlargement of wage differentials, which turns out to be crucial to his whole argument: again his theory of wages emerges as the heart of his whole theory.

9.4 METHODS OF PRODUCTION

The second main plank in Emmanuel's argument linking unequal exchange to real development, is that high wages lead to a high organic composition of capital and also a high 'organic composition of labour'. (The latter phrase is Emmanuel's own invention.) Again, unequal exchange is important primarily as a mechanism that permits relatively high wages in one country without a corresponding relative depression of profits.

As far as the organic composition of capital is concerned, the basic point is simple. Capitalists try to minimize costs (competition forces them to do so) by substituting means of production for labour when wages are high. More exactly, they use more of those means of production produced in low-wage countries, since those produced in the high-wage area itself will also be increased in price. The effect, therefore, is to reduce employment in the high-wage country in much the same way as substitution of lower-priced for higher-priced products does, and to reduce the attraction of capital to the production of non-traded goods in high-wage areas. It is not, then, at all clear why mechanization caused by wage increases should be beneficial to capitalist development in the country where the wage increase takes place. One can, of course, say that mechanization *is* development, and thus define the problem away (I don't think Emmanuel quite did this, though he came close to it at times), but the real question is whether it provides a further impulse for sustained or cumulative development. Emmanuel's answer is to argue that mechanization alters the social character of work and of production and thus lays the foundations for further wage increases. This links up both with his theory of wages (above) and with the organic composition of labour, to which I now turn.

High wages, according to Emmanuel, bring about a high 'organic composition of labour'. By this he means a high proportion of skilled workers, professionals, and so on, in the total labour force. Even if basic wage rates and the scale of wages were the same everywhere, areas with a large proportion of high paid skilled workers would have a higher level of per capita income and therefore larger markets. Why should there be a connection between high basic wage rates and a high proportion of skilled workers? A casual comparison of rich and poor countries suggests that these two factors do, in practice, go together, but what is needed is a relation of cause and effect, not just a statistical association which might well be the result of a some third factor.

It is possible to argue that mechanization is the result of high wages (see above), and that mechanization, in turn, leads to the training and employment of engineers, technicians, and so on. However, Marx argued that mechanization tends to eliminate skills, and Braverman (1974) has re-emphasized this aspect of Marx's thinking. Braverman also argued that conventional classifications of skills are seriously misleading; farm workers and others usually classified as unskilled, are, in fact, highly skilled. This does not directly undermine Emmanuel's position, since he was concerned with the proportion of socially recognized skills, recognized by being paid above the rates for other workers. It does, however, suggest the possibility that certain skills are recognized and rewarded because they are particularly important in high-wage countries, while traditional craft skills may be badly rewarded precisely because they are practised in low-wage areas. If this is so, then a high or low organic composition of labour becomes merely the way high or low wages are manifested, rather than being a distinct result of high or low wage levels with its own distinct effects. I conclude that Emmanuel has not succeeded in demonstrating this part of his case.

9.5 CRITIQUE OF THE THEORY

Before going on to the main criticisms of the theory, it is worth looking at some historical examples which Emmanuel presented to show how the theory can be elaborated to deal with the complexities of the real world. First, consider England in the period of the industrial revolution. England made a decisive advance during this time, laying the foundations of a century of dominance in the world economy. Real wages, however, did not rise to any substantial extent until after the major advances had been made, contrary to Emmanuel's theory in which wages are the independent variable and high wages lead to development. Emmanuel claimed that wages in England were relatively high even before the industrial revolution got under way, and that the Corn Laws (import restrictions on grain), by raising the price of subsistence goods, raised money wages even though real wages failed to rise; the mechanism of unequal exchange depends, as we have seen, on relative levels of money wages. Instead of the workers being the beneficiaries of unequal exchanges, the benefits went to landowners in the form of a 'super-rent'.

This is an ingenious argument, but there are still criticisms to be made. First, the conquest of world markets for cotton textiles, which provided a crucial opportunity for industrialization, was the result of reduced prices, not high prices. The price cuts were made possible by technical advances, and while Emmanuel can say that the Corn Laws held prices higher than they would have been otherwise, this still leaves technical advance, increased productivity stemming from mechanized production, as the main driving force of the industrial revolution. High money wages followed the break-through in development: they did not cause it. Second, it is not clear how the 'super-rent' accruing to the landlords fuelled economic development. In so far as it was saved, and became a source of capital accumulation, it should not have contributed to a relative advance in England if capital were internationally mobile (which it was not, to any great extent, at that date, but which the theory requires). In so far as the extra revenue was spent, it created extra local demand, though how much of landlords' extra revenue was spent on industrial products must be doubtful.

A second example is the colonies of European settlement. Emmanuel argued that the USA, Canada and Australia became rich, while Latin American countries did not, mainly because the social conditions under which migration took place, together with the form of appropriation of land (which was relatively freely available in the USA, by comparison with Latin America), favoured high wages, and this set the mechanisms of unequal exchange into operation. South Africa, he argued, developed to a lesser extent precisely because of the availability of cheap local labour. Tariff pro-tection, according to Emmanuel, played an essential role, but only in excluding imported goods, especially industrial products, from the enlarged market created by high wages. This argument is attractive, since the relative success of the USA, Canada and Australia is a major historical problem that calls out for a Marxist analysis. There must, however, be doubts about this explanation. The major export products of the USA, Canada and Australia were also produced in other parts of the world where wages were much lower. Where countries with different wage levels produce the same commodities and trade them on the world market, the high-wage country must have correspondingly higher levels of productivity (or lower profits). So, again, advances in prod-uctivity appear as the driving force, with high wages the result rather than the cause of development. High produc-tivity in agriculture, in these cases, must have been at least partly the result of favourable natural conditions and plentiful land. In any case, US exports in the early stages were quite largely produced by cheap (slave) labour in the plantations of the southern states.

Emmanuel's theory of unequal exchange can be viewed on two levels. One could argue simply that he has filled a gap in the Marxist analysis of the world economy by providing an analysis of the determination of international prices and by developing some of its consequences. This is my view of it, and it amounts to a substantial and important contribution. Emmanuel, however, made a stronger claim.

> Even if we agree that unequal exchange is only one of the mechanisms whereby value is transferred from one group of countries to another, and that its direct effects account for only a part of the difference in standards of living, I think it is possible to state that unequal exchange is the elementary transfer mechanism and that, as such, it enables the advanced countries to begin and regularly give new emphasis to that unevenness of development that sets in motion all the other mechanisms of exploitation and fully explains the way that wealth is distributed. (*UE*: 265)

As Emmanuel knew, the disparities in standards of living and productivity between advanced and underdeveloped countries are far larger than can be explained by unequal exchange in itself. There are many commodities that are produced in both groups of countries and there are enormous differences in productivity between countries.

We must therefore look at the connection between unequal exchange and the process of capitalist development in a broader sense. I have argued that Emmanuel's arguments mainly come down to asserting that high wages are the key to development, and that unequal exchange is important in permitting wage disparities to exist without corresponding inverse differences in profit rates. High wages, we are told, promote development, first, by creating a larger local market and, second, by encouraging mechanization. There is considerable merit in both of these arguments, though it is not clear that either would explain a cumulative growth of inequality between countries. Cumulative divergence can, however, be explained if we follow Emmanuel in saying that wages will increase further in high-wage countries as an indirect, long delayed response to industrialization and that they will remain low in low-wage countries in the absence of this stimulus. His wage theory is therefore critical, and I have argued that it is plausible, but by no means beyond criticism.

There is a further major criticism of Emmanuel's model. I have presented it throughout in terms of a given division of activities between countries, or groups of countries, so high wages in a particular country mean a correspondingly high price of production for its products. The objection is very simple: why should the high-wage, high-price products go on being produced in the high-wage countries? Given free mobility of capital between countries why should any investment go to the high-wage countries at all? For some products the answer is clear: oil will be extracted from Alaska, the North Sea and so on because it is a scarce natural resource which must be extracted where it is found. But the advanced countries specialize mainly in the products which are least tied to the location of natural resources: manufactured goods, especially high technology products whose raw material content is very small relative to total cost.

Emmanuel was aware of this problem, and made several attempts to meet it. One attempt is to argue that there are so many different products that 'a high wage country can never find itself in a position where it cannot discover a specialization that . . . is free from competition on the part of the low wage countries'. Thus India, having taken up textiles, displacing Britain, could now move into producing textile machinery, and so on, but 'if India were to specialize one day in metallurgy and engineering . . . Britain would find no difficulty in taking up [textiles] again' (*UE*: 145-6). This argument is simply wrong. Countries do not choose what to specialize in (and if they did, they could choose to do everything). In Emmanuel's model, production is in the hands of competing capitalist enterprises, which are free to move capital between countries, and are driven by the blind forces of competition to produce wherever costs are lower. If they are free to produce all goods in low-wage countries, with productivity and other costs equal, then they will do so. Emmanuel met this problem in a rather roundabout way: he recognized that, on his own arguments, the underdeveloped countries would do better if they only traded amongst themselves, and discussed whether they might decide, collectively, to do so, concluding that they would benefit by not trading with high-wage countries and, instead, producing the goods that they (collectively) import at the moment. However, he thought that this would involve setting up a state monopoly of foreign trade, while his theory assumes free competition. However, as I have argued above, the real problem is to explain why free competition itself should not produce the outcome without any need for a foreign trade monopoly (cf. Brewer 1985). Free competition clearly has not done so, but it remains to explain why.

His strongest argument is presented almost as an afterthought. The rich countries are benefiting from an existing specialization. If production is to start up in poor countries, it will have to suffer the handicaps of an infant industry: 'during this "acclimatization" period of the new branch, the ratio between the costs of the old producers and the new is not one that can be deduced from merely calculating the effect of the difference in wages' (*UE*: 151). During this time, he says, the high-wage countries have time to 'adjust their aim'. These points are still rather doubtful, since the establishment of 'prices of production', the theoretical basis of his whole argument, requires a sufficient timespan for the mobility of capital to take effect, and if it is difficult and costly for a poor country to take up a new branch of industry, it should be equally hard for a high-wage country. In practice, it is probable that the advanced countries have more flexible economic structures, but this implies a greater technological capacity, not simply a difference in wages.

Emmanuel's final argument does carry conviction: the period of adaptation when a new branch of industry is introduced into a country is 'too long for the relatively short view taken by private capital, which under a competitive system is the exclusive agent of the introduction and establishment of the new branch' (*UE*: 51). The foundation of the argument, then, comes down to this: to set up production in a new location takes longer than to alter the scale of production in areas where a line of business is well established. The period required is long enough for private capital to be unwilling to do the job, despite the profits it would reap at the end of the day. In theoretical terms, there is no doubt that this is a good argument (and a fairly well known argument too – it is the basic argument for tariffs to protect infant industries). It does not seem to me to be enough in itself to explain the pattern of development of the world economy over the last two centuries, though it may be an important part of the explanation.

The first thing that has to be explained is the rapid development of areas of European settlement (the USA, Canada, etc.) in the nineteenth century. Private capital did flow into these areas, and established new industries there. Why were 'infant industry' problems overcome in some places, while in low-wage areas, where export production should have been very profitable, the problems of establishing new industries were insuperable? Second, in Emmanuel's framework it does not matter what branches of production the high-wage countries specialize in since they will benefit from unequal exchange anyway. However, in practice, the rich countries are those which have a large, modern industrial sector, even where they export primary products as well, while the poor countries are those which have a large peasant or pre-capitalist agricultural sector. The 'rich' countries are also those that are 'advanced' in a more general sense. This has to be explained, and I do not believe that wage differences are the primary cause.

Lewis's version of unequal exchange (1969: 17-22) makes an interesting contrast with Emmanuel. In Lewis's model, labour is the only cost, and all countries produce food, which is traded, and hence has a single world price. Underdeveloped countries have much lower productivity in food production than advanced countries, so they must have correspondingly lower wages. Other goods are produced only in advanced countries (manufactures) or only in underdeveloped countries (products of tropical agriculture), so their prices must reflect the different wage levels in those areas. Exchange in non-food goods is 'unequal' in a sense rather like Emmanuel's, and for very much the same reasons; prices reflect wage differences. In Lewis's model, however, wage differences stem from productivity differences in the industries which exist in both areas.

9.6 SUMMARY

Emmanuel's essential contribution was to extend the analysis of prices of production (equilibrium prices in a capitalist system) to the determination of international prices, when capital is mobile between countries and labour is not. His analysis hinges on the existence of a given, predetermined, pattern of international specialization. (In this, as in other aspects of his work, Emmanuel had much in common with dependency theorists.) The major weakness in Emmanuel's arguments is that he was unable to explain why all capital does not flow into low-wage areas. He argued the contrary, that high wages attract capital (since markets are large) and induce the use of more mechanized methods of production. I have argued that this analysis can only be justified on rather special assumptions.

APPENDIX TO CHAPTER 9

In this appendix, I will briefly set out the algebra of prices of production, first with a single wage rate (the usual case) and then with different wages in different sectors (assumed to represent different countries). I will not use Emmanuel's notation (*UE*, appendix V), which is based on that of Sraffa and seems to me to be rather clumsy. Instead I will use my own notation based on that of Morishima (1973) which is now fairly widely used. I will also alter Emmanuel's model in some technical matters to simplify the exposition. I assume that all means of production are used up in a single period of production, in order to avoid complications connected with depreciation. Emmanuel did not make this simplifying assumption, and disputed Sraffa's treatment of depreciation (in a note added to the English edition). As far as I can see, Emmanuel's method is simply a different way of writing Sraffa's equations. I also assume that the purchasing power of the wage is given as a list of physical quantities of different goods. This is one alternative considered by Emmanuel, who favoured a model in which wages are fixed as a quantity of the 'money commodity'. He noted that the commodities actually bought by workers depend on prices, so both of these devices are somewhat artificial.

The basic problem is as follows: given the technical conditions of production and the real wage, find a set of prices such that the rate of profit is the same in all industries. First, define some notation. Number all goods, 1 to n. Let a_{ij} be the quantity of good i required, as means of production, to produce one unit of good j, and l_j the amount of labour. These coefficients are assumed to be fixed. Let the wage per hour of labour be w, and the prices (as yet unknown), p_1, p_2, ..., p_n. The wage, we assume, must be sufficient to buy quantities of goods given as $b_1, b_2, \ldots, b_n$, so

$$w = p_1 b_1 + p_2 b_2 + \ldots + p_n b_n$$

If, say, the ith good is used only as a means of production, then $b_i = 0$, and if it is used only in consumption then $a_{ij} = 0$ for all j. Luxuries, goods which do not enter into the real wage and are not used as means of production, can be ignored. Wages are assumed to be advanced at the beginning of the period of production (following Marx and Emmanuel, but not Sraffa). Let r stand for the rate of profit (as yet unknown).

We can now write down the equations. Capital advanced (per unit of product) is the same as the cost of production, because capital is simply the sum the capitalist has to lay out in order to produce. Cost plus profit must be equal to price, and the profit must equal the capital advanced multiplied by the general rate of profit, so.

$$p_1 = (p_1 a_{11} + \ldots + p_n a_{n1} + w l_1)(1 + r)$$
$$p_2 = (p_1 a_{12} + \ldots + p_n a_{n2} + w l_2)(1 + r)$$
$$\ldots\ldots\ldots\ldots\ldots\ldots\ldots\ldots\ldots\ldots\ldots\ldots$$
$$p_n = (p_1 a_{1n} + \ldots + p_n a_{nn} + w l_n)(1 + r)$$

Incorporating the equation for the wage gives:

$$p_1 = [p_1(a_{11} + b_1 l_1) + \ldots + p_n(a_{n1} + b_n l_1)](1 + r)$$
$$p_2 = [p_1(a_{12} + b_1 l_2) + \ldots + p_n(a_{n2} + b_n l_2)](1 + r)$$
$$\ldots\ldots\ldots\ldots\ldots\ldots\ldots\ldots\ldots\ldots\ldots\ldots$$
$$p_n = [p_1(a_{1n} + b_1 l_n) + \ldots + p_n(a_{nn} + b_n l_n)](1 + r)$$

There are n equations with $n + 1$ unknowns (n prices and the rate of profit). However, only relative prices matter, so we can fix the price of one good arbitrarily and solve for the remaining $n - 1$ prices and the rate of profit. Counting equations is a rather primitive approach; any mathematician knows that it ensures neither that a solution will exist nor that it will be unique. Fortunately, it can be shown that prices will indeed be determinate and positive, if the real wage is set at a level that permits a profit to be made at all.

The analysis can be written more compactly in matrix form. Let A be the matrix with elements (a_{ij}), B the real wage vector; L the vector of labour requirements and P the price vector. We can write the equations as

$$P = P(A + BL) (1 + r)$$

where BL is the matrix (not the scalar) product. This is a (slightly) disguised form of a standard problem, finding the eigenvalues and corresponding eigenvectors of a matrix.

Now for Emmanuel's main subject: pricing with different wages in different sectors. Let w_j be the wage in the jth sector, corresponding to a real wage vector $B_j = (b_{1j}, \ldots, b_{nj})$. The equation for good j must now be written as

$$p_j = [p_1(a_{1j} + b_{1j} l_j) + \ldots + p_n(a_{nj} + b_{nj}l_j)](1 + r)$$

The structure of the equations is not changed in any essential way. There is, of course, no need to have a different wage in each sector; there could be just two wages for two countries.

Notice that changed b_{ij} coefficients enter into the equations in much the same way as a change in methods of production. An increased real wage in any sector is equivalent to a cost-increasing change in technical coefficients. It can be shown (e.g. Himmelweit 1974) that any change which reduces costs (at the prices ruling before the change) will increase the rate of profit, and conversely that cost increases reduce the profit rate. Hence an increase in wages in any sector reduces profits, and low wages anywhere raise profits.

10

Classes and Politics
in the Third World

It is almost an axiom of Marxism that international relations
(political or economic) can only be understood in terms of the
internal structure of the states concerned, conceptualized by
Marxists in terms of *classes* and *modes of production*. In the
1960s and 1970s an upsurge of interest in Marxist theory and
a rediscovery of the Marxist classics provoked a series of
debates about the appropriate way to analyse social and
economic structures in underdeveloped countries, surveyed
to the mid-seventies (the most active period of debate) by
Foster-Carter (1976). I shall concentrate on those aspects of
the debate relevant to theories of imperialism.

Advanced capitalist countries all have a rather similar
structure; 'the country that is more developed industrially
only shows, to the less developed, the image of its own
future' (Marx, *Capital I*: 91). The transition to fully developed
capitalism, however, takes very different forms in different
places, depending on the previous stage of development, the
pre-existing mode of production, on whether it comes early
or late in the development of capitalism on a world scale, and
so on. Class structures and class alliances are particularly
complex during the transition, now under way in the Third
World. Study of classes and politics in the Third World must
therefore take the form of case studies; there is no sign of any
general theory to cover all cases. Section 10.1 surveys the
Marxist tradition and the idea of the *articulation of modes of
production*, developed by P. P. Rey. Section 10.2 describes
debates over Indian agriculture, and 10.3 to 10.5 outline three
influential case studies of African societies: G. Arrighi on the

difference between southern and tropical Africa, Rey (again) on Congo-Brazzaville, and C. Leys on the development of a national bourgeoisie in Kenya. Finally, 10.6 presents a very different, non-Marxist, view of the relation between imperialism and Third World politics in the work of J. Gallagher and R. Robinson.

10.1 MODES OF PRODUCTION

Until recently, most Marxists thought of modes of production as successive stages in the evolution of human society, following each other in a predestined order. In a transitional period, the old mode decays, while the new mode first emerges within the previous system, and then replaces it. The development of new forms of organization actively undermines the old and accelerates their decay. At some stage, a revolution reconstructs the political and legal superstructures to fit the needs of the new mode of production. The relation between the two modes is therefore one of contradiction, and the new ruling class establishes itself through class struggles in which it is irreconcilably opposed to the old order. Each nation must go through the sequence of stages, though external influences may accelerate or slow the process, or even allow a stage to be skipped. This brief summary is, of course, a caricature, but I think it brings out the key ideas that underlie more sophisticated accounts. There is some warrant for it in Marx's own writings (especially the *Preface to the Critique of Political Economy*).

Trotsky had a somewhat different view. Although his thinking remained in essence bounded by a 'stages' perspective, he stressed the importance of (relative) backwardness, and argued that the structure of societies that started to develop late was not the same as those that had led the way. This thesis, as applied to Russia, is scattered through his works (see Knei-Paz 1978, for Trotsky's views and for detailed references; also Szymanski 1981: 55). Russia, he argued, came under pressure, military and economic, from the more advanced West, and the Russian state, reacting to this pressure, took the initiative in promoting both industrial development and (limited) measures of social and administrative modernization designed to increase the military efficiency of the state. The state machine had a larger, and the bourgeoisie a smaller, relative weight than in the countries of western Europe, and there were massive disparities between the industrial cities and the impoverished and backward countryside. This is summarized in the phrase 'uneven and combined development', meaning that nations, sectors, and areas develop at different rates, but do not do so in isolation from each other. What is distinctive about Trotsky's view is his emphasis on the role of the state. As it stands it is difficult to think of many areas except Russia, Japan, and parts of south-east Europe to which it is relevant; in other areas national states went under when confronted with western pressure. Ex-colonial territories frequently exhibit a rather similar enlarged state apparatus, though they have reached this condition by a different route.

The classic account of a transition from feudalism to capitalism is Lenin's *The Development of Capitalism in Russia* (1974, first published 1899). Russia was in the middle of the transition, and Lenin, grappling with the problems of political strategy in a relatively backward country, looked in detail at the process of transition and at the transitional forms created. The issues he focused on are substantially those that concern Marxists in the underdeveloped world today: the prospects for capitalist development and the class struggles and possible class alliances inherent in the situation.

Lenin identified four main processes at work in the countryside. First, commodity production and exchange were emerging through the progressive separation of successive 'industrial' activities from agriculture. These activities formed distinct industries, perhaps organized on a craft basis but rapidly penetrated by capitalist relations of production, linked to each other and to agriculture by exchange (recall Marx's similar analysis). Second, there was a progressive differentiation of the peasantry, as the 'middle peasantry' of relatively self-sufficient family units broke down into a rural bourgeoisie (the *kulaks*) and a rural proletariat. Third, the role of the landlord was transformed as the (feudal) *corvée* or labour-service system was supplanted by capitalist agriculture based on the employment of wage-labour. Capitalist agriculture emerged by two routes: the rise of a rural bourgeoisie from the peasantry, and the conversion of the landlords' economy into capitalist estates. Finally, there was a developing pattern of specialization within agriculture itself, and thus a development of commodity exchange within agriculture as well as between agriculture and industry.

In this process a great variety of transitional forms were created; 'the systems mentioned are actually interwoven in the most varied and fantastic fashion' (Lenin 1974: 197). Lenin was able to make sense of them only by setting them in the context of a process of transition from one fairly well-defined system (feudalism) to another (capitalism). I suspect that at least part of the debate about contemporary underdeveloped countries is bedevilled by a desire to link immediately observable features of society (the 'fantastic form' that Lenin described) directly to the defining features of various modes of production without setting them adequately in the context of a historical process.

The classical Marxist analysis has had considerable success in analysing European history, when applied in a creative and undogmatic way. Whether it can be used with the same success in dealing with non-European societies is a matter of dispute. In a 'stages' perspective, one must either say that underdeveloped countries are pre-capitalist, that they are capitalist, or that they are in transition (thus implying that they are becoming capitalist). In the orthodox Marxist view, the capitalist stage has three main characteristics: first, commodity production, second, the relation between wage-labour and capital, and third, the pressure to accumulate and to introduce new methods of production. In underdeveloped countries the penetration of commodity production went ahead rapidly but, for a long time, wage-labour and best practice levels of productivity were confined to small sectors. Either these countries are not becoming capitalist (in which case what are they?) or capitalism has quite different laws of motion in underdeveloped areas (in which case, what use is the concept of capitalism?). Some attempts to solve these problems have already been discussed.

Frank and Wallerstein took the most drastic line. Capitalism, they argued, is a world system, defined in terms of production for the world market, whether wage-labour is employed or not. This is a fundamental shift of definition. Its laws of motion, too, are quite unlike those analysed by Marx. Capitalism does not promote general development; it promotes the development of some areas at the expense of others. I have criticized Frank and Wallerstein for the lack of any well-worked-out theoretical analysis to back up their sloganistic generalizations. Amin's analysis is an advance, using more traditional concepts of modes of production in an overall framework derived from dependency theory; it is open to criticism, but on other grounds.

An alternative to Frank and Wallersein, more faithful to Marx, is to treat the wage relation as the defining feature of capitalism, as Laclau suggested (section 8.3 above), and argue that different modes of production can coexist within a single society, either permanently (abandoning the 'stages' perspective) or over a very long-drawn-out transition. Various phrases have been used in this context; one can talk of a 'conservation–dissolution' relation (between capitalism and the subordinated mode), of a 'blocked' transition (preserving a 'stages' view, at least verbally) or, as Bettelheim does in another context, of a transition 'between' two stages without implying movement in one direction or another. All these devices seem to be essentially semantic; what matters is the substance of the analysis.

The case for focusing on the relation between the direct producers and their exploiters, and thus on the wage relation as the defining characteristic of capitalism, was put most forcefully by Brenner (1977), in work on the origins of capitalism in Europe (see also Brenner 1985, and discussion reported in Aston and Philpin 1985). He argued that the production of relative surplus value and the tendency to increase productivity differentiates capitalism from all previous modes of production:

> The logic of [Wallerstein's] position ... is that capitalist underdevelopment is as much the cause of capitalist development, as capitalist development is the cause of capitalist underdevelopment. Such an argument is not compatible with the view of capitalist economic development as a function of the tendency towards capital accumulation via innovation, built into a historically developed structure of class relations of free wage labour. For from this vantage point, neither economic development nor underdevelopment are directly dependent upon, caused by, one another. Each is the product of a specific evolution of class relations, in part determined historically

'outside' capitalism, in relationship with non-capitalist modes. . . . Wallerstein resorts to the position that both . . . are essentially the result of a process of transfer of surplus. . . . He must thus end up by . . . ignoring any inherent tendency of capitalism to develop the productive forces. (Brenner 1977: 60-1)

The existence of free wage-labour matters for two reasons. First, because only in a system of free labour can labour be reallocated from one task to another and gathered into ever larger and more complex productive organizations. Capital can only be genuinely mobile where it can gather labour and means of production freely in the market. Second, and perhaps more important, in a wage-labour system all the needs of reproduction have to be bought in the market and competition then acquires coercive force. Any enterprise that fails to keep up with socially established levels of productivity is driven out of business; the process of concentration and centralization, an essential part of the development of capitalism, thus depends on the wage relation. Labour-saving innovation allows costs to be cut by making workers redundant, an option not open in feudal systems in which peasants are tied to a particular estate. Competition forces capitalists to minimize costs, constantly recreating a mobile reserve army of labour.

In a feudal system, the needs of reproduction are met by peasant plots, so the *demesne* product, which may be sold on the market, is all surplus product. A feudal lord, maximizing short-run profit, will attempt to restrict peasants' mobility (to keep them under his control) and to reduce the land and labour time devoted to the peasants' plots, not by increasing productivity, but by increasing absolute surplus value, even to the point where the long-run reproduction of the system is threatened. An extension of market opportunities can even intensify feudal exploitation and promote regression in the forces of production. Brenner had a telling example; in the Poland of the 'second serfdom' (one of Wallerstein's favourite examples), 'despite the orientation of the entire economy to exports, it could send out at best 5 per cent to 7 per cent of its total grain produce' (Brenner 1977: 69-70). Peasant plots were more productive than *demesnes*, and could generate a larger marketable surplus per acre, but they were ruthlessly cut down to expand the lord's profits. Here profitability (for the rulers) generated regression. A switch to wage-labour would only be profitable for the lords in the very long run, if at all. Wage-labour was only used where serfdom had decayed beyond possibility of restoration.

An alternative system in agriculture is small peasant proprietorship. Here again the market lacks coercive force if peasants can produce their own subsistence (cf. Luxemburg), and here again the attachment of producers to the means of production inhibits flexibility and thus technological advance. England was the one place in Europe where serfdom had been eliminated without small peasant proprietorship taking its place. There are also cases in which the producers are wholly dependent on the market for their subsistence, without labour-power, as such, becoming a commodity. Peasant producers of industrial raw materials are an example. In these cases fully capitalist production can penetrate relatively easily.

The mode of production, defined by the relation between the direct producers and the owners of the means of production, is thus not a purely formal characteristic of the social system, nor does it define classes opposed to each other in purely distributive terms. It is of crucial importance in determining the evolution of the forces of production, and in determining development and underdevelopment. Brenner displayed the mechanisms linking structural features of the mode of production to its dynamics, and thus demonstrated their relevance rather than merely asserting it. Development and underdevelopment are the product of class structures which are themselves the outcome of a historical process of development that cannot be analysed in the abstract.

Perhaps the most important and sophisticated discussion of the role of modes of production is by P. P. Rey. It predates Brenner's work, and is more directly aimed at the analysis of contemporary underdeveloped countries; the rest of this section will be devoted to a discussion of Rey's theoretical framework, while his case study of Congo-Brazzaville will be dealt with in section 10.4. In *L'articulation des modes de production*, which makes up the bulk of *Les alliances de classes* (Rey 1973, cited below as *Alliances*), Rey set out his main theoretical perspective and discussed the transition from capitalism to feudalism in Europe. *Colonialisme, neo-*

colonialisme et transition au capitalisme (Rey 1971, cited below as *Colonialisme*) is a detailed study of the transition from the 'lineage mode of production' to capitalism in Congo-Brazzaville. *Capitalisme negrier* (Le Bris, Rey and Samuel 1976) is a collection of studies of migration by African workers, both within Africa and between Africa and France. The 'theoretical introduction' by Rey is a good concise summary of his views. One of the starting points for Rey's work was a debate among Marxist anthropologists about the nature of social relations in the part of Africa which Rey studied; for these debates see Meillassoux (1964), Terray (1972) and Rey (1975), as well as *Colonialisme*. There are useful discussions of Rey's work in English in articles by Bradby (1975) and Foster-Carter (1978). On the notion of an 'articulation' of modes of production, see Wolpe (1980) and Miles (1987).

Rey's starting point was the distinction between a *mode of production* and a *social formation*, drawn by Althusser and Balibar. The best statement of these concepts and their inter-relations is to be found in Balibar's essay 'The basic concepts of historical materialism' (Althusser and Balibar 1970, part III), and in the glossary in the English translation of the same book. Put simply, they insisted that a mode of production (capitalism, feudalism, etc.) is an abstract, timeless concept, defined by a particular, exactly specified, relation connecting two classes (except, of course, for classless modes). A social formation is also a conceptual construction, but of a more concrete kind; a real society can be thought of as a social formation. (There are some tricky philosophical issues here, concerning the relation between abstract concepts and reality, which I will not pursue; cf. Ruccio and Simon 1986.) Both mode of production and social formation must be analysed from the point of view of their reproduction, that is to say that their different components must interlock to produce a functioning system which can maintain itself in existence, at least for a time. For a critical discussion of these concepts, see Cutler, Hindess, Hirst and Hussain (1977).

What is most relevant in understanding Rey's work is the idea that a social formation (like Laclau's 'economic system') may contain more than one mode of production. Althusser and Balibar insisted that one mode of production dominates, defining a dominant or ruling class, except during brief periods of transition. Rey's concept of the *articulation of modes of production* is firmly set in a classical Marxist analysis of transition, analysed in Althusserian style. As noted above, the classical Marxists conceived of modes of production as stages of development which succeed each other in turn. Since one mode cannot replace another overnight, there must be a long process of transition in which the old mode dominates at first, while allowing the new to grow up, then the new mode comes to dominate, while the old persists for a further period. Rey's originality is in insisting that this process takes so long that transition is the normal state of affairs, and analysing the process with the rigour usual in the study of 'pure' modes.

In a transitional social formation the two modes of production are not independent of each other, just sitting side by side. There is an interaction, in which each affects the workings of the other, so the evolution of a transitional social formation cannot be understood by analysing the logic of one mode of production in isolation. The two modes are in contradiction, in the sense that one will replace the other but, during the transition, each must be reproduced, so the conditions of their reproduction must be compatible. This Rey called the 'articulation' of two modes.

In all the cases Rey dealt with, the expanding mode is capitalism. Like Luxemburg he insisted that capitalism has an inherent tendency to expand at the expense of the pre-capitalist societies it finds around itself. This insistence on what Foster-Carter (1978) called the 'homofience' of capitalism (literally, 'having the same effect') put him firmly in the classical Marxist tradition and led him to reject any explanation of underdevelopment in terms of restrictive behaviour by capitalists, as proposed by Baran and Frank:

> Let us cease to reproach capitalism with the one crime that it has not committed, that it could not think of committing, constrained as it is by its own laws always to enlarge the scale of production. Let us keep firmly in mind that all the bourgeoisies of the world burn with desire to develop the 'underdeveloped' countries. (*Alliances*: 16)

Why then have some areas advanced, while others have not? If capitalism by itself has the same effect everywhere, the difference must be in the other half of the articulation, in the pre-capitalist modes that are the 'medium and soil' (in

Luxemburg's words) of capitalist development. Rey criticized Luxemburg for not taking the internal workings of these modes seriously. Capitalism prospered where it succeeded feudalism, while 'generally speaking, non-Western countries, apart from Japan, have shown themselves and still show themselves to be wretched environments for the development of capitalist relations of production' (*Alliances*: 11).

Rey proceeded by considering the conditions required for the expanded reproduction of capital. The first is a class of free wage-labourers, so the articulation with the pre-capitalist mode must be such as to exclude a growing section of the population from pre-capitalist production (or at least to ensure that they have to spend a part of their time or a stage in their lives working for a wage). Capitalism is relatively slow to establish itself in agriculture, especially in the production of basic foods. The capitalist sector must, therefore, obtain means of subsistence for its workers by trading with pre-capitalist agricultural producers. In the heartlands of capitalism, where it succeeded feudalism as the dominant mode, these needs were met by the expulsion of peasants and the sale of a surplus product extracted as rent, as Marx showed in his account of primitive accumulation.

In the rest of the world, however, pre-capitalist modes did not evolve naturally to meet the needs of capitalism, so capitalist relations of production could not arise from within. These areas could (and did) engage in exchange, and were drawn into the world market, but exchange reinforced the hold of pre-capitalist ruling classes and strengthened resistance to the implantation of capitalist relations of production. This is really the most crucial part of Rey's argument; he argued it in detail only for a particular area in Congo-Brazzaville (section 10.4), and it is not at all clear that the argument generalizes to other areas.

Since the preconditions for capitalist production did not arise naturally in most parts of the world, they were imposed by external force. To open up these areas for capital, it was necessary to displace the existing ruling class and reorganize indigenous societies. Direct military and administrative coercion was used to recruit workers and to compel villagers to sell cash crops (especially food crops). Rey called this system of administrative coercion the *colonial mode of production*. Once the pre-capitalist framework has been transformed to fit the needs of capital, it can be left to itself. Capitalist reproduction and growth can be assured by economic means and by the local state: the 'neo-colonial' pattern of the underdeveloped world today. Formal decolonization is no threat to the economic interests of capital. The expansion of capitalist relations of production is, however, hindered by the persistence, in a modified form, of pre-existing modes, since capitalist mechanisms cannot, for a long time, provide for reproduction on their own.

Rey deduced his central political conclusions from this account. Capitalism and the restructured pre-capitalist modes of production need each other and sustain each other. It is therefore impossible to try to abolish pre-capitalist forms of oppression without at the same time seeking to overthrow capitalism, while anti-capitalist revolutions (Russia, China) have been able to abolish these archaic restrictions in a very short space of time.

On a world scale, the development of capitalism went ahead in previously feudal areas, but was blocked elsewhere. Capitalist and non-capitalist areas were linked by exchange, but pre-capitalist societies did not respond well to market signals, since exchange does not alter the basic relations of production and does not provide any strong stimulus to a more rational organization of production. There were thus good reasons for capitalist expansion into non-capitalist areas, but the means were lacking. The blockage was broken when central capitalism reached the stage of finance capital, according to Rey, because it was only at this stage that capital could impose capitalist relations of production from the outside. This part of the argument is not very clear. European states did, in fact, reorganize the mode of production in colonial territories much earlier (e.g. Latin America from the sixteenth century), but they imposed pre-capitalist, not capitalist, modes of production. Rey's whole chronology is geared to Africa. The epoch of finance capital is thus also the age of imperialism and colonial conquest, but for reasons rather different from those proposed by Lenin. (See Michalet, 1976, for a reinterpretation of Lenin on similar lines; Michalet and Rey differ on most other points.)

Gathering the story together, it goes as follows. Capitalism emerged in previously feudal areas, and went through a whole process of development there (the capitalism–

feudalism articulation), with a corresponding, massive, development of the forces of production; the rest of the world was drawn into relations of exchange without the transformation of relations or forces of production. The rise of finance capital was the signal for forcible conquest and transformation of 'underdeveloped' areas, followed (in the end) by decolonization, leaving capitalist relations of production dominant, but with development still retarded by the persistence of pre-capitalist modes alongside capitalism.

Rey drew heavily on the classical Marxists. Like Rosa Luxemburg, he emphasized the role of coercion in the expansion of capitalist relations of production, but he distinguished between the transition from feudalism to capitalism (coercion by the feudal ruling class itself) and other transitions (coercion from outside), and also between the transformation of a 'natural economy' into a commodity-producing system (which need not involve coercion) and the transformation of relations of production by the creation of a proletariat. His argument has obvious (and acknowledged) roots in Marx's treatment of primitive accumulation, of the Asiatic mode of production, and of merchant capital. The aspects of Marx's work that Rey built on had been substantially neglected in the intervening period, so to point to these roots in Marx is not to decry Rey's contribution. More important, he provided an explanation for a 'neo-colonial' stage following colonialism, connecting the present stage of development to its predecessors and to a coherent account of the history of capitalism.

10.2 INDIAN DEBATES

At about the same time as the Frank–Laclau debate (about Latin America), and the work of Rey, Arrighi and others on Africa, there was a debate in India over rather similar ground. The point at issue was ostensibly whether Indian agriculture should be described as capitalist, a rather uninteresting semantic question, but the real question was whether the backwardness of Indian agriculture was caused by capitalism or by the absence of capitalist relations of production. Rudra (1969, 1970) provoked the debate with a rather naive statistical survey of large farms in the Punjab, from which he concluded that there was no clearly defined class of capitalist farmers. Patnaik (1971a, b; 1972) criticized this conclusion, and Chattopadhyay (1972a, b) criticized both for being insufficiently Marxist. A general *melée* ensued (Banaji 1972, 1977; Frank 1973; Sau 1973; Alavi 1975). The debate has been surveyed by McEachern (1976) and Foster-Carter (1976).

There was general agreement that the 'green revolution' (the introduction of high-yielding varieties of cereals) was associated with increased differentiation among the peasants, since rich farmers were better able to pay for the necessary irrigation and fertilizers. All the participants in the debate (except Rudra) seem to have agreed that this represented a development of capitalism in agriculture. The point at issue was whether agriculture in India had been capitalist during the colonial (pre-1949) period (as Chattopadhyay argued), making the 'green revolution' a stage of development within capitalism, or whether agriculture had not previously been capitalist (as Patnaik and others claimed). The basic facts were common ground: the agricultural sector had been producing for the market for a long time, a fraction (30-40 per cent) of the rural population consisted of agricultural wage-labourers, but development in methods of production had been very slow, with little reinvestment of surplus. (See Alavi 1975, for a useful review of the facts and their historical context.)

It is convenient to start with Chattopadhyay (1972a, b), ignoring the chronological order of debate. He argued that Indian agriculture had long been substantially capitalist, though still in transition, since commodity production and wage-labour constitute capitalism. India was in substantially the same position as Russia in Lenin's time. The slow pace of development was not a problem (for the theory) since the early development of capitalism had been slow everywhere else as well. In short, he restated a traditional Marxist analysis in which each nation, in its turn, passes through substantially the same stages of development. McEachern (1976) generally supported Chattopadhyay's diagnosis of India in terms of a classical Marxist analysis of transition, with more emphasis on the external dimension. He was unwilling to accept any idea that modes of production may be 'combined', except during relatively brief periods of transition, and argued that surviving pre-capitalist forms in India conceal the real (capitalist) relations of production.

Patnaik (1971a, b; 1972), with Sau (1973) and Banaji (1972, 1977) also distinguished apparent forms and underlying reality, but to support the opposite conclusion. The existence of wage-labour, she claimed, is not conclusive evidence that Indian agriculture was capitalist, since workers were not really free, given the lack of employment opportunities. Further, one should not speak of capitalism unless the surplus is productively invested within the same sector or even the same enterprise. There are two issues here: whether to define capitalism in terms of accumulation, the third major characteristic of capitalism in the classical Marxist view (commodity production and wage-labour are the other two), and whether the definition applies at the level of a firm or farm, or at some higher level. Brenner (discussed above) argued in the European context that the introduction of capitalist relations of production led to capitalist development and increased productivity; the Indian debate hinged on the apparent failure of this connection in India. Frank (1973) remarked that the surplus was indeed invested, in England.

The question of definition is semantic. What matters is to discover the necessary and sufficient conditions for accumulation to take place, and the forms it takes. Patnaik had an explanation for the stagnation of agriculture in the colonial period. Industry failed to develop because of British competition, backed by the colonial state, so markets for agricultural products were stagnant. Agriculture was exploited by 'antediluvian forms of capital' (merchant capital, usury) and 'generalized commodity production . . . led to a prolonged disintegration of the pre-capitalist mode without its reconstitution on a capitalist basis' (Patnaik 1972: A-149). Independence led to (state-sponsored) industrial development, and hence to scope for investment in agriculture. Patnaik, then, argued that Indian agriculture, in the colonial period, had not been capitalist, but she did not offer any definite alternative classification.

Banaji (1972) and Alavi (1975) proposed a concept of a 'colonial mode of production' to cover colonial India and other colonial territories. Banaji subsequently abandoned the idea, so I will concentrate on Alavi's arguments. (It is worth noting that this concept is not the same as Rey's 'colonial mode' though there are common features.) Alavi's main idea was to restore the classical conception of modes of production as stages of development. He argued that colonial India was neither feudal (since there was widespread commodity production) nor capitalist (since there was little accumulation). He was unwilling to talk of a combination of modes, because different modes of production can only co-exist in a state of contradiction, and no one has 'demonstrated that there is any conflict between the rural "capitalist" class and the "feudal" landlords'. (He did not, apparently, notice that one could say much the same of early modern England.) Colonialism does not correspond in any simple way to a capitalist or to a feudal stage, so it must be something else, a 'colonial' stage. His colonial mode is characterized by colonial bourgeois state power, internal disarticulation, generalized commodity production, a transfer of surplus to the metropolis, and a lack of accumulation (cf. Baran's 'typical' underdeveloped country or Amin's peripheral capitalism). Alavi is entitled to call this a mode of production, if he chooses, but it is not remotely like any other Marxist concept of a mode of production. It has no defining relation of production, and it does not define any specific class opposition. It is difficult to see what can be gained by calling it a mode of production.

Banaji (1977) developed the idea that capitalism is identified with capital accumulation. Modes of production are 'a definite totality of historical laws of motion' which must be discovered by analysis, and cannot be reduced to 'simple abstractions' (such as commodity production, or wage-labour). Any given mode of production may be compatible with a variety of 'forms of exploitation'. How then are the 'laws of motion' of the various modes to be distinguished? They seem to amount to different (socially determined) motivations or purposes on the part of those who control production. Capitalism is production directed to accumulation, feudalism is directed to meeting the (socially determined) luxury consumption needs of the landlords, and the 'patriarchal-peasant' mode is governed by the subsistence needs of the peasant family. The *latifundias* of Latin America are, he argued, feudal estates, while superficially similar production units in plantation agriculture are capitalist, since they are orientated to the accumulation of capital, albeit 'only in the long run, as a relatively slow and mainly sporadic tendency dominated by feudal modes of consumption' (Banaji 1977: 16); I find this distinction hard to grasp. Although there are many incidental felicities in this provocative article (such as the demonstration that wage-labour was as common in thirteenth-century England as in present day rural India), the main argument seems to remain very much up in the air. Where do 'laws of motion' come from? The political economy of consumption and the social bases of motivation are important and neglected topics, but they must be explained, not introduced as a *deus ex machina* to define different modes of production. To trace them back to their roots in relatively permanent features of social structure would, I suspect, lead back to relations of production.

Two major issues emerge from the Indian debates. The first is the role of 'forms of exploitation' (wage-labour, serfdom, etc.). Many writers have pointed out that superficial or juridical relations may be misleading; a nominally independent peasant, for example, may depend on advances from a merchant and receive a price for the product that is more like a piece-rate wage than a genuine market price. This is no problem; Marxists commonly distinguish between juridical and real relations. It is a quite different matter to claim, for example, that a slave plantation can be capitalist, when the slaves really are slaves who can be bought and sold in slave markets. There are strong reasons, explained by Brenner, for thinking that (real, not juridical) relations of production are important. The second question concerns the appropriate level of analysis: world system, nation state, unit of production, or whatever. This is a non-problem. There can be no question of choosing to analyse at one level and ignore the others; any adequate account of the world system must incorporate them all, and their interrelations. The only problem is semantic: to what kinds of entities can the adjectives capitalist, feudal, and so on be attached? Can one talk of a capitalist farm, or a feudal nation? In isolation, these are meaningless questions.

10.3 ARRIGHI

Some of the most original work on the persistence and transformation of pre-capitalist modes of production emerged from studies of Africa, perhaps because capitalism penetrated much of Africa more recently than most other parts of the world. I shall discuss three writers on Africa: Arrighi, Rey, and Leys, starting with Giovanni Arrighi. His most important contributions, some written in collaboration with John Saul, are collected in *Essays on the Political Economy of Africa* (Arrighi and Saul 1973, cited below as *EPEA*; page references are to this collection, though the original articles are listed in the bibliography). The best known of these papers is 'Labour supplies in historical perspective: a study of the proletarianisation of the African peasantry in Rhodesia', which is rightly regarded as a classic.

Arrighi studied the penetration of capitalism in Africa south of the Sahara. He argued that this area divides into two regions with very different histories: tropical Africa and southern Africa. In his analysis of both areas the implicit (sometimes fairly explicit) basis is an account of the articulation of the indigenous modes of production with capitalism. From Arrighi's description, it is clear that he regarded the indigenous societies of tropical and South Africa as essentially primitive-communal:

> The vast majority of the population of tropical Africa consists of independent producers. . . . Individuals can customarily acquire land through tribal or kinship rights. Only comparatively rarely is land acquired or disposed of through purchase or sale. . . . Market exchanges were . . . peripheral. . . . Feudal elements, landowning classes and national bourgeoisies are either nonexistent or not sufficiently significant, politically and/or economically, to constitute the power base of the state. (*EPEA*: 13-14, 141)

The indigenous peasantry has, however, been very responsive to market stimuli, supplying goods and working for wages whenever it paid them to (though not otherwise). In contrast to Rey, Arrighi did not see the indigenous mode of production as a substantial obstacle to capitalist development. The lagging development of tropical Africa is due to the failure of capitalist development to expand the demand for labour-power and for the products of pre-capitalist agriculture, not to a deficient supply of either.

The main characteristics of tropical Africa derive from the limited extent to which capitalism has supplanted pre-capitalist modes of production. In the earlier stages of capitalist penetration the main demand was for unskilled labour, and was not met by the creation of a distinct proletariat, but by migrant labourers who kept a foothold in the pre-capitalist mode of production, where their families could produce a large part of their subsistence and where reciprocal obligations guaranteed the individual's security in illness and old age. A low-wage, low-skill pattern developed. Arrighi argued that this migrant labour force was part of the peasantry, not a proletariat (as subsistence was guaranteed in the pre-capitalist sector) so there was a capitalist mode of production without any substantial proletarian class.

Modern international corporations, however, use capital-intensive methods of production requiring a smaller number of semi-skilled workers. To make it worthwhile to train workers even for semi-skilled work requires a stabilization of the labour force, which requires, in turn, a substantial increase in wages above the migrant level, to induce workers to sever their ties with the traditional economy. At the same time, the state apparatus, taken over substantially unaltered from the colonial powers, supports a relatively well paid élite and sub-élite. These groups, together, Arrighi called a 'labour aristocracy' (while admitting some unease about the term). In the absence of any substantial indigenous bourgeoisie or landowning class, this labour aristocracy forms the political basis of the state (cf. Leys's account, section 10.5). State policies understandably favour relatively high wages, which encourage the use of capital-intensive methods of production and correspondingly low levels of employment.

The result is 'growth without development', in which the (small) modern sector offers relatively few opportunities of employment, and buys relatively little from the traditional sector, since the relatively highly paid proletariat proper spends its income largely on the products of the modern sector or on imports. The high demand for imports, together with the lack of a substantial capital goods sector, leads to balance of payments constraints which inhibit any acceleration of growth in the modern capitalist sector, while the pre-capitalist peasant sector stagnates for want of any stimulus from demand. The relative impoverishment of the peasantry may lead to differentiation and the formation of a *kulak* class of capitalist farmers, but the slow growth of demand for agricultural products 'restrains the incentive for, and financial ability of, the emerging *kulaks* to expand wage employment so that . . . it tends to produce an impoverished peasantry without fostering its absorption in capitalist agriculture' (*EPEA*: 126).

This formulation is strikingly similar to Patnaik's (section 10.2) and to the 'dependency theorists'. Arrighi was mainly concerned with the effects of a particular pattern of economic development on class structure, and therefore did not explain in detail why foreign investment should take the particular form he described. In addition, he assumed almost without discussion that there was no scope for small-scale, locally based development; Leys's discussion of the formation of an indigenous bourgeoisie in Kenya (section 10.5) suggests that the prospects for development may be better than Arrighi thought. (See also chapter 11 below, for more general discussion of capitalist development in the Third World.)

De Janvry's (1981) analysis of agriculture and development in Latin America makes an interesting contrast with Arrighi's description of tropical Africa. De Janvry argued that there was an alliance between the industrial bourgeoisie and the landowners in most Latin American states. Protection raises the price of industrial products, while a number of policy measures (including food imports) keep down the prices of staple foodstuffs, allowing wages to be kept down. Food production is unprofitable, and is left to the peasantry, while large estates concentrate on non-food agricultural exports. Policy is designed to support the export agriculture sector, in order to keep the support of the landlords and bolster the balance of payments; the export sector also benefits from cheap food and low wages. Investment in food production is unprofitable, so food production has grown slowly, storing up trouble for the future. The class structure is different from that in Africa (wages are kept low, not high, because of the power of the local bourgeoisie and the landed élite), but the results are rather similar: the peasant sector loses out in both cases, and agricultural growth suffers.

Southern Africa, by contrast, is distinguished by the much larger scale of capitalist penetration in the nineteenth and early twentieth centuries (the result of mineral discoveries) and also by the presence of a substantial settler-colonial bourgeoisie drawn by the opportunities (real and imagined) created by this earlier boom. The difference between tropical and southern Africa thus arises from the different opportunities that capital found in the two areas, not from any important difference in the pre-capitalist mode of production. Arrighi studied Rhodesia (Zimbabwe), though he argued that developments in South Africa were similar.

During the early stages of capitalist penetration it proved difficult to recruit a sufficient labour force locally, not because of any unwillingness by Africans to respond to market incentives, but because producing goods for sale gave a better cash return on effort than wage-labour, at the rates the mines were prepared to offer. At this stage, the African peasantry could meet their subsistence needs without participating in the cash economy; sales of produce or labour-power were a use of surplus labour time to increase living standards.

The solution to this 'problem' was, in essence, simple; the African peasantry was expelled from the land, the classic centrepiece of a process of primitive accumulation. There are, however, some distinctive aspects of primitive accumulation in Rhodesia that make it worth looking at in a little more detail. The expulsion of the peasantry from the land could not take place at once, since there was a need for food supplies for the mining sector. Most of the land in Rhodesia was expropriated at a very early stage (by 1902; *EPEA*: 195), but the African peasantry was left in occupation since land was plentiful but labour scarce. European owners of land initially exploited the Africans through the establishment of 'semi-feudal' relations: the exaction of labour services, or rents in money or kind. Rent and tax charges forced Africans into the cash economy, but did not force them to sell their labour-power rather than their products. Extra-territorial African workers from what is now Zambia and elsewhere were essential to capitalism in Rhodesia until the slump of 1921-3.

During this first stage various counteracting tendencies were at work. African peasants invested in improved means of production, mainly of a 'land-using' type (draught animals, ploughs), increasing their capacity to produce, but at the same time they developed new consumption habits, became more dependent on the cash economy, and were progressively excluded from the best lands by European capitalist farmers. Supplies marketed by capitalist farmers drove down the prices Africans could get for their products, while their capacity to produce was reduced by land scarcity and subsequent loss of fertility due to over-farming. The slump of 1921-3, when agricultural prices fell sharply, marked the turning point. From then on the African population was essentially a proletariat, dependent for subsistence on the sale of labour-power, and in a quite different position from the peasantry of tropical Africa.

The foothold African workers retained in the peasant economy allowed the wage to be held down to the subsistence of a single worker, with the costs of reproduction of labour-power met by the work of the rest of the family in the tribal reserve areas. After the Second World War, average African wages rose as oligopolistic industry introduced more modern techniques and 'stabilized' sections of the labour force, while the wages of other sections of the proletariat remained at the single-man-subsistence level. Arrighi summed up in a much quoted sentence: 'Real wages remained at a level which promoted capitalist accumulation not because of the forces of supply and demand, but because of politico-economic mechanisms that ensured the "desired" supply at the "desired" wage rate' (*EPEA*: 214).

Arrighi's analysis is a superb application of the Marxist analysis of primitive accumulation in a particular case. It has often been misunderstood as illustrating some specifically colonial mechanism; what strikes me is how similar it is to the origins of capitalism in, say, England. The 'semi-feudal' stage, and the expulsion of peasants by individual landowners converting themselves into capitalist farmers are strikingly familiar. The really interesting question is why other places where superficially similar 'semi-feudal' structures existed (e.g. the Latin American *latifundia* system) have so far evolved in a very different way. Arrighi's explanation seems to be that Rhodesia's economy expanded rapidly because of the implantation of competitive capitalism with a numerous national (settler) bourgeoisie.

10.4 REY

Rey's general theoretical framework has already been discussed. His analysis of the impact of capitalism outside its homelands rests essentially on a single case study of 'lineage' societies in Congo-Brazzaville (Rey 1971). It can have few equals in its combination of rigorous and creative Marxist theory with detailed study of a pre-capitalist society and its penetration by capitalism. Rey claimed, first, that he could define a *lineage mode of production* (in a strictly Marxist sense), which was dominant before the installation of capitalism in the area studied and, second, that the history of the area could be understood by looking very carefully at the inter-action of capitalist and lineage modes of production. Specifically, the lineage mode of production was very well suited to generating a supply of slaves for export during the period of the slave trade, rather poor at producing goods for export, and quite incapable by itself of generating either a proletariat or a marketable supply of food to support a pro-letariat. These facts conditioned the history of its interaction with capitalism.

According to Rey, the lineage mode of production defines two classes: chiefs (or elders) and their dependents (or juniors). Each chief has a group of dependents; individuals are allocated to positions in the system by (real or notional) kinship relations. Subsistence production is carried out in groups of various sizes, the chief's subsistence being prod-uced mainly inside his own household. Groups are connected by a network of exchanges, carried out by the chiefs; the class status of chiefs, and the lineage mode of production are defined by the chiefs' role in these exchanges. 'Prestige goods', obtained in previous exchanges or produced by the surplus labour of dependents, are exchanged for each other, for slaves (until 1920), or for women (as brides for group members, for whom a *dot* or 'bride price' is paid).

Other writers have described this (or similar systems) as primitive-communal, that is, classless. Rey presented a very careful definition of class:

> We shall speak of class conflict in any society in which a particular group controls a surplus product, the partial or total use of which is for the reproduction of the relations

of dependence between the direct producers and this group. (Rey 1975: 60)

Capitalism too is defined by an exchange relation (the sale of labour-power) and in the capitalist mode, as in lineage societies, the surplus product may not be devoted to the personal consumption of the ruling class. It has been argued that chiefs (elders) are not a distinct class, because juniors succeed in their turn, but Rey retorted that the majority of the population (slaves and their descendants, women, most free males) are excluded.

Slavery and the exchange of slaves are clearly of vital importance to the history of this area. It should be understood that slavery within lineage societies was quite different from slavery in the plantations of the Americas. When an offence was committed (theft, witchcraft) the offender could be handed over to the chief of the offended group, so enslavement always took an individual outside his group of origin. The receiving chief could pass the slave on in a further exchange or settle him in his own group. Once settled, he was no longer saleable and acquired a status little different in practice from other members of the group. Slave production did not exist, nor did a permanent status of chattel slavery. Rey argued that this 'circulation of men' together with the 'circulation of women' (as wives) functioned to redistribute population from over-populated to under-populated groups, in a society in which population was the main resource.

It is easy to see how this system fitted in with the slave trade. It is often argued that commodity exchange with merchant capital has a dissolving effect on pre-capitalist societies, and one would think at first sight that the export of literally millions of slaves (from Africa as a whole) over a period extending from the sixteenth to the late nineteenth century would have had the most appallingly destructive effects. Rey argues, on the contrary, that lineage societies remained in good shape during this period, since the trade in slaves was no more than an extension of the normal functioning of these societies.

European traders acquired slaves through the coastal kingdoms, hierarchical lineage societies each of which monopolized one of the few usable harbours. Traders bought slaves through the chiefs of important lineages, so trade with Europeans was assimilated to the system of exchanges be-tween chiefs. Coastal lineage societies received considerable revenues (in commissions and the like) from the slave trade which could be used to acquire slaves, over and above the number exported, who could then be settled and incor-porated into the society. 'Throughout the whole period of the slave trade the kingdom of Loango enriched itself both in goods and in men' (*Colonialisme*: 279). Much of the same goes for lineage societies further in the interior, which served as a transmission belt moving slaves towards the coast, and European products inwards. The category of 'prestige goods' came, during this period, to consist almost exclusively of European products. The wealth and power of the dominant chiefs increased and the network of exchange relations between them was extended rather than being undermined. 'The depopulation of lineage societies [was] slowed down by the mechanisms of control over the circulation of men, and above all compensated by the mechanisms of reinsertion of a part of the slaves who came into them' (*Colonialisme*: 279). The main areas of depopulation were far inland, in areas without a lineage structure or where the lineage mode of production was weak, and failed to provide for a net acquisition of slaves. This illustrates Rey's general thesis that exchange relations with capitalism do not necessarily break down pre-capitalist societies or pave the way for the estab-lishment of capitalist relations of production.

As the slave trade declined (for reasons external to Africa), European merchants tried to develop trade in products as a substitute. The products involved were primarily ivory and rubber, products of hunting and gathering obtained in traditional and extremely wasteful ways, which threatened to destroy the natural sources of these products. In 1898-1900, the French state, having taken formal authority over the area, tried to establish 'rational' production for export by dividing the territory between 'concessionary companies' (*sociétés concessionaires*). This episode is important in Rey's argument, since the failure of this initiative is his main piece of evidence for the incapacity of capitalism to establish itself by primarily economic means. The concessionary companies found they had to deal with local chiefs, since French colonial power had not, in practice, been imposed. Attempts to introduce capitalist production proved unprofitable since wages (paid to the chiefs) were high, and supplies of labour-power and provisions for the workers were unreliable. The companies ended up continuing the traditional pattern of trade by barter, on a limited scale, from trading posts in the interior instead of at the coasts. Trade was restricted in volume, since lineage society only met its needs for prestige goods through exchange. Subsistence continued to rest on traditional production outside the sphere of the market. Because of the wasteful methods of production, supplies dried up and the companies effectively ceased to exist.

The period from the completion of military conquest in 1920, to 1934 was characterized, according to Rey, by the dominance of a *colonial mode of production*, defined by the forced recruitment of labour and the forced sale of products. This was the first stage in the articulation of the capitalist and lineage modes of production, corresponding to the stage of primitive accumulation in the homelands of capitalism; the previous contacts between capitalist and lineage societies were wholly external, and did not constitute an articulation. The centrepiece was the construction of the Congo–Ocean railway by forcibly recruited labour, an enterprise that cost fifteen or twenty thousand lives.

In the beginning, after the failure of the concessionary companies, a 'subsistence' society only exchanging with commercial capital to meet its needs for prestige goods. Afterwards, in the period from 1934 (or even 1932) to today, 'free' sale of labour power ... and continually growing sale of products. This is because, during the period of construction of the railway, workers who had lived in the self sufficient subsistence economy became simultaneously wage earners, and buyers; while the men who remained in the villages and above all the women became sellers of provisions. The unity of the producers and consumers was broken. ... During a first stage workers on the one hand, products on the other were obtained by force, because the society did not know what to do with the money that was forced on it in 'payment'. ... But soon enough the situation was reversed and money became the intermediary, not only for goods, but also for ... the bride price. (*Colonialisme*: 365-6)

The colonial mode of production was not set up deliberately to transform lineage society, though the administration certainly had in mind a 'civilizing mission' (for civilization read capitalism). They had little choice in the circumstances they found themselves in.

In 1921, the administration were forced by facts to use the only form of intervention which was adequate to the scale of their projects: the reorganisation of the mode of production itself.... We consider that a very large number of economic and even technical choices which were made had the essential function of transforming the social mode of production (whether or not that was the conscious aim of those in charge – G. Sautter does not judge them to have been intelligent enough to have consciously attempted such an intervention). (*Colonialisme*: 367)

The lineage mode of production adapted to the needs of capitalism through the monetarization of the *dot* (bride price). Rey stressed that the social relations of the lineage mode of production are expressed in money form, just as money rent is, according to Rey, a monetary expression of a feudal relation of production. Money circulating among chiefs of lineages as bride-price payments is generally not diverted to other purposes. At the same time, the chiefs require young men to make money payments to them as a contribution to the bride price. The sums of money available for payment in the form of bride price have thus continually increased, and the level of the bride price has inflated correspondingly. Young men are forced to work for wages or sell products in order to pay their share, so the lineage relation of production, the control of chiefs over the circulation of women, serves the needs of capitalism by forcing products and, above all, labour-power on to the market. Simultaneously, the inflation of the bride price keeps it out of reach of a wage earner unless it is augmented by the accumulated hoard of the chief, so the chiefs keep their hold; the lineage relation is maintained.

During the colonial period, the political structure of lineage society was first disregarded and disrupted, then reconstituted, in much the same way as the economic-social structure. The traditional system of chiefs was absorbed into the administration, and previous patterns of dominance between tribes, clans and lineages reappeared. The nascent indigenous bourgeoisie and the political leadership of the independent state of Congo-Brazzaville are derived from the same group who controlled and profited by the slave trade, a *comprador* group with centuries of experience in acting as intermediaries between capitalism and native society.

The stage is set for the neo-colonial period. In this stage, capitalism can see to its own reproduction by purely economic means, but needs a pre-capitalist mode alongside it to provide a source of additional labour-power and also to provide food for the capitalist labour force. There is less to be said about this period than about its predecessors, since the capitalist mode of production now dominates, and the workings of capitalism are relatively well understood. In Congo-Brazzaville this stage got fully under way in the 1950s, after an interlude of twenty years in which first depression and then world war held up development. The dominant motive force in this period is investment by metropolitan finance capital in the export sector. Only metropolitan capital has the means to invest on a large scale: the colonial period had created a suitable environment for capitalism, but had not formed any substantial capitalist class. The transformation of the lineage mode had ensured the availability of plentiful, cheap labour, and the natural resources of the region were now open to capitalist exploitation. The external market dominated, since the internal market, created by the separation of producers from the means of production, was primarily a market for food, met by small-scale production.

Rey's most important claim about the neo-colonial period is that development is still held up by the persistence of the pre-capitalist (lineage) mode of production. This is no longer a matter of labour scarcity, but of the dominance of 'tribalist' politics in the newly independent state of Congo-Brazzaville (though this is asserted rather than demonstrated):

> The reinforcement of the lineage system is undoubtedly an obstacle to 'development'. Many well-intentioned European observers believe that the capitalist states of the West could, from a technical point of view, have an interest in supporting the development of an efficient modern bureaucracy as against the tribalist bureaucracy.

251

> They forget one thing, that capitalism is not interested in the technical aspect of development (production of use values), but in the social aspect (development of capitalist relations of production and above all the extraction of surplus value). (*Colonialisme*: 462)

For this reason, capitalist states support tribalism and maintain the lineage mode of production and, in other parts of the world, maintain other pre-capitalist forms. 'Throughout the world, capitalism today plays a fundamentally counter-revolutionary role: it keeps the most archaic forms in existence; it restores them when they are threatened (see for example the sultanates of Chad)' (*Colonialisme*: 463). Pre-capitalist forms of exploitation are maintained by capitalism and stand or fall with it. Capitalist expansion will not remove the burden of these archaic forms except at a snail's pace. Only a socialist revolution can remove the double burdens suffered by the workers of underdeveloped countries; victory over capitalism will sweep away pre-capitalist forms as well.

Rey's analysis is open to criticism. First, it can be argued that lineage societies are in fact classless, primitive-communal systems. This criticism would harm Rey's claim that analysis must be founded on the defining relations of production of the dominant mode, but would otherwise leave his account untouched. Second, the notion of a 'colonial' mode of production is profoundly unsatisfactory. The idea seems to be a product of Rey's Althusserian structuralism (which he later rejected); there must be a dominant mode, and it could not at that stage be capitalism since the conditions of capitalist reproduction were not yet assured. This is only a problem on the local level; capitalism had a secure base for its reproduction in its homelands. Rey insisted, in other contexts, that a mode of production must be defined by a relation between classes which reproduces the domination of one class over the other. What is this relation in the colonial mode of production? What classes does it connect? The colonial organization clearly did not reproduce itself: rather it produced the conditions of capitalist domination. There is no need to describe colonialism as a mode of production at all. We can simply describe forced recruitment of labour and forced sale of products as a form of state intervention generated by the articulation of the capitalist and lineage modes of production at a certain stage of development, and serving the interests of capital.

A more serious question is whether the area in Congo-Brazzaville studied by Rey is typical even of other parts of Africa, let alone of other continents (cf. Crummey and Stewart 1981; van Binsbergen and Geschiere 1985). Rey's assertion that lineage societies could absorb the impact of the slave trade and survive with their essential structures intact does not seem to apply to other parts of Africa. The destructive effects of the slave trade in many areas are fairly well documented (e.g. Amin 1976: 319-22, and references cited there; for a more general discussion of slavery in the history of capitalism, see Miles 1987). Arrighi found that in other parts of Africa the indigenous inhabitants were willing from the start to sell agricultural products and labour-power, though only if the price was right. Force was used in southern Africa to displace Africans from the land and force down the price of labour-power, as it was in Europe; it was not used to force the population into the market, but to impose the desired terms on them. It remains true, however, that force was used, and that it came from outside and not from an indigenous ruling class, so Rey's analysis is not wholly undermined.

10.5 LEYS

The first wave of writing on modes of production and classes in the Third World understandably concentrated on the persistence of pre-capitalist relations of production in agriculture. In so far as changes in class structure came into the picture, the stress was on the formation of a proletariat from the agricultural population. Many writers accepted the dependency theorists' pessimism about the prospects for capitalist development, and explained what they assumed to be slow development in terms of the persistence of pre-capitalist economic systems. Amin (discussed in chapter 8) is a paradigm example of the way analysis of modes of production can be slotted into a dependency framework.

Leys's study of the formation of a national bourgeoisie in Kenya (1978) marked a new stage in the debate, particularly as he had previously established himself as a leading exponent of dependency theory in the African context (Leys 1975), a perspective he now explicitly rejected. Kenya, he argued, had experienced fairly rapid growth over a substantial period, accompanied by a steady extension of capitalist relations of production, increasing productivity in industry, and a (small) net inflow of capital. Dependency theorists had claimed that examples of growth in the Third World were 'exceptional'; the Kenyan case could not be explained away so easily. At the same time, Leys did not go all the way with Warren's claim that a general process of capitalist development was under way (on Warren, see chapter 11 below); instead he argued for the study of specific cases to establish why development proceeds more rapidly in some places than in others.

Before colonization, a class of 'accumulators', in what is now the central region of Kenya, had gained control of land and livestock through migration to new territories, raiding, and trade. Installed as 'chiefs' by the colonial state, they found access to land curtailed by settlers, but were able to defend and even advance their status through education, wage-labour, and commerce. They also established a dominant position in the nationalist movement, and emerged as the leaders of an effective power bloc when the country achieved independence. This group, who became a nascent 'national bourgeoisie', were able to transmit capital accumulated before conquest through the colonial period, and emerge as the dominant class at the end of it. (Leys credited M. Cowen for laying the basis of this analysis, mainly in unpublished papers.)

The state played a crucial role in the next stage: 'the state apparatus superintended a series of measures which rapidly enlarged the sphere and rate of indigenous capital accumulation' (Leys 1978: 250). Settler capitalism had created the preconditions for capitalist development (a proletariat, infrastructure). The national bourgeoisie, sponsored by the state, displaced settlers in sector after sector, starting with agriculture, then urban real estate, commerce, and finally manufacturing. Leys insisted that the state did not play an independent role in this process, but 'reflected the existing class power of the indigenous bourgeoisie, based on the accumulation of capital they had already achieved' (1978: 251). He rejected as 'mystification' the idea of a 'modernising élite' and equally of the state as mediator between foreign and domestic capital. While one can see his point, he may have overstated it; surely the state has some degree of autonomy, and a political élite has to balance conflicting pressures and construct a workable power bloc. It seems too crude to treat the state as no more than the passive instrument of a dominant class.

In the 1970s, primitive accumulation continued through 'modern forms of plunder', winked at by the state, but there was also a movement of indigenous capital from commerce, with its quick returns, to manufacturing, where returns are slower but more secure, because there is less competition. The national bourgeoisie stabilized its position and started to develop all the appurtenances of an established bourgeois class: the emergence of different fractions of capital, of associated adjutant groups (lawyers, accountants, and so on), of a distinct bourgeois culture and life style (private schools, magazines, and the like), and of class organizations (the Federation of Kenyan Employers) and class consciousness.

Leys did not claim that the Kenyan case was typical; it depended on certain special features of Kenyan experience, notably the existence of a pre-capitalist class of accumulators sufficiently developed to survive the colonial era, and the existence of a settler class which established the pre-conditions for capital accumulation ready for the national bourgeoisie to take over. Other cases would have their own special features (Lubeck 1987 contains studies by various writers of different parts of Africa). Leys did claim

> that capitalist production relations may be considerably extended in a periphery social formation, and the productive forces may be considerably expanded within and through them, for reasons having primarily to do with the configuration of class forces preceding and during the colonial period: and that the limits of such development cannot be determined from the sort of general considerations advanced by underdevelopment and dependency theory. (Leys 1978: 261)

10.6 GALLAGHER AND ROBINSON

The history of empire and of imperialism has, of course, been studied extensively, but most non-Marxist historians have been very unwilling to theorize or generalize about imperialism as a whole. Refusal to see the wood for the trees is almost an occupational qualification for historians. One very notable exception is the work of John Gallagher and Ronald Robinson; I shall argue that they anticipated some of the themes discussed in other sections of this chapter, albeit using a very different style and terminology, and that Marxists can learn from their work. The seminal article on the 'imperialism of free trade' (Gallagher and Robinson 1953) was followed by a full-scale study of *Africa and the Victorians* (Robinson and Gallagher 1961). Some more recent articles (Robinson 1972, 1986) summarize what Robinson now calls the *excentric* view of imperialism; for a full bibliography of his work to 1988, see Porter and Holland (1988).

The 1953 article started by rejecting the idea that the 'free trade' era of the mid-nineteenth century was a period of indifference to empire. As Gallagher and Robinson pointed out, Britain did not abandon any territory in this period, indeed the formal empire expanded significantly, while the area of informal control was extended even further. A second theme, stressed more strongly by Robinson in his later writings, is a rejection of the Eurocentrism of existing theories, that is, of the idea that the major developments in the history of empire must be explained by corresponding developments in the imperial centres, and that the colonies were simply passive victims of events at the centre. The excentric theory ('excentric', centred outside Europe, is a manufactured opposite of Eurocentric) emphasized the role of local collaborators with imperialism (*compradors*, in Marxist and radical terminology), an idea reminiscent of Frank's (later) notion of a chain of metropolis satellite relations.

Imperialists aimed to get 'empire on the cheap', the maximum return for the minimum cost and risk. They therefore preferred to manipulate rather than to control directly, and they relied on local collaborators wherever possible, and used local resources. The imposition of formal empire represented a failure of this policy, and was adopted reluctantly when informal control broke down. Different non-

European societies had different structures, and hence offered different opportunities for manipulation and different sorts of potential collaborators. Differences in the history of imperialism in different areas can be explained by differences in the structures of indigenous societies, and the evolution of imperialism by the evolution of politics and society in the periphery, not by changes in the centre.

Robinson (1972, 1986) drew a distinction between areas of European settlement, on the one hand, and Africa and Asia, on the other. White colonists were ideal collaborators: tied culturally to Europe, ready and willing to seek out mutually profitable patterns of trade and investment. Hence the informal British empire in Latin America and the steady shift of power to local administrations in Canada, Australia, and so on. By contrast, in Africa and Asia, the 'institutional barriers to Europeanisation proved intractable' (1972: 276), a local bourgeoisie was lacking, and the imperial powers had to turn to ruling oligarchies and local élites. As these areas were drawn into the net, local political systems were destabilized, and sooner or later the imperialists were forced to choose between retreat or taking over and 'reconstructing collaboration from the inside' (1986: 278). The exact pattern still depended on the available local resources. At one end of the scale, where the imbalance of power was at its greatest, pro-consuls 'demolished indigenous structures' and 'imposed the most inordinate terms' (1986: 278); interestingly, Robinson named Congo-Brazzaville as an example (cf. Rey on the colonial stage, section 10.4 above). More often, local structures could be reconstructed but retained and made to bear most of the costs, and provide most of the personnel, of empire; divided India conquered itself, and paid the costs into the bargain.

The end of (formal) empire is explained in similar terms. Imperialism depended on a series of 'contracts': between European powers (the conventions dividing Africa, for example); between imperialists and collaborators; between collaborators and the mass of the subject population. After 1940, these broke down fairly rapidly, with the rise of nationalist movements and the decline in the power of the European colonial powers relative to the USA and USSR. Empire became too expensive to maintain (cf. Szymanski 1981: 119-20).

What are we to make of this account? I see little or nothing in it that is incompatible with Marxism (if that matters), at least as far as the main outline is concerned. Robinson was surely right to remark that the 'endless debate as to whether imperialism is economically or politically motivated seems ultimately futile' (1986: 281). It is true that accepting the Gallagher and Robinson story would involve abandoning the idea that imperialism entered a new and quite different stage at the turn of the century, but that idea looks fairly thread-bare anyway. On the other hand, I suspect that Gallagher and Robinson took the 'excentric' element of their theory a bit too far. They simply took the expansive impulse of (capitalist) Europe for granted, seeking to explain everything by the obstacles it found in its way in the periphery. Robinson (1972), for example, asserted almost casually that Europe was the source of a drive to integrate non-European economies into the system as markets and investments and to secure them against rivals, and assumed without discussion that Europe had a great advantage in economic and military power over other areas throughout the process, allowing it to assert control, at a cost, wherever and whenever needed. The extent and character of the European lead surely varied over time, which may help to explain the relative costs of different options, while the opportunities of gain from (formal or informal) control also varied over time as a result of economic and political changes in the capitalist centres. If the history of imperialism is to be explained by the balance of costs and benefits (to the imperialists) offered by different courses of action, it must be recognized that costs and benefits were affected by developments in the centre as well as in the periphery.

10.7 SUMMARY

The classical Marxists defined modes of production in terms of the relation between the direct producers and their immediate exploiters, and treated them as successive stages of social development. This approach can still be defended, but it does not seem to work well when applied to modern underdeveloped countries. One alternative is to redefine modes of production as stages of development on a world level and to deny the relevance of production relations, but this leaves little to put in their place. Another possibility is to modify the conception of modes of production as successive stages by arguing that a variety of relations of production can coexist within a single society, either permanently or during a very prolonged transition, an 'articulation' of modes of production. In itself, this only provides a framework for analysis, but a number of writers have used it to construct illuminating accounts of development in particular places.

Two main questions emerge from the debate. First, how important are relations of production in explaining development or underdevelopment? For some authors they are central, while others explain the persistence of underdevelopment in terms of factors which can occur in a variety of social systems, such as the extraction of surplus, or by unequal exchange in a wholly capitalist world. My own view is that a single explanation is unlikely to apply to all cases at all stages of development, so a complete theory may draw on both views. State policy matters: an important and growing body of literature links analysis of modes of production to class alliances and state policy. Political independence is important, because it greatly increases the scope for action by local political forces, though it does not by itself guarantee national political autonomy. Second (and this is a very closely related issue), how can changes in the relations of production be analysed? Some writers regard production relations as very durable, only subject to alteration as a result of catastrophic events (such as conquest) or of protracted class struggles. Others regard 'forms of exploitation' or 'modes in which labour is recruited and compensated' as fairly easily altered in response to economic conditions. Again, it is not clear to me that one can safely generalize.

11

After Imperialism?

The classical Marxists thought of capitalism as an engine of change, advancing in a generally predictable direction through a series of crises and disturbances. There was no presumption that whoever was on top at any particular stage would stay on top, because capitalism generates *uneven* development. Marx, for example, expected full capitalist development in India, once independence was achieved, and Lenin expected that the centres of accumulation would shift from more advanced to less advanced areas in search of cheap labour, accessible natural resources and higher profits. The end of formal empire might be a crucial turning point, seen in this framework. By contrast, many post-war Marxist theorists assumed that capitalism always accentuates existing differences in levels of development. In Frank's picture, a chain of metropolis-satellite relations ensures development for the metropolis and underdevelopment for the satellites, reinforcing the chain. This leads to a prediction that the United States, as the most powerful imperialist centre, will continue to dominate the system, and that underdeveloped countries are bound to remain subordinate unless they break away from the capitalist world system altogether through socialist revolutions. The end of formal empire is of no significance, in this view (which was, after all, first advanced to account for the poor performance of independent Latin American countries).

The classical Marxist view, never completely lost, returned to prominence in the 1970s and 1980s. The modes of production debate (chapter 10 above), with its emphasis on internal causes of underdevelopment, is part of the revival of a classical perspective. This chapter deals with recent trends in the development of capitalism, and with the way they have been analysed in the new climate of opinion among Marxists. The first section is a brief discussion of the multinational corporation, the latest form of capitalist enterprise. The second section surveys debates about the future of central capital: is US domination assured, or is a return to rivalry between relatively equal capitalist centres likely? The final section is concerned with the future of capitalism in the periphery: is the Third World doomed to remain underdeveloped, or is the complete capitalist industrialization of the world a real possibility?

11.1 MULTINATIONAL CORPORATIONS

Multinational corporations are capitalist firms which operate in more than one country. There is no clear line between multinational and national firms, since all multinationals started as national firms and expanded their operations abroad by degrees. Multinationals are generally thought of as large; this need not necessarily be so, but most of the world's largest firms are multinational and larger multinationals are the principal subject of concern. Some writers restrict their attention to firms with production activities in more than one country, excluding commercial and financial companies, which are also rapidly becoming multinational. Multinationals may alternatively be referred to as transnational or international firms; the terms are (usually) synonymous.

By far the most important fact about multinationals is that they are *capitalist* firms. Both national and multinational firms sell products and buy means of production in markets that are usually fairly well integrated on a world scale, and both buy labour-power at wages substantially determined by local labour markets. Both are subject to the same competitive imperative to minimize costs and to accumulate. Not surprisingly these circumstances, determined by the working of the capitalist system on a world scale, place close limits on their behaviour. Consider, for example, a system without multinationals, in which firms in several different countries compete in selling, say, raw materials. The lowest cost supplier will generally succeed, while the others fail. All try to reduce costs to the minimum. Now compare that with a multinational firm operating in all the different countries concerned. It, too, will concentrate production in the lowest cost location, and try to minimize costs. The outcome is likely to be exactly the same. It is pointless to attack foreign firms for 'disregarding the needs of the national economy' when there is no reason to suppose that domestic capital would behave any differently. Criticism must be directed at the system. This example also suggests that state control of industry is likely to be relatively ineffective as long as the imperatives of competition in a world market remain. The second important fact about (large) multinationals is that they are large, and may have a degree of monopoly power. Large firms have the organizational resources to control operations scattered over several countries and to deal with the legal and financial complications involved. Much of the literature, especially on multinationals in underdeveloped countries, conflates the effects of capitalism, of monopoly capitalism, and of foreign capital under a single heading: the impact of multinational companies. This does not make for analytical clarity.

It would be a mistake to overstate the novelty of multi-nationals. Merchant capital has operated internationally since its beginnings. The organization and financing of mines and plantations abroad also goes back to the beginnings of capitalism. By the late nineteenth century, international flows of capital were occurring on a large scale, and a noticeable part of this flow of capital took the form of direct investment, that is the investment of capital in productive activity abroad by a firm already engaged in production in its home country. Multinational firms even today often have the bulk of their activities located in the state where they have legal domicile and their head office. Nevertheless, it is possible to speak today, if only as a tendency, of companies which have a 'global perspective', and look over the whole world for potential locations for production.

The emergence and significance of multinationals cannot be adequately analysed at the level of the firm; it must be seen as part of a much wider process of internationalization of production and of capital (see Palloix 1973). Multinational firms can be seen as organizations that channel the inter-national movement of goods, of capital, of technical knowledge and organizational capacity, and of skilled personnel. They are not by any means the only channel for any of these flows. Relations between capitalist firms (within a single country or in different countries) can range across a whole spectrum from impersonal market exchange to incorporation under a single ownership; there are, for example, licensing arrangements for the use of technology and brand names, joint ventures, management contracts, and 'turnkey' contracts for the supply of complete industrial plants together with the necessary training.

The emergence of multinationals is a result of the concentration and centralization of capital on a world scale, in the context of the continuing internationalization of capitalism. It would be very surprising if the formation of giant firms were confined within national boundaries. Bukharin analysed these processes (chapter 6 above), but expected the formation of national blocs of capital to predominate; it has not turned out quite that way. The multiplication of links between capitalist firms across national boundaries represents the internationalization of the 'relations of mutual dependence and domination' described by Hilferding at the level of a single national economy (chapter 5 above).

Michalet (1976) argued that the development of multinationals is the defining feature of the imperialist stage of capitalism. Orthodox economic theory deals with relations between distinct nation states, assuming free mobility of capital and labour within but not between nations. This approach he called 'international economics'. Many Marxists (Marx, Luxemburg, Amin) have adopted this approach. The alternative approach, 'world economics', conceives of production and capitalist relations of production as international, or rather world-wide. Lenin was not guilty of adopting the first of these approaches (even Bukharin does not completely escape the charge) but was incomplete and ambiguous in his analysis. Michalet thus felt free to 'reread' (rewrite?) Lenin, making capital export the fundamental characteristic of Lenin's imperialist stage, but insisting that the essential element is not the export of money capital but the export of capitalist relations of production. Capitalist relations of production on a world scale are created by direct investment by firms or financial groups which create subsidiaries abroad (as opposed to 'portfolio' investment through loans, or the purchase of shares as purely financial assets). The emergence of large monopoly firms and of finance capital is a necessary precondition for the creation of overseas subsidiaries. Michalet thus identified imperialism (in Lenin's sense) directly with capital export and the emergence of multinational firms. He dated the start of this trend to around 1900, though it was held back by depression and war, so it appears even now as a novel phenomenon.

He described three main forms of capital export. First, capital export in Lenin's time was aimed mainly at obtaining raw materials. This is of declining relative importance now. Second, it may be aimed at penetrating markets that cannot be effectively penetrated by exports, generating a structure in which production facilities are replicated in several different countries. This is the dominant form today, as a result of oligopolistic rivalry (and, possibly, general 'realization' problems; Michalet's argument is unclear). Third, and of increasing importance, capital export may be aimed at exploiting cheap labour to produce goods for re-export to the 'home' country or to third markets. Michalet particularly stressed this form, which leads to the creation of integrated production organizations cutting across national boundaries. There is a real movement to transfer production to the low-wage periphery, not merely by way of 'import substitution' (the second motive above) but to produce for the markets of the centre and the whole world. I have already mentioned this possibility and argued that it has been neglected by most Marxist writers. Michalet, however, argued that it will not eliminate the centre–periphery gap, since capital-intensive methods of production keep employment in the periphery low and hence keep wages down. He did not, however (except in passing; 1976: 154), note the possibility that wage and employment levels in the centre might be dragged down towards those in the periphery.

Like many other writers, Michalet argued that the growth of multinational companies and of relations of production on a world scale represents a lessening of the importance of the nation state. Here I think he went wrong. The internationalization of capital makes a conception of the world system in terms of distinct *national economics* increasingly irrelevant, but it does not follow that the *nation state* is unimportant as a site of class conflict, of political integration, and of a state apparatus that has at its command more potent weapons than those of monetary and fiscal policy. I shall argue below that the nation state in this sense is a very important and durable institution.

I shall not give a complete survey of the literature on multinationals; it is rather scrappy and much of it is irrelevant to the topic of imperialism. It is better to look at the effect of multinationals, along with other aspects of capitalism, in the context of more specific problems. Radice (1975) provides a useful collection of articles, which also has a bibliography. Perhaps the most influential writer on the subject has been Hymer, who started out writing from a critical position within the mainstream of economics, then adopted a Marxist standpoint not long before his tragic death (see Hymer 1972, 1976; Hymer and Rowthorn 1970). The most important result of the emergence of multinationals is that the expansion of the national capital of a particular country (i.e. of the firms based there) is no longer tied directly to the expansion of the national economy. The implications of this are explored in the next two sections.

11.2 CENTRAL CAPITAL: UNITY OR RIVALRY?

Multinational corporations, by definition, operate in several nation states. Other capitalist firms are involved in the world economy though production for export, through the use of imported materials or components, through the use of technology licensed from abroad, through the sale of licenses to others, and so on. Commercial and financial capital is also internationalized. None of this means that any specific capital lacks a nationality, a definite base in a particular capitalist nation state. The idea that multinational firms are somehow above the petty conflicts of nation states is a fiction. Virtually all multinationals have a very clear national base; each company has historical roots in a particular country, and in most cases its top management is recruited in its home country, and the largest part of its capital and production is still located there. The few exceptions include firms based in small countries (e.g. Nestlé of Switzerland) and two Anglo-Dutch giants (Shell and Unilever), which have dual nationality.

Capitalism and the nation state grew up together. The analytical primacy, in Marxist theory, of the economic over the political does not imply a historical order, nor does it imply that the division of the world into distinct nation states and the determination of their boundaries can be explained at the economic level. At the beginnings of capitalism, and for a long time after, the productive activities of industrial capital were locally based, while the markets it served were as often local or international as national. It would be a mistake to think of an integrated national economy or national 'social formation' coming into existence and then conjuring up a state to match. Rather, the existence of a state (and the extension of its boundaries to the point where the resistance of other nation states limited further expansion) created and delimited national interests, national markets, and so on. Each capital looked to its 'own' state for support against other capitals forming in other nation states and, through the common need for state support, formed an alliance with other regional capitals within the same nation. The need for compromise between different sectional interests within the capitalist class, and the need to contain conflict with other classes, created a dense network of political and ideological links, which is what constitutes a 'nation'.

As capital extends outside national boundaries, it must, of course, create links with other states as well, at least to the extent that it needs conditions that can only be provided by state action (a legal framework, a monetary system, infrastructure). Murray (1971) discussed these questions, and drew the general conclusion that internationalization weakens the nation state *vis-à-vis* private capital, a conclusion contested by Warren (1971) and (briefly but cogently) by Rowthorn (1971), who argued that the key question is not about the power of the state *vis-à-vis* particular capitals, but about how a state can support its own capital when it operates abroad. The essential point is that capital needs the support of a home state to protect its interests. The whole range of needs that are met internally by the state (protection of property, enforcement of contracts, and so on) are met internationally by negotiations and agreements between states. A large part of the diplomatic apparatus through which nation states deal with each other (in time of peace) has grown up precisely to negotiate the regulation of commercial activities. A stateless corporation, while not in principle impossible, would be at a disadvantage, since it would have no representation in this system.

Rowthorn (1971) took the analysis further, looking at the particular example of Britain. British capital is relatively strong, while the British national economy is relatively weak. Individual firms respond by shifting more of their activities abroad, where growth prospects are better, thus further weakening the British economy. In the end this weakens the British state's capacity to defend their interests, while 'nationalist' policy measures to improve the performance of the national economy are blocked by the threat of retaliation against the vulnerable foreign interests of British capital. 'Leading sections of the British bourgeoisie have been effectively "denationalised", not through their own weakness, but through the weakness of the British state and their own home base' (Rowthorn 1971). Hence the anxiety of British capital that Britain should joint the EEC, which may provide, ultimately, a more substantial home base. The strength of a particular nation state and its capacity to defend the interests of its national capital thus depends on the strength of the national economy as well as the national capital.

The history of the capitalist world economy has seen periods of acute rivalry between capitalist powers, separated by periods of relative peace. Marx wrote at a time when it seemed reasonable to predict the obsolescence of the nation state, while Lenin and his contemporaries analysed a period when inter-imperialist rivalry was at its most violent. After the Second World War, the United States emerged as very much the strongest capitalist power, and when Marxist discussion of imperialism revived it was generally assumed, almost without debate, that inter-imperialist rivalry had been superseded by US dominance. This seemed particularly obvious to those American writers who took a special interest in Latin America, the area most clearly within the American sphere of influence. However, the rapid recovery of the European and Japanese economies, the weakness of the US dollar and the American defeat in Vietnam raised doubts about this view of the present stage of imperialism, and provoked a fresh debate in the 1970s.

A number of writers anticipated a fusion of national capitals within the European Community (EC), to form a unified European capital. Mandel (1967, 1975) predicted such a development, which was also discussed, more cautiously, by Rowthorn (1971). It must be said that the formation of truly European companies (as opposed to the takeover and absorption of a company from one country by another from a different country) did not progress at the pace that these authors expected; it was not until the 1980s that any number of European companies started to emerge, and then only rather slowly. Fusion of capital on a European scale would strengthen European capital *vis-à-vis* that of America, while continued divisions in Europe correspondingly favour American capital. The prediction of Europe-wide fusion of national capitals is of course bound up with the possible evolution of the EC into something closer to a nation state; again development has proceeded, but only very slowly. The slow development of European unity reinforces the argument above that nationality is a very deeply rooted thing; the dense network of political links that constitutes a nation state represents the institutionalization of a multitude of compromises between classes, fractions of classes and other interest groups, which is very difficult to reconstruct on a new basis.

An alternative possibility raised in the 1970s debate was that national capitals would merge under US dominance, as American multinationals absorb enterprises from other states or subordinate them through licensing agreements, subcontracting arrangements and so on. This seems to be Poulanzas's position (1975, chapter 1). This case, however, differs little from one in which national capitals remain distinct, but in which other imperialist nations accept a subordinate role because they know that any challenge to American domination would be sure to fail; this prospect was presented forcefully by Nicolaus (1969). Many writers thought that US capital was overwhelmingly dominant in modern imperialism, without spelling out the details (for example, Magdoff and Sweezy 1969; Magdoff 1969). At that time, American corporations predominated in the listings of the world's largest firms and American domestic production and overseas investments were much larger than those of any other country. The size and growth of American investments in Europe seemed particularly significant. The breaking up of European colonial empires enabled American capital to penetrate areas of the world formerly denied to it (hence American 'anti-colonialism' in the post-war period). American military dominance in the non-communist world was, and is, obvious.

The trend of development was less clear. America clearly enjoyed a quite exceptional superiority immediately after the Second World War, and one would expect some relative recovery by other powers. Some writers argued that more rapid growth in Europe and Japan as compared to America was no more than a return to the trend (e.g. Poulanzas 1975), while others claimed that it was a real threat to American dominance, presaging an epoch of relative equality between the main capitalist powers. Mandel (1967, 1975) and Rowthorn (1971) both predicted a narrowing of the gap between America and other imperialist centres and a consequent intensification of rivalry. Rather oddly, on both sides of the debate attention focused on the relative strength of American and European capital. The relative failure of moves towards European unity hampered the competitive strength of European capital; it was justly said that the largest beneficiary of the formation of the EC was American capital in Europe, which was much quicker to treat Europe as a single market. However, even in the 1970s it should have been clear that Japanese capital was the most formidable rival; it is not divided on national lines, and maintained a rate of growth quite unprecedented in the history of capitalism for some three decades.

The debate centred on the interpretation of the large flow of capital from America to Europe and the consequent rapid growth of American capital in Europe. Ironically, the 1980s have seen a massive reversal of this flow, with American nationalists expressing the same fears about foreign ownership that were heard in Europe in the 1970s. Poulanzas (1975) saw American investment in Europe as decisive evidence of American hegemony, on the grounds that the export of capital is the dominant factor in the expansion of capital in the imperialist period, but offered little evidence for this assertion beyond a reference to Lenin. Rowthorn, drawing on his work with Hymer (Rowthorn and Hymer 1971), countered ingeniously, pointing out that American capital still operated predominantly in America, European capital in Europe. Since European markets were expanding more rapidly than American, American capital had to increase its penetration of the European market simply to maintain its relative position. (Expansion in other markets could not offset the loss of ground relative to Europe, since the Japanese market proved difficult to penetrate, and other markets were very small by comparison.) Combining the effects of market growth rates and changing market shares, 'big American firms are having and will have increasing difficulty in keeping ahead of their foreign rivals' (Rowthorn 1971; 163).

Rowthorn thus agreed that American investment in Europe was, in itself, a gain by American capital relative to its rivals, offset by the fact that European companies still had the larger share of the more rapidly growing European market. Mandel (1967) similarly argued that American expansion in Europe was a 'defeat' for European capital. They are open to criticism, because the relative rate of growth of different markets cannot be taken as given. Not only was the more rapid growth in Europe the result as well as the cause of the greater dynamism of European capital, but the inflow of investment from America may well have contributed to European growth, helping rather than hindering the growth of European capital. In more general terms, the expansion of one capital may complement, rather than compete with, the expansion of others.

If we accept that there is a trend towards relative equality between a small number of capitalist centres, as Mandel and Rowthorn argue, we must ask what kind of relation between them is likely. Rowthorn took rivalry and antagonism for granted: 'Relations between capitals are always to some extent antagonistic, the degree of antagonism depending both on the area of actual or potential competition and on its intensity' (Rowthorn 1971). This is undoubtedly true of individual capitals at a micro-economic level; the overall rate of expansion of the market in which they are competing with other firms is beyond their control, and they are struggling over shares of a given market. However, it is not clear that similar antagonism must exist between capitalist states (Jenkins 1987 distinguished between inter-firm and inter-state rivalry). Once the overall rate of expansion of the whole economy is treated as a variable, the expansion of one capital may be complementary to that of another. The state is in a position to try to reconcile the two aspects of the relation between capitals, complementarity and antagonism. It may thus be possible to resurrect Kautsky's notion of 'ultra-imperialism'; imperialist powers could agree to co-operate and exploit the world jointly. The choice is not simply between predicting inter-imperialist rivalry on the one hand or ultra-imperialism on the other; it is more relevant to ask how far the recognition of common interests can contain the antagonisms generated by other, divergent interests.

That some degree of co-operation, some limits to conflict, are taken for granted is indicated by the fact that few post-war writers have even considered the possibility of inter-imperialist war (which Lenin and Bukharin regarded as inevitable). Sutcliffe (1972) mentioned the possibility in passing, as did one or two others. My own opinion is that if states really did act rationally in the interests of their national capital as a whole, as some rather simple Marxist analyses have assumed, then it would not be difficult for them to co-operate. Kautsky would be proved right. However, state policies are the outcome of real political practice, which has to reconcile the interests of different groups and is deeply affected by a long history of compromises and of the ideologies that go with them (this is the 'relative autonomy' of the state). As a result, state policies are not necessarily rational in any simple sense.

Since the date of the main writings discussed here, the world capitalist system has been subjected to a succession of tests, in the two oil crises and the subsequent world recessions, and in the debt crisis. Although co-operation between the major capitalist states has clearly not been perfect, most commentators predicted far more severe rivalry than in fact occurred. In the 1970s, the measures taken by oil companies to redirect supplies when some oil importing states were embargoed by Arab suppliers, and the surprisingly successful expedients taken to preserve the world monetary system from potentially disruptive movements of 'petro-dollars', were examples of private sector adaptability based on inter-state co-operation, and the rescheduling of debt in the 1980s, if rather more conflict-ridden, has (so far) proved enough to stave off the worst fears of international

271

financial collapse. Although the dominance of the United States is visibly coming to an end, it would be unwise to expect rivalry between capitalist states to lead to any immediate breakdown of the world capitalist system.

11.3 CAPITALIST DEVELOPMENT IN THE THIRD WORLD

Perhaps the most important single question about the future of the world system is whether capitalist development in the Third World can start to close the gap between the developed and underdeveloped countries, as the classical Marxists expected. In the first half of the twentieth century, there were relatively few signs of capitalist development in under-developed countries, and many Marxists came to argue a position almost diametrically opposed to that of the classics. Where it had been argued that capitalist development had to come first to create the possibility of a socialist revolution, it was now argued that the absence of capitalist development made socialist revolution necessary.

When Europe and North America industrialized, the world economy was relatively unintegrated. Transport was expensive and risky, so goods were only traded where production costs were very different in different areas. Most basic subsistence goods and means of production were produced locally, by craft techniques. There was therefore scope for local development of capitalist production at the expense of older methods, while competition from more advanced centres was limited. Capital was relatively immobile, and technology was embodied in the skills and experience of the labour force. Thus any capitalist development that did take place created an independent local bourgeoisie and a local concentration of skills and technical knowledge. Independent capitalist development in many centres was possible and its progress was determined largely by local conditions (except where it was suppressed by a colonial state). Frank and Wallerstein would not accept this analysis; they have argued that an integrated capitalist world economy existed from an early stage. The facts are against them. Up to the industrial revolution the bulk of intercontinental trade was in luxuries such as sugar (slaves are an exceptional case), and the impact of European colonial dominance was primarily through its effects (often direct and brutal) on the mode of production in the subordinated areas.

During the later part of the nineteenth century transport costs fell dramatically, organizational forms were found that permitted large-scale international capital flows, and the systematization of technical knowledge made international transfers of technology much easier. All this, of course, was the result of capitalist development, and it led to the progressive creation of a relatively integrated world capitalist economy. The situation facing an underdeveloped country today is therefore quite different from that of earlier periods. One can ask whether industrialization on the pattern set by, say, Britain is possible today. One can also ask whether industrialization on that pattern is a relevant standard to set in present day conditions.

On the one hand, underdeveloped countries now starting a process of industrialization face competition from advanced centres with centuries of capital accumulation and technical progress behind them. As a result, a world pattern of specialization has been established in which the underdeveloped areas export mainly primary products (or did until recently), and import industrial products. Industrialization means displacing imports (or breaking into export markets) rather than displacing primitive craft industries. On the other hand, capital and technology can now be imported, and rising wages in the advanced countries offset the advantages of high productivity there.

There has been a substantial amount of industrial development in the Third World in recent years, typically in the form, to begin with, of import substitution, starting with the production of relatively 'light' consumer goods using imported capital equipment, often using at least some imported funds and with some sort of involvement of multi-national companies (wholly or partly owned subsidiaries, joint subsidiaries, licensing arrangements, and so on). The central issue in debate is whether this merely reproduced relations of dependence between centre and periphery in new forms (as Amin, Frank, Sutcliffe and others argue) or whether it marks the beginning of a breakdown of the centre–periphery division (as Warren claimed).

Sutcliffe (1972) was one of the few writers who tackled the question of the prospects for development in under-developed countries explicitly, and recognized clearly how different the present Marxist orthodoxy is from classical Marxism. (Barratt-Brown 1972 covered some of the same ground.) Sutcliffe recognized the facts of industrial growth in the periphery, but argued that the evidence did not answer the critical question: can there be a full independent ind-ustrialization like that of Japan, or, failing that, can there be enough development to create 'progressive socio-political forces' (a proletariat like that of Russia in 1917)? Apart from some problems of measurement (the figures may overstate the extent of development) he gave two reasons for dis-counting the observed industrial growth. First, growth has often been by import substitution concentrated in the production of luxury consumer goods for which the demand is limited, and this type of industrialization reinforces the unequal income distribution and social structure which limits demand. This is the argument of the dependency theorists (see Furtado 1973); to be acceptable it needs to be supported by some explanation of the failure of industrialization to penetrate into other branches of the economy or into export markets. Second, growth of industrial output may not be matched by growth in employment, since high productivity, capital-intensive methods are used. With production in the hands of foreign capital, the result is 'the absence of a bourgeoisie and the absence of a proletariat' (cf. Arrighi, chapter 10 above). Hence capitalist development may not create the kind of class structure that Marx described, in which the vast majority of the population is drawn into the proletariat. This 'marginalization' of masses of people has been stressed by many writers. It should be remarked that Marx in fact predicted a growing 'relative surplus pop-ulation', and it could be said that the underdeveloped countries fit Marx's model of capitalist accumulation more closely than do the advanced countries.

Sutcliffe proposed various criteria for 'independent' industrialization, which, he says, 'does not mean autarky, but carries with it the idea that industrialization is not merely "derived" from the industrialization of another economy' (1972: 174). His criteria for economic independence are that production should be orientated principally to the domestic market, that investment funds should be raised locally or at least should be under local control, that there should be a diversified industrial structure, and that technology should, in some (not very clearly defined) sense, be independent. The basis of these criteria is not clear; they show the rather nebulous character of the concept of dependence. In any case, why should it matter where development is 'derived' from? The results are surely more important.

Economic independence also has its 'social and political counterparts'. Here Sutcliffe's argument seems stronger:

> Economic development only happens when the surplus gets into the hands of those who will use it productively. ... This partly implies the need for an industrial bourgeoisie supported by a state that is capable of defending its interests. ... The state must be largely independent both of those local social interests opposed to industrialisation and also of foreign interests. (Sutcliffe 1972: 176-7)

This is the nub of the matter: is an independent national bourgeoisie formed? Independence in this sense does require that development be (mainly) financed locally and under local control, but it requires 'technological independence' only in the sense that use of foreign technology may lead to effective foreign control through conditions attached to licensing agreements, and the like. (See P. Patnaik 1973, for a detailed case study of the dependence that can result from reliance on imported technology through joint subsidiaries.) I see no reason why an independent capitalist class should not be formed on the basis of export-led industrialization or copying of techniques; in an interdependent world, a degree of specialization, together with large-scale exchanges of goods, capital and technology, are to be expected.

Sutcliffe's concern with technological independence seems to stem mainly from a different concern. He evidently thought that 'foreign' technology (can technology have a nationality?) is unsuitable because it is too capital-intensive (1972: 176). This line has been widely argued; capital-intensive technology means relatively little employment, which has further consequences for the structure of demand. However, it is likely that capitalist firms, whether foreign or national, will adopt the technique that maximizes profits. Underdeveloped countries constitute a large enough market for capital goods for it to be profitable to adapt technology to prices and wage rates there. It is thus unlikely that local firms using locally devised techniques would make very different choices. There are, in any case, reasons to think that a choice of technique that maximizes reinvestable surplus may be the optimum choice from the point of view of long-run growth (Dobb 1955, 1960; Sen 1968; Amin 1976: 320). Emmanuel (1982) has argued forcefully that underdeveloped countries should welcome inward investment as a way of acquiring technology, and should adopt 'best practice' techniques.

Sutcliffe argued that independent development (in the sense in which he defined it) was unlikely, unless the links between metropolis and satellite are disrupted by inter-imperialist war or acute capitalist crisis. The prospects of development are limited by the relative backwardness of the underdeveloped countries, by monopolistic control based on technological superiority, and by the pumping of surplus out of underdeveloped countries by repatriation of profits and by unequal exchange. These are all familiar arguments.

By the 1970s and 1980s, the tide was running very strongly against Sutcliffe's kind of dependency theory, and classical Marxist ideas were making a strong comeback. One of the most important contributions to this trend was Bill Warren's *Imperialism, Pioneer of Capitalism* (1980), left incomplete by his tragically early death, and published posthumously. The main lines of his argument had already emerged in a number of earlier articles (Warren 1971, 1973). For a trenchant critique of Warren, see Ahmad, who describes Warren's work as 'shallow and wrongheaded' (1983: 65); a more measured attempt by Foster-Carter (1985: 21) to preserve some of dependency theory seems to empty it of most of its content.

Warren's writings are very much in the spirit of the *Communist Manifesto* and of Marx's writings on India (see chapter 2 above). Capitalism is a progressive mode of production, which differs from all preceding forms of society by generating continuous technical advance, freeing individual creativity and at the same time allowing economic gains from large-scale production. The 'humanistic side' of capitalist culture promotes equality, justice, generosity, and the spirit of inquiry and adventure, and has done so since the beginnings of capitalism. It is a 'bridge to socialism', not only economically, but also culturally and politically, since Parliamentary democracy, the normal political form of a capitalist state, provides the best political environment for the socialist movement. 'The process of expanding Parliamentary democracy ... has thus far proved to have a powerful and irresistible momentum *within capitalism*' (Warren 1980: 30).

He defined imperialism as 'the penetration and spread of the capitalist system into non-capitalist or primitive capitalist areas of the world' (1980: 3). Given his strong emphasis on the progressive role of capitalism, it is not surprising that he treated imperialism as historically progressive, since 'the devastatingly superior productivity and cultural attributes of capitalism are bound, in the end, to subordinate all other modes of production and eventually eliminate them entirely' (1980: 40). As Warren defined it, imperialism can continue after decolonization, but it is inherently self-limiting. Once the whole world becomes capitalist (or socialist), the spread of capitalism must come to an end.

Colonialism, direct political and military control over subject territories, is a specific stage of imperialism. It is, as Warren recognized, hard to support the undemocratic imposition of outside control on a subject population, but he argued that it was time to shed liberal feelings of guilt, and recognize the positive achievements of colonial regimes. The most dramatic evidence of the benefits of colonialism is the improvement in health which followed colonial conquest, measured by improved life expectancy and the resulting population explosion. Like Marx, Warren took a very positive view of population growth as a stimulus to economic development, and dismissed Malthusian fears more casually than most commentators feel able to do. He also stressed the improvement of education under colonial rule, which transmitted both the technical and the cultural achievements of capitalism into new areas of the world. This does not mean that he dismissed democratic, anti-colonial struggles. Modern anti-colonialism is itself a product of the transmission of capitalist culture into the colonies, and is both inevitable and desirable. What he did argue was that Marxists should not deny the achievements of colonialism, that they should have no truck with sentimental and backward-looking opposition to capitalist penetration, and that they should not confuse bourgeois nationalism with socialism.

Warren's essential argument was that development based on foreign (or foreign controlled) capital is complementary to the development of national capital (1973: 39), given a state apparatus which exerts pressure on foreign business and promotes national capitalist development. He argued the case, in his 1973 article, largely in the context of resource-based international enterprises (fuel and materials), showing that local governments have successfully extracted greater shares of revenue and greater control. Since then, of course, the OPEC countries have gone much further in this direction. The same developments, he argued, were taking place in manufacturing. In particular, the position of the host country is strengthened as its nationals acquire greater experience and knowledge in particular industries, as a result of the simple presence of the industry and even more as a result of government pressures to employ and promote local residents. Partly-owned subsidiaries of multinational companies tend to come more and more under the control of local shareholders, who thus form the basis of a national capitalist class. Multinationals transfer technology, and, more generally, modern capitalism into the Third World.

What of imperialism as a system for draining surplus value from the periphery to the centre? Warren argued forcefully that even if the outward flow of repatriated profit exceeds the inward flow of investment, this does not demonstrate that the economic effect is harmful since 'what exactly is done with the capital "in between", so to speak, is ignored ... under capitalism exploitation is the reverse side of the advance of productive forces' (1973: 39). Capitalism both exploits and promotes development.

If the extension of capitalism into non-capitalist areas of the world created an international system of inequality and exploitation called imperialism, it simultaneously created the conditions for the destruction of this system by the spread of capitalist social relations and productive forces throughout the non-capitalist world. Such has been our thesis, as it was the thesis of Marx, Lenin, Luxemburg and Bukharin. (Warren 1973: 41)

There is an obvious objection to this view of imperialism. There have been few examples of successful capitalist industrialization since Lenin's time. (Japan was well on the way before the First World War.) Over much of the period, the gap between advanced and underdeveloped countries has been widening. Warren replied that the period since the Second World War has seen the breakup of colonial empires and the establishment of independent states in the Third World. We must presumably see the history of imperialism in stages: first the creation of a basis for national (political) independence, and then full capitalist development.

National independence was crucial, according to Warren, both because it provided a political framework for popular pressures for higher living standards, compelling governments to promote industrial development, and because it broke the monopoly hold of the colonial power, permitting newly independent states to take advantage of inter-imperialist and East–West rivalries to bargain for favourable treatment. Capitalist development does not require the prior existence of a 'national bourgeoisie'; other ruling classes can and must promote industrialization. 'These "industrialisers" may themselves become industrial bourgeoisies or may be displaced by the industrial Frankensteins they have created or they may become fused with them' (1973: 42-3; cf. Szymanski 1981: 120, Jenkins 1984, and Leys 1978, discussed in chapter 10 above). In addition, imperialist states have positively supported development (by right-wing, nationalist regimes) to contain socialism.

In terms which must have been calculated to provoke, he asserted:

> Imperialism was the means through which the techniques, culture and institutions that had evolved in Western Europe over several centuries – the culture of the Renaissance, the Reformation, the Enlightenment and the Industrial Revolution – sowed their revolutionary seeds in the rest of the world. (Warren 1980: 136)

Defending himself in advance against charges of ethnocentricity and arrogance, he argued that societies do not develop at the same rate, so some must logically be ahead of others at any given moment, and that to refuse to use the standards of the most advanced is to abandon any conception of human progress. In this, as in most of his argument, Warren followed Marx, who never hesitated to pass judgement on systems and societies he regarded as backward.

If Warren's argument seems shocking and perverse to many Marxists (as it does) despite its close resemblance to Marx's own views, it is natural to ask what had happened to Marxism in the interim. A substantial part of Warren's book is devoted to a critique of the course of Marxist thinking on imperialism, from Lenin onwards, designed to answer this question. I shall summarize it briefly. Lenin is the villain of the piece. His earlier work, especially his *Development of Capitalism in Russia*, escapes censure; indeed, his attack on the backward-looking ideas of the *Narodniks* fits Warren's case well, and is cited approvingly. In *Imperialism, the Highest Stage of Capitalism*, however, Lenin emphasized the 'parasitism and decay' of monopoly capitalism, presented capital export as the result of a lack of investment opportunities at home, and conveyed an impression of a world in which the prosperity of a few countries was based on the exploitation of half the world. By doing this, he was able to present imperialism as the last stage of a capitalism which had become retrogressive everywhere, so immediate revolution was the only hope. (I am not convinced that Lenin painted quite as gloomy a picture of the prospects for capitalist development in relatively backward areas as Warren made out, though some of his followers certainly did.)

According to Warren, Lenin's picture is the reverse of the truth. Imperialism is the work of young and vigorous capitalist economies. Capital export is not an alternative to investment at home, but is complementary to it. High rates of growth at home created demands for materials, and hence for investment in raw material producing areas. Rapid technical change created new investment opportunities at home, and also opportunities to apply the new techniques in other countries (railways are an example). In any case, capital export expanded before the rise of monopoly, and declined after the First World War (and after Lenin wrote), when monopoly was more widespread.

The first congress of the Comintern, in 1919, restated the classical Marxist view that the emancipation of the colonies must follow socialist revolutions in the metropolitan countries. However, as the 1920s wore on and hopes of immediate revolution in western Europe faded, communists from colonial countries pressed to be let off the leash. By degrees, Comintern policy shifted towards encouraging alliances with bourgeois nationalists, and towards seeing socialism as an alternative path to modernization, by-passing capitalist industrialization altogether. In 1928, the Comintern declared formally that imperialism was economically retrogressive in the colonies. (The idea that a political organization could settle such a question by decree is itself revealing.) From then on, according to Warren, Marxism allowed itself to be captured by bourgeois nationalist ideas, in which all ills were blamed on foreigners, and the goals of national independence and socialism were conflated. The notion of neo-colonialism is a letout for nationalist governments; if independence fails to bring the hoped-for benefits, it must be because the hated foreigners are still conspiring to undermine real independence.

Warren's attitude to dependency theory is summed up by his chapter heading: 'Dependency theory as nationalist mythology'; his own view could hardly be more different:

> Empirical observations suggest that the prospects for successful capitalist development ... of a significant number of major underdeveloped countries are quite good; ... that the period since the Second World War has been marked by a substantial upsurge in capitalist social relations and productive forces (especially industrialisation) in the Third World ... that the imperialist countries' policies and their overall impact on the Third World actually favour its industrialisation; and that the ties of dependence ... have been and are being markedly loosened. ... None of this is meant to imply that imperialism has ceased to exist.... What we wish to indicate are elements of change. (Warren 1973: 3-4)

To justify his position, Warren had to show that capitalism has been, and still is, progressive in underdeveloped areas. He claimed that the evidence shows unprecedented improvements in productive capacity and in the material welfare of the bulk of the population of the Third World, in the period after the Second World War. This development has been very uneven, so some countries, sectors and regions have advanced much more than others; indeed, he questioned whether the Third World can be regarded as a valid category at all.

There is no need to reproduce the mass of data marshalled by Warren to support his case; the main features of the case can be summarized quite briefly. For capitalist under-developed countries as a whole, the rate of growth of per capita GNP has accelerated since the Second World War. The Third World is growing faster now than the developed capitalist countries did at any stage in their history. Per capita GNP is not a perfect measure of welfare, but it is closely correlated with other measures of welfare and development, so the observed growth of per capita GNP does represent a real growth of welfare. There is no evidence of any general increase in inequality (though it has to be said that the evidence is so shaky that it would be unwise to draw any conclusions at all from it). There is also little evidence of the alleged 'marginalization' of large sectors of the population; open unemployment shows little trend, and there is equally little evidence of underemployment, at any rate in the sense that individuals are unable to work as much as they want (hours of work are often very long). Poverty, of course exists, and much work is still wasted by low productivity, but both are declining. The Third World's share of world output and of exports of manufactured goods has grown over the period. Agricultural performance has not been so good, but this is largely the result of mistaken policies; improvement is possible. The 1980s, it is true, have been more difficult than the earlier periods covered by Warren, and the heavy debt burden of some Third World countries will hold back gains in welfare, if not in output, but these are minor qualifications. China and India, the two most populous countries in the world, did well in the 1980s.

Warren's tone is at times irritatingly Panglossian, but his main conclusions cannot be denied; capitalist growth in the Third World in the post-war period has been a striking success. Socialists have often implicitly defined development in such a way that capitalist development is effectively ruled out. If development is defined by reference to the 'needs of the masses', then Marxists are unlikely to accept that capitalist development can fit the bill, but this leaves us unable to distinguish between continued stagnation, and development that is successful, in capitalist terms, in that it creates conditions for continued reproduction of capital.

Two more substantial criticisms of Warren's arguments remain. First, he was too ready to generalize about the whole of the Third World. As he admitted in passing, the record of development is strikingly uneven. Some countries have grown at quite unprecedented rates, but there are others, notably in sub-Saharan Africa, where per-capita incomes have actually fallen over substantial periods of time. This should not give any comfort to dependency theorists or to those who blame capitalism for failures of growth, since the low-growth countries are, in the main, those least involved in the capitalist world system, but it does suggest that it is more important to explain exactly why capitalism has succeeded so dramatically in some cases and not in others, than to insist that it is equally effective everywhere.

Second, his claim that capitalism generates development conveys, and I think must have been intended to convey, a further message, that *only* capitalism can carry development to the point where a genuine socialist revolution is possible. Throughout the book, the implication is that there is a single mainstream of historical development, running through the development of capitalism in Europe and spreading to encompass the whole world through the agency of imperialism. Now this may be true (it is certainly consistent with Marx's views, give or take some famous but lightweight remarks about the possibility of a distinctively Russian route), but it is clearly a case that needs more discussion than Warren gave it. It is possible, for example, to argue that capitalist development is taking place, but socialism offers a better alternative. One cannot blame Warren for not arguing the case more explicitly, since he did not live to do so.

11.4 SUMMARY

In the 1960s and 1970s, Marxist writers generally predicted continued United States dominance in the capitalist world, and saw little chance of underdeveloped countries improving their relative position without a complete break with the world capitalist system. Both predictions look pretty doubtful now. Multinational corporations are subject to the same market pressures as any other capitalist firms. The only way they can evade the imperatives of competition is by turning to their home state for support, but the capacity of the state to help them has been drastically curtailed. US hegemony in the capitalist world is clearly over, so the fiercely independent states of the Third World can play off one capitalist power against another. The most important limitation on the growth of any one Third World country is likely to be competition from others, so growth will continue to be very uneven, as capitalist growth always has been. Established industries in advanced countries are threatened by the continued development of industrial centres in low-wage areas; perhaps it is the centre, not the periphery, which now has most to lose from participation in the capitalist world system. The world order created by imperialism is changing quite rapidly.

Bibliography

ʻAdam, G. (1975) 'Multinational firms and worldwide sourcing', in Radice (1975); first published 1973.

Addo, H. (ed.) (1984) *Transforming the World Economy: Nine Critical Essays on the New International Economic Order*, London: Hodder & Stoughton.

——— (1986) *Imperialism: the Permanent Stage of Capitalism*, Tokyo: The United Nations University.

Ahmad, A. (1983) 'Imperialism and progress', in Chilcote and Johnson (1983).

Alavi, H. (1975) 'India and the colonial mode of production', in R. Miliband and J. Savile (eds) *The Socialist Register 1975*, London: Merlin.

Allett, J. (1981) *New Liberalism: the Political Economy of J. A. Hobson*, University of Toronto Press.

Althusser, L. and Balibar, E. (1970) *Reading Capital*, London: New Left Books; first published in French 1968.

Amin, S. (1966) *L'Economie du Maghreb*, 2 vols, Paris: Editions de Minuit.

——— (1971) *L'Afrique de l'ouest bloquée*, Paris: Editions de Minuit.

——— (1974) *Accumulation on a World Scale*, New York: Monthly Review Press; first published in French 1970.

——— (1976) *Unequal Development*, Hassocks: Harvester Press, and New York: Monthly Review Press; first published in French 1973.

——— (1977) *Imperialism and Unequal Development*, Hassocks: Harvester Press, and New York: Monthly Review Press; first published in French 1976.

——— (1978) *The Law of Value and Historical Materialism*, New York: Monthly Review Press; first published in French 1977.

——— (1980) *Class and Nation: Historically and in the Present Crisis*, New York: Monthly Review Press; first published in French 1979.

Anderson, P. (1974) *Lineages of the Absolutist State*, London: New Left Books.

Andreff, W. (1976) *Profits et structures de capitalisme mondial*, Paris: Calmann-Lévy.

Arrighi, G. (1966) 'The political economy of Rhodesia', *New Left Review*, Sept.-Oct.

——— (1970a) 'International corporations, labour aristocracies and economic development in tropical Africa', in Rhodes (1970).

——— (1970b) 'Labour supplies in historical perspective: a study of the proletarianisation of the African peasantry in Rhodesia', *Journal of Development Studies*, 3; first published in Italian 1969.

——— (1978) *The Geometry of Imperialism*, London: New Left Books.

——— and Saul, J. S. (1968) 'Socialism and economic development in tropical Africa', *Journal of Modern African Studies*, 2.

285

—— and —— (1969) 'Nationalism and revolution in sub-Saharan Africa', in R. Miliband and J. Savile (eds) *The Socialist Register 1969*, London: Merlin.

—— and —— (1973) *Essays on the Political Economy of Africa*, New York: Monthly Review Press.

Aston, T. H. and Philpin, C. H. E. (eds) (1985) *The Brenner Debate: Agrarian Class Structure and Economic Development in Pre-Industrial Europe*, Cambridge University Press.

Avinieri, S. (1969) 'Introduction' to Marx (1969).

Bagchi, A. (1986) 'Towards a correct reading of Lenin's theory of imperialism', in P. Patnaik (1986).

Banaji, J. (1972) 'For a theory of colonial modes of production', *Economic and Political Weekly*, Bombay, VIII, 52, December.

—— (1977) 'Modes of production in a materialist conception of history', *Capital and Class*, 3, Autumn.

Baran, P. (1973) *The Political Economy of Growth*, Harmondsworth: Penguin; first published 1957.

—— and Sweezy, P. (1968) *Monopoly Capital*, Harmondsworth: Penguin; first published 1966.

Bardhan, B. (1985) 'Marxist ideas in development economics: a brief evaluation', *Economic and Political Weekly*, Bombay, March 30.

Barone, C. (1982) 'Samir Amin and the theory of imperialism: a critical analysis', *Review of Radical Political Economics*, 14.

—— (1985) *Marxist Thought on Imperialism*, Houndmills and London: Macmillan.

Barratt-Brown, M. (1972) 'A critique of Marxist theories of imperialism', in Owen and Sutcliffe (1972).

—— (1974) *The Economics of Imperialism*, Harmondsworth: Penguin.

Bleaney, M. (1976) *Underconsumption Theories: A History and Critical Analysis*, London: Lawrence & Wishart.

Bowles, S. (1981) 'Technical change and the profit rate: a simple proof of the Okishio theorem', *Cambridge Journal of Economics*, 5.

Bradby, B. (1975) 'The destruction of natural economy', *Economy and Society*, IV, 2.

Braverman, H. (1974) *Labor and Monopoly Capital*, New York: Monthly Review Press.

Brenner, R. (1977) 'The origins of capitalist development: a critique of neo-Smithian Marxism', *New Left Review*, 104, July/August.

—— (1985) 'Agrarian class structure and economic development in pre-industrial Europe' and 'The agrarian roots of European capitalism', in Aston and Philpin (1985).

Brewer, A. (1980a) 'On Amin's model of autocentric accumulation', *Capital and Class*, 10, Spring, also correction of printing errors, 11, Summer.

—— (1980b) *Marxist Theories of Imperialism: a Critical Survey*, first edn, London: Routledge & Kegan Paul.

—— (1984) *A Guide to Marx's Capital*, Cambridge University Press.

—— (1985) 'Trade with fixed real wages and mobile capital', *Journal of International Economics*, 18.

—— (1986) 'Theories of imperialism in perspective', in Mommsen and Osterhammel (1986).

Bukharin, N. (1972a) *Imperialism and World Economy*, London: Merlin; first published in Russian, 1917.

—— (1972b) *Imperialism and the Accumulation of Capital* (edited by K. Tarbuck), London: Allen Lane; first published in Russian.

Cain, P. J. (1978) 'J. A. Hobson, Cobdenism, and the radical theory of economic imperialism', *Economic History Review*, 31.

—— (1985) 'J. A. Hobson, financial capitalism and imperialism in late Victorian and Edwardian England', *Journal of Imperial and Commonwealth History*, 13.

Chandler, A. and Redlich, F. (1961) 'Recent developments in American business administration and their conceptualisation', *Business History Review*, Spring.

Chattopadhyay, P. (1972a) 'On the question of the mode of production in Indian agriculture, a preliminary note', *Economic and Political Weekly*, Bombay, VII, 13.

—— (1972b) 'The mode of production in Indian agriculture, an anti-kritik', *Economic and Political Weekly*, Bombay, VII, 53.

Chilcote, R. H. and Johnson, D. L. (eds) (1983) *Mode of Production or Dependency?*, Beverly Hills: Sage.

Crummey, D. and Stewart, C. C. (eds) (1981) *Modes of Production in Africa: the Pre-Colonial Era*, Beverly Hills: Sage.

Cutler, A., Hindess, B., Hirst, P., and Hussain, A. (1977) *Marx's Capital and Capitalism Today*, 2 vols, London: Routledge & Kegan Paul.

De Janvry, A. (1981) *The Agrarian Question and Reformism in Latin America*, Baltimore: Johns Hopkins University Press.

Dobb, M. (1940) *Political Economy and Capitalism*, 2nd edn, London: Routledge & Kegan Paul, first edn published 1937.

—— (1955) *On Economic Theory and Socialism*, London: Routledge & Kegan Paul.

—— (1960) *Economic Growth and Planning*, London: Routledge & Kegan Paul.

—— (1963) *Studies in the Development of Capitalism*, London: Routledge & Kegan Paul; first published 1946.

Dos Santos, T. (1970) 'The structure of dependence', *American Economic Review*, LX, May, and in Wilber (1973).

Dumont, R. and Mazoyer, M. (1973) *Socialisms and Development*, London: Deutsch; first published in French 1969.

Edelstein, M. (1982) *Overseas Investment in the Age of High Imperialism: the U.K. 1850-1914*, London: Methuen.

Emmanuel, A. (1972) *Unequal Exchange: A Study of the Imperialism of Trade*, London: New Left Books, and New York: Monthly Review Press; first published in French, 1969.

—— (1974) 'Myths of development versus myths of underdevelopment', *New Left Review*, 85, May/June.

—— (1982) *Appropriate or Underdeveloped Technology?*, Chichester: Wiley.

Etherington, N. (1984) *Theories of Imperialism: War, Conquest and Capital*, Beckenham, Kent: Croom Helm.

Fann, K. and Hodges, D. (eds) (1971) *Readings in U.S. Imperialism*, Boston: Porter Sargent.

Foley, D. (1986) *Understanding Capital: Marx's Economic Theory*, Cambridge, Mass: Harvard University Press.

Foreman-Peck, J. (1983) *A History of the World Economy: International Economic Relations since 1850*, Brighton: Wheatsheaf.

Foster-Carter, A. (1976) 'From Rostow to Gunder Frank: conflicting paradigms in the analysis of underdevelopment', *World Development*, IV, 3, March.

—— (1978) 'The modes of production controversy', *New Left Review*, 107, Jan./Feb.

—— (1979) *Marxism vs. Dependency Theory? A Polemic*, University of Leeds, Department of Sociology, Occasional Paper no. 8.

—— (1985) *The Sociology of Development*, Ormskirk: Causeway.

Frank, A. G. (1969a) *Capitalism and Underdevelopment in Latin America*, revised edn, New York and London: Modern Reader Paperbacks; first edn 1967.

—— (1969b) *Latin America: Underdevelopment or Revolution*, New York: Monthly Review Press.

—— (1972) *Lumpenbourgeoisie: Lumpendevelopment*, New York and London: Monthly Review Press.

—— (1973) 'On feudal modes, models and methods of escaping capitalist reality', *Economic and Political Weekly*, Bombay, VIII, 1.

—— (1978) *Dependent Accumulation and Underdevelopment*, London: Macmillan.

—— (1981) *Reflections on the World Economic Crisis*, London: Hutchison.

—— (1983) 'Crisis and transformation of dependency in the world system', in Chilcote and Johnson (1983).

—— (1984) *Critique and Anti-Critique: Essays on Dependence and Reformism*, London: Macmillan.

Friedman, A. L. (1977) *Industry and Labour*, London: Macmillan.

Furtado, C. (1973) 'The concept of external dependence', in Wilber (1973).

Gallagher, J. and Robinson, R. (1953) 'The imperialism of free trade', *Economic History Review*, 2nd series, 6.

Gibson, B. (1980) 'Unequal exchange; theoretical issues and empirical findings', *Review of Radical Political Economics*, 12.

Griffin, K. and Gurley, J. (1985) 'Radical analyses of imperialism, the Third World and the transition to socialism: a survey', *Journal of Economic Literature*, 23.

Harris, N. (1986) *The End of the Third World: Newly Industrializing Countries and the Decline of an Ideology*, London: I. B. Tauris.

Hay, D. and Morris, D. (1979) *Industrial Economics: Theory and Evidence*, Oxford University Press.

Hilferding, R. (1981) *Finance Capital: a Study of the Latest Phase in Capitalist Development*, London: Routledge & Kegan Paul; first published in German, 1910.

Himmelweit, S. (1974) 'The continuing saga of the falling rate of profit – a reply to Mario Cogoy', *Bulletin of the Conference of Socialist Economists*, 9, Autumn.

—— and Mohun, S. (1978) 'The anomalies of capital', *Capital and Class*, 6, Autumn.

Hobson, J. A. (1938) *Imperialism: a Study*, 3rd edn, Allen & Unwin, London; reprinted Ann Arbor: University of Michigan Press, 1965; 1st edn 1902.

Hodgson, G. (1974) 'The falling rate of profit', *New Left Review*, March/April.

Howard, M. C. and King, J. E. (1985) *The Political Economy of Marx*, 2nd edn, London: Longman.

Hymer, S. (1972) 'The multinational corporation and the law of uneven development', in J. Bhagwati (ed.) *Economics and the World Order from the 1970s to the 1990s*, New York: Collier-Macmillan, and in Radice (1975).

—— (1976) *The International Operations of National Firms*, Cambridge, Mass: MIT Press; written as a PhD thesis, 1960.

—— and Rowthorn, R. (1970) 'Multinational corporations and international oligopolies: the non-American challenge', in C.P. Kindelberger (ed.) *The International Corporation*, Cambridge, Mass: MIT Press.

Jalee, P. (1972) *Imperialism in the Seventies*, New York: Okpaku Publishing, The Third Press; first published in French 1970.

Jenkins, R. (1984) *Transnational Corporations and Industrial Transformation in Latin America*, London: Macmillan.

—— (1987) *Transnational Corporations and Uneven Development: the Industrialisation of the Third World*, London: Methuen.

Kautsky, K. (1970) 'Ultra-imperialism', *New Left Review*, 59, Jan./Feb.; first published in German, 1914.

Kay, G. (1975) *Development and Underdevelopment*, London: Macmillan.

Kemp, T. (1967) *Theories of Imperialism*, London: Dobson.

Knei-Paz, B. (1978) *The Social and Political Thought of Leon Trotsky*, Oxford: Clarendon Press.

Krader, L. (1975) *The Asiatic Mode of Production*, Assen, Netherlands: Van Gorcum.

Laclau, E. (1971) 'Feudalism and capitalism in Latin America', *New Left Review*, 67, May/June; reprinted, with postscript, in Laclau (1977).

—— (1977) *Politics and Ideology in Marxist Theory*, London: New Left Books.

Le Bris, E., Rey, P. P., and Samuel, M. (1976) *Capitalisme Negrier*, Paris: Maspero.

Lenin, V. I. (1950) *Imperialism, the Highest Stage of Capitalism*, in *Selected Works*, vol. I, Moscow: Foreign Languages Publishing House; first published in Russian 1917.

—— (1964) *Collected Works*, vol. 19, Moscow: Progress Publishers.

—— (1974) *The Development of Capitalism in Russia*, Moscow: Progress Publishers; first published in Russian 1899, 2nd edn 1908.

—— (1989) *Lenin's Economic Writings*, ed. M. Desai, London: Lawrence & Wishart.

289

Lewis, W. A. (1969) *Aspects of Tropical Trade*, Stockholm: Almqvist & Wiksell.

Leys, C. (1975) *Underdevelopment in Kenya*, London: Heinemann.

—— (1978) 'Capital accumulation, class formation and dependency – the significance of the Kenyan case', in R. Miliband and J. Savile (eds) *The Socialist Register 1978*.

Little, I. (1982) *Economic Development: Theory, Policy, and International Relations*, New York: Basic Books.

Lubeck, P. (ed.) (1987) *The African Bourgeoisie: Capitalist Development in Nigeria, Kenya, and the Ivory Coast*, Boulder, Colorado: Lynne Rienner.

Luxemburg, R. (1951) *The Accumulation of Capital*, London: Routledge & Kegan Paul; first published in German 1913.

—— (1972) *The Accumulation of Capital: an Anti-Critique*, in Bukharin (1972b); first published in German 1921.

McEachern, D. (1976) 'The mode of production in India', *Journal of Contemporary Asia*, 6.

McMichael, P., Petras, J., and Rhodes, R. (1974) 'Imperialism and the contradictions of development', *New Left Review*, 85, May/June.

Magdoff, H. (1969) The *Age of Imperialism*, New York: Monthly Review Press.

—— and Sweezy, P. (1969) 'Notes on the multinational corporation', *Monthly Review*, Oct./Nov.; and in Fann and Hodges (1971).

—— and —— (1975) 'The economic crisis in historical perspective', *Monthly Review*, March/April; and in Magdoff and Sweezy (1977).

—— and —— (1977) *The End of Prosperity*, New York: Monthly Review Press.

Mandel, E. (1967) 'International capitalism and "supranationality"', in R. Miliband and J. Savile (eds) *The Socialist Register 1967*, London: Merlin.

—— (1975) *Late Capitalism*, London: New Left Books; first published in German 1972.

Marx, K. (1957) *Capital*, vol. II, ed. F. Engels, Moscow: Foreign Languages Publishing House; first published in German 1885.

—— (1961) *Capital*, vol. I, ed. F. Engels, Moscow: Foreign Languages Publishing House; first published in German 1867.

—— (1962) *Capital*, vol. III, ed. F. Engels, Moscow: Foreign Languages Publishing House; first published in German 1894.

—— (1969) *On Colonialism and Modernisation*, ed. with introduction by S. Avinieri, New York: Doubleday Anchor; collection, various dates.

—— (1976) *Preface and Introduction to a Contribution to the Critique of Political Economy*, Pekin: Foreign Languages Publishing House; preface first published in German 1859.

—— and Engels, F. (1950) *Manifesto of the Communist Party*, in *Selected Works*, vol. 1, Moscow: Foreign Languages Publishing House; first published in German 1848.

—— and —— (1971) *On Ireland*, London: Lawrence & Wishart; collection, various dates.

—— and —— (no date) *On Colonialism*, Moscow: Foreign Languages Publishing House; collection, various dates.

Matthews, R. C. O. (1959) *The Trade Cycle*, London: Nisbet, and Cambridge University Press.

Meillassoux, C. (1964) *Anthropologie economique des Gouro de Cote d'Ivoire*, Paris: Mouton.

Michalet, C. A. (1976) *Le capitalisme mondiale*, Paris: Presses Universitaires de France.

Miles, R. (1987) *Capitalism and Unfree Labour: Anomaly or Necessity?*, London: Tavistock.

Mitchell, H. (1965) 'Hobson revisited', *Journal of the History of Ideas*, 26.

Mommsen, W. and Osterhammel, J. (eds) (1986) *Imperialism and After: Continuities and Discontinuities*, London: Allen & Unwin.

Morishima, M. (1973) *Marx's Economics*, Cambridge University Press.

—— (1974) 'Marx in the light of modern economic theory', *Econometrica*, 42.

—— (1976) 'Positive profits with negative surplus value – a comment', *Economic Journal*, 86.

Mummery, A. and Hobson, J. (1889) *The Physiology of Industry*, reprinted New York: Kelley & Millman, 1956.

Murray, R. (1971) 'The internationalisation of capital and the nation state', *New Left Review*, 67, and in Radice (1975).

Myrdal, G. (1957) *Economic Theory and Underdeveloped Regions*, London: Duckworth.

Nicolaus, M. (1969) 'Who will bring the mother down?', *Leviathan*, 1, and in Fann and Hodges (1971).

Okishio, N. (1961) 'Technical changes and the rate of profit', *Kobe University Economic Review*, 7.

—— (1963) 'A mathematical note on Marxian theorems', *Weltwirtschaftliches Archiv*, 91.

Owen, R. and Sutcliffe, B. (eds) (1972) *Studies in the Theory of Imperialism*, London: Longman.

Palloix, C. (1969) *Problèmes de croissance en économie ouverte*, Paris: Maspero.

—— (1973) *Les firmes multinationales et le procès d'internationalisation*, Paris: Maspero.

Patnaik, P. (1972) 'Imperialism and the growth of Indian capitalism', in Owen and Sutcliffe (1972).

—— (ed.) (1986) *Lenin and Imperialism*, London: Sangam Books.

Patnaik, U. (1971a) 'Capitalist development in agriculture, a note' *Economic and Political Weekly*, Bombay, VI, 39.

—— (1971b) 'Capitalist development in agriculture, further comments', *Economic and Political Weekly*, Bombay, VI, 52.

—— (1972) 'On the mode of production in Indian agriculture, a reply', *Economic and Political Weekly*, Bombay, VII, 40.

Porter, A. and Holland, R. (1988) *Theory and Practice in the History of European Expansion Overseas: Essays in Honour of Ronald Robinson*, London: Cass.

Porter, B. (1968) *Critics of Empire; British Radical Attitudes to Colonialism in Africa, 1895-1914*, London: Macmillan.

Poulanzas, N. (1975) *Classes in Contemporary Capitalism*, London: New Left Books; first published in French 1974.

Radice, H. (ed.) (1975) *International Firms and Modern Imperialism*, Harmondsworth: Penguin.

Rey, P. P. (1971) *Colonialisme, néo-colonialisme et transition au capitalisme*, Paris: Maspero.

——— (1973) *Les alliances de classes*, Paris: Maspero.

——— (1975) 'The lineage mode of production', *Critique of Anthropology*, 3, Spring.

Rhodes, R. I. (ed.) (1970) *Imperialism and Underdevelopment, a Reader*, New York: Monthly Review Press.

Ricardo, D. (1951) *Principles of Political Economy and Taxation*, Cambridge University Press; first published 1817.

Robinson, R. (1972) 'Non-European foundations of European imperialism, sketch for a theory of collaboration', in Owen and Sutcliffe (1972).

——— (1986) 'The excentric idea of imperialism, with or without empire', in Mommsen and Osterhammel (1986).

——— and Gallagher, G. (1961) (with A. Denny) *Africa and the Victorians: the Official Mind of Imperialism*, London: Macmillan.

Roemer, J. (1981) *Analytical Foundations of Marxian Economic Theory*, Cambridge University Press.

——— (1982) *A General Theory of Exploitation and Class*, Cambridge Mass.: Harvard University Press.

Rowthorn, R. E. (1971) 'Imperialism in the 1970s – unity or rivalry', *New Left Review*, 69, and in Radice (1975).

——— and Hymer, S. (1971) *International Big Business 1957-67: a Study of Comparative Growth*, Cambridge University Press.

Ruccio, D. and Simon, L. (1986) 'Methodological aspects of a Marxian approach to development; an analysis of the modes of production school', *World Development*, 14.

Rudra, A., *et al.* (1969,1970) 'Big farmers of the Punjab', in three parts, *Economic and Political Weekly*, Bombay, IV, 39 and 52, and V, 26.

Sau, R. (1973) 'On the essence and manifestation of capitalism in Indian agriculture', *Economic and Political Weekly*, Bombay, VIII, 13.

Semmel, B. (1970) *The Rise of Free Trade Imperialism: Classical Political Economy, The Empire of Free Trade and Imperialism, 1750-1850*, Cambridge University Press.

Sen, A. K. (1968) *Choice of Techniques*, 3rd edn, Oxford: Blackwell.

Shaikh, A. (1982) 'Neo-Ricardian economics: a wealth of algebra, a poverty of theory', *Review of Radical Political Economics*, 41.

Simon, L. and Ruccio, D. (1986) 'A methodological analysis of dependency theory: explanation in Andre Gunder Frank', *World Development*, 14.

Solow, R. (1956) 'A contribution to the theory of economic growth', *Quarterly Journal of Economics*, 70.

Sraffa, P. (1960) *Production of Commodities by Means of Commodities: Prelude to a Critique of Economic Theory*, Cambridge University Press.

Steedman, I. (1975) 'Positive profits with negative surplus value', *Economic Journal*, 85; and in Steedman (1989).

—— (1976) 'Positive profits with negative surplus value: a reply', *Economic Journal*, 86.

—— (1977) *Marx after Sraffa*, London: New Left Books.

—— (1989) *From Exploitation to Altruism*, Cambridge: Polity Press.

Stolper, W. and Samuelson, P. (1941) 'Protection and real wages', *Review of Economic Studies*, 9.

Sutcliffe, B. (1972) 'Imperialism and industrialisation in the Third World', in Owen and Sutcliffe (1972).

Sweezy, P. (1942) *The Theory of Capitalist Development*, New York: Oxford University Press.

Szymanski, A. (1981) *The Logic of Imperialism*, New York: Praeger.

Taylor, J. G. (1979) *From Modernization to Modes of Production: a Critique of the Sociologies of Development and Underdevelopment*, London: Macmillan.

Terray, E. (1972) *Marxism and Primitive Societies: Two Studies*, New York: Monthly Review Press.

Turner, B. S. (1978) *Marx and the End of Orientalism*, London: Allen & Unwin.

van Binsbergen, W. and Geschiere, P. (eds) (1985) *Old Modes of Production and Capitalist Encroachment: Anthropological Explorations in Africa*, London: Kegan Paul International.

Wallerstein, I. (1974a) *The Modern World System*, New York: Academic Press.

—— (1974b) 'The rise and future demise of the world capitalist system', *Comparative Studies in Society and History*, 16, 4, and in Wallerstein (1979).

—— (1979) *The Capitalist World Economy*, Cambridge University Press and Paris: Editions de la Maison des Sciences de l'Homme.

—— (1980) *The Modern World-System II: Mercantilism and the Consolidation of the European World-Economy 1600-1750*, New York: Academic Press.

—— (1983) *Historical Capitalism*, London: Verso.

—— (1984) *The Politics of the World Economy: the States, the Movements and the Civilisations*, Cambridge University Press.

Warren, B. (1971) 'How international is capital?', *New Left Review*, 68, July/August, and in Radice (1975).

—— (1973) 'Imperialism and capitalist industrialisation', *New Left Review*, 81, September/October.

—— (1980) *Imperialism, Pioneer of Capitalism*, London: New Left Books.

Wilber, C. K. (ed.) (1973) *The Political Economy of Development and Underdevelopment*, New York: Random House.

Wolpe, H. (ed.) (1980) *The Articulation of Modes of Production: Essays from Economy and Society*, London: Routledge & Kegan Paul.

Wright, E. O. (1979) 'The value controversy and social research', *New Left Review*, 116, July/August.

Index

Notes: 1. Because of differences in terminology between writers, the actual word or phrase indexed may not appear in the corresponding text. Conversely, related material may be indexed under several headings. 2. Places and historical events are very sparingly indexed, because this is a book about theories.